ART THINKING

ALSO BY AMY WHITAKER

Museum Legs: Fatigue and Hope in the Face of Art

ART THINKING

How to Carve Out
Creative Space
in a World of Schedules,
Budgets, and Bosses

AMY WHITAKER

HARPER
BUSINESS

An Imprint of HarperCollins*Publishers*

HarperCollins books may be purchased for educational, business, or sales promotional use. For information, please e-mail the Special Markets De-partment at SPsales@harpercollins.com.

All art care of the author.

Parts of this book are adapted from work that appeared previously in *Art21*, *The Millions*, and *Fast Company*, as well as in an essay called "Own-ership for Artists" within a collection called *The Social Life of Artistic Property* (Hudson, New York: Publication Studio, 2014).

Chapter 5 includes a drawing that reproduces, with the author's permis-sion, Vijay Kumar's diagram from Vijay Kumar, *101 Design Methods: A Structured Approach for Driving Innovation in Your Organization* (Hoboken, New Jersey: Wiley, 2012), 8.

The appendix reproduces a list of academic degrees at Cambridge Uni-versity in the eleventh, eighteenth, and twenty-first centuries, with per-mission, from Bryan Boyer, Justin Cook, and Marco Steinberg, *In Studio: Recipes for Systemic Change* (Helsinki, Finland: SITRA, 2011), 30.

FIRST EDITION

Designed by Meghan Day Healey

Library of Congress Cataloging-in-Publication Data has been applied for.

ISBN: 978-0-06-235827-1

16 17 18 19 20   OV/RRD   10 9 8 7 6 5 4 3 2 1

For Beverly, Elaine, Jeff, and Stacey
and for anyone who has ever asked,
"Wouldn't it be cool if . . . ?"
and followed up.

I don't remember when I became an artist
but I remember when everyone else stopped being one.

—Vik Muniz, artist

CONTENTS

Saving Lives vs. Making Lives Worth Saving

I just want to encourage people not to wait for an ideal state of awareness. They must begin with the current means and with their mistakes.

—Joseph Beuys, artist

I grew up not completely understanding what a job was. My parents had an almost peculiar passion for what they did. My father was a neurologist so enamored with his work that he numbered his ATM pin code for a protein sequence in his "favorite enzyme." He skipped lunch every day because it slowed him down too much. My mother, a medievalist, skipped lunch every day of graduate school to pore over illuminated manuscripts.

Someone once asked my father how he and my mother got along so well being in such different fields. He said that he was in the business of saving lives and she was in the business of making lives worth saving. The differences between their vocations were not as great as they first appeared. The truth was, they flipped roles all the time. He helped people with quality-of-life issues like debilitating headaches or nerve damage that made it unpredictable and scary to walk. She taught people basic survival skills like how to write in complete sentences.

That idea of "saving lives versus making lives worth saving" describes the general relationship between literature and science in the case of my parents, and art and business in the case of this book. At first, one looks like leisure and the other necessity, one like imagination and the other analysis—except that it is often hard to know which one is which.

On January 17, 2008, a British Airways pilot named John Coward was bringing a Boeing 777 in to land at London's Heathrow Airport. The plane had been in the air for more than ten hours on its way back from China. In the last two minutes of the flight, within two miles of the end of a five-thousand-mile journey, the engines failed. Working swiftly with the captain who adjusted the wing flaps, Coward pulled the plane just over the perimeter fence and landed it on its belly in the grass. No one was gravely injured.

In describing the incident, the aviation expert Philip Butterworth-Hayes said the pilots were dealing with a situation for which "[t]here is no training . . . and the instruments are of no help whatsoever." In uncharted territory, they acted in a way that was both analytic and imaginative. The 150-metric-ton aircraft is a masterpiece of technology, but to land it safely they had to negotiate the physics of flight with the more human tools of ingenuity and split-second response. As the British Airline Pilots Association said, the crew, including the cabin crew who evacuated the plane, were "ordinary people who did an extraordinary thing."

THE MFA IS THE NEW MBA

Like many children of specialist parents, my siblings and I became generalists. My brother became a COO/CFO type, warm and dry-witted with a vaguely militaristic streak. Our sister went into marketing and business development. I became a jack-of-all-trades kind of person. In some other life, I might have been a scientist or a policy wonk but I became an artist instead, in the general DIY life-assembly sense.

Despite our parents' different fields, ours was a household of epic and unspoken Calvinist work ethic. I had always loved to draw but found it hard to see the public service in making art. Even with the saving-lives-vs.-making-lives-worth-saving moral complexity, if elected officials had to rank-order giving money to road repair, cancer research, and art education, it wasn't hard to see which came in third.

It was easy to see the immediate need to help the sick and repair what was broken. But in the long run, art is aligned with imagination, which is aligned with the cure for cancer itself. Creativity is also behind the economic successes that make the roads possible. And the roads are worthwhile for getting places besides the beige-cubicled world. Making lives worth saving has its own claim on necessity. Art and science, leisure and work, invention and execution are all parts of the same system.

After college, I went to work in art museums because I thought they were public libraries for imagination. It turned out their inner workings were decidedly economic and I went to business school in hopes of becoming a museum manager. The plot of my life splintered in 2001, the summer after business school. Within a month, our father died suddenly, the corporate job I had taken was canceled, and 9/11 happened. A year later, I made a life decision as much as a career one and enrolled in an MFA in painting program at the Slade School of Fine Art in London.

In 2004, the year I finished art school, Daniel Pink declared in the *Harvard Business Review* that the MFA was the new MBA. James J. Cramer wrote that Wall Street analysts should get fine art degrees so that they could, like the great modernists, spot undervalued AT&T stock before everyone else.

On the ground, the cultures were almost comically different. Business school was full of frameworks so general we could apply the same one to population control and toothpaste marketing. My navy interview suit felt so generic I taped plastic airline wings to the lapel and wore it for Halloween.

Art school, by contrast, overflowed with patternless and singular events. One day I crested the grand, worn marble staircase of the Slade building. On the landing, someone had placed a banana on which they had written, "Please put me in your ass." The only person in art school who wore a suit was fellow painter Nick Brown, and only once when he had been out all night at a burlesque strip club and then come into the studio directly to paint still wearing three-piece, pin-striped tails.

Having an MFA and MBA as of 2004 made me somewhat exotic, but what was surprising was to realize how intertwined creativity and commerce actually are for all of us.

This book is a meditation and a manual, a manifesto and a love story, for how art—creativity writ large—and business go together. It is about how to construct a life of originality and meaning within the real constraints of the market economy. It is about how to make space for vulnerability and the possibility of failure within the world of work, with its very real and structural pressures to get things done, to win praise and adulation, and to contribute to bottom-line growth.

My perspective is not as a captain of industry but as someone who has spent more than a decade working and playing in two very different worlds—art and business—and thinking about how they come together.

Ultimately, business represents strength, art, and flexibility. To be an athlete—a whole person—you need both power and range of motion. The particular ways in which you decide to combine art and business—invention and execution—will stem from many different questions that we will come to address by the end of this book.

THE A-WORD

To really talk about art and business together, the first thing we need is a more versatile, Swiss Army knife definition of what art is.

Art traditionally means objects like paintings or sculptures. The term more recently includes the highly conceptual or "deskilled" works that people puzzle over in museums and galleries. That confusion about art is not new. In 1926, Constantin

Brancusi's sculpture *Bird in Space* got stopped in customs and labeled as "Kitchen Utensils and Hospital Supplies." In 1974, the German artist Joseph Beuys—who famously proclaimed that everyone is an artist—made an artwork that consisted of locking himself in a room with a live coyote, a wool blanket, a cane, and daily delivery of the *Wall Street Journal.* Our remit here is more universal, and does not require you to lock yourself in a room with a news source and a predatory animal.

The German philosopher Martin Heidegger attempted to define the category of art in a 1947 essay called "The Origin of the Work of Art." In a testament to how difficult that is to do, Heidegger worked and reworked his argument from 1930 until 1960, republishing it periodically. I like to think that defining art is so hard, he only stopped working on it in 1976, when he died.

To adapt a definition from Heidegger:

A work of art is something new in the world that changes the world to allow itself to exist.

(You can simulate the experience of reading the original Heidegger essay by pausing and reading that sentence a couple of times.)

CHANGING THE WORLD TO ALLOW SOMETHING TO EXIST

In this model of progress, you move forward not just by winning a game, but by creating the game itself.

If you are making a work of art in any area of life, you are not going from a known point A to a known point B. You are inventing point B. You are creating something new—an object, a company, an idea, your life—that must make space for itself. In the act of creating that space, it changes the world, in however big or small a way.

By this definition, art is less an object and more a process of exploration. Many things outside the art world are art—computers and 747s, counterinsurgency manuals and business models, afternoons and lives inventively spent. And, conversely, many things inside the art world are high-end, branded commodity products that trade on an art market—objects that are just recognizable enough and just scarce enough to function as alternative currencies.

GETTING THE PLANE OFF THE GROUND

Business prizes being able to put prices on things and to know their value ahead of time. Yet, if you are inventing point B—in any area of life—you can't know the outcome at the moment you have to invest money, time, and effort in the point-A world.

This is the central paradox of business: The core assumptions of economics—efficiency, productivity, and knowable value—work best when an organization is at cruising altitude, but they won't get the plane off the ground in the first place. That is to say, the history of business—the way we got here—follows from the kind of creative and open-ended work that the structure of business makes hard.

Innovation has long been part of business theory. In 1942, Joseph Schumpeter coined the term "creative destruction" to describe the constant need for change and reinvention. Schumpeter argued that capitalism rests on change; corporations that keep doing the same thing eventually go out of business. Invention is necessary for survival. Following patterns, rather than inventing new ones, will only get you so far. The people who devised those patterns didn't have a template when they started. Seeing how someone else started a $100 million company won't promise you the same outcome. The power fades in the copy.

Change and reinvention are essential to longer-term success. The *Economist* magazine calculates growth of economies by tracking inputs—labor and capital—against outputs, measured as gross domestic product. The amount of GDP not accounted for by capital and labor is attributed to innovation. In the United States and the United Kingdom, that unexplained amount accounts for more than half of GDP. "In short, it is innovation—more than the application of capital and labour—that makes the world go round."

Another way of saying that is that companies can grow by two means. They can grow by scaling up to the most efficient level of production. Or they can grow artistically by the alchemy of invention.

THE RIDDLE OF THE PIN AND THE PENCIL

The friction between business structures and open-ended process comes from two allegories, one about a straight pin and

one about a pencil, the first about efficiency and the second about known value.

In his 1776 book, *The Wealth of Nations*, Adam Smith, the godfather of economics, visits a pin factory and finds that if a single worker makes an entire pin by himself, he can make twenty in a day, but if ten men divide pin-making up into steps, they can make the equivalent of 4,800 pins per person per day—240 times as many. The division of labor helps you make pins faster, but it doesn't help you make a better pin or figure out how to make a pin from scratch—whatever the "pin" is.

The story of the pencil comes from Leonard Read's 1958 essay, "I, Pencil"—a charming tour of how a pencil is made, from the point of view of the pencil. The upshot is that no one person could ever make a pencil. Only the "magic of the price system"—to quote Milton Friedman's 1980 retelling—lets all the different actors—loggers, graphite miners, kiln operators, lacquer painters, and so on—combine efforts.

The reason the pricing system works is the belief that price represents value. But if you are making something for the first time, you often can't know the value ahead of time when you're getting started.

The pin is a story about depth—about how to do one thing quickly if it is the only thing you do. The pencil is a story of breadth—about how to coordinate with other actors to assemble your small parts into a whole. Together, they describe the efficiencies of execution and the possibilities of trade. They do not, however, describe the messiness of starting and the uncertainty of trying that are required to invent a point B.

Traditionally defined, art itself has a long history of scrambling the idea of efficiency. Ever since the invention of photography, making a painting at all is an act of willful inefficiency.

The information age also changes what it means to be efficient in the first place. The successful fashion brand Zara does not run its factories at full capacity; it reserves 50–85 percent of its own factories so that it can be responsive to trends in midseason. The company can get feedback from its stores as to what is selling well and then use the extra capacity to make more of those pieces. Efficiency becomes lateral. Being able to coordinate complex systems becomes as valuable as producing things quickly.

The stories of the pencil and the pin can lead to forms of magic that wring value out of scarce resources, or they can act like a steamroller that keeps you head-down making your part of the straight pin or the pencil. Art thinking bends the stories of the pencil and the pin so that you can protect and inhabit the "before" picture—the time before the pencil or the pin was designed—or the time when not even Watson and Crick knew what a double helix was or why it mattered. Championing that space is a human process, but one that also requires the tools of the market, in surprising ways.

THE ART THINKING FRAMEWORK

Art thinking is a framework and set of habits to protect space for inquiry. It will help you to dream big in ways that are completely lifted above yet still tethered to reality. It is about how to structure and set aside space for open-ended, failure-is-possible exploration and to move forward by asking the big, messy, important questions, whether you know they are possible to answer or not. It is a form of optimism in the face of uncertainty.

With these mindsets you'll see clearly and make progress through the clunky process of making anything truly new. Art thinking then draws on tools of risk and return and investment management, within the frameworks of operating a business. Those mindsets and tools come together to support the process of art, and all of the vulnerability, risk of failure, *actual* failure, negotiation, and surprise involved in open-endedly and openheartedly creating the life—and the working life—you want.

The chapters of this book trace the steps along this path, from the mindsets of art through the tools of business.

1. From a Wide Angle: Zoom out and see everything from a wide-angle view.

Economic theory models an object-based method of producing a product efficiently, but your life is really the entire ecosystem around the object. Your work and leisure are not always separate. As in the case of Thomas Fogarty, the inventor of the balloon catheter, a breakthrough idea can come from anywhere. You need to develop habits of what I will call "studio time"—ways of setting aside empty space in the landscape of your life. Paradoxically, in order to fully access these advantages, you may need to relax your hold on goal completion and efficiency enough to even feel like you're wasting time.

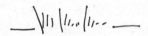

2. In the Weeds: Change your focus from outcome to process and from comparing your work in progress to other people's completed projects.

After it was completed, Harper Lee's book *To Kill a Mockingbird* came to look like a masterpiece that sold 40 million copies, won the Pulitzer Prize, and became a film with Gregory

Peck. While Lee was writing it, she worked for many years as a reservations agent for the airlines and, in her words, wore through three pairs of blue jeans sitting at a desk. When you look at other people's creative projects, you see them from the outside, after the fact. When you look at your own, you see them from the inside, in the weeds. To counteract this bias, you need to change your relationship to judgment and to adopt tools for sitting with the vulnerability of not yet being at the end.

3. To the Lighthouse: Trade outcome goals for questions that guide you forward.

Given the realities of being in the weeds, the way to navigate is not toward a solution but from a question. The question becomes a lighthouse that guides you forward, toward your point B. That question can arise from a general sense of "Is this possible?" as it did for Roger Bannister running the first sub-four-minute mile, or it can stem from the purpose of your organization, from your own expertise, or from your general experiences as a person.

In a film, the question that propels the plot forward is deeper than the storyline itself. In screenwriting parlance, it is called an MDQ, or "major dramatic question." Your lighthouse question has this deeper nature. It drives the plot of your life forward by connecting your personal authenticity and your external circumstance.

4. To Make a Boat: Manage risk by taking a portfolio view and by owning the upside of what you create.

Even having a guiding question, you still have to take on risk and to invest time and resources to explore anything. How do you make those decisions? Here, you need the tools of the market. You need to think in terms of a portfolio of projects around your lighthouse. In the short term, income from one area can support investment in another. Over a longer period of time, the collection of projects functions like a diversified portfolio, with gains in one area balancing out losses in another.

Like many artists, you may need to self-fund in the early stages, as an individual or a company, in order to get something off the ground. To reap those gains, you will need to own some form of shares in what you make.

Planning for gains is critical because, in the case of creative work, risk usually gets framed in terms of failure. But failure is only one kind of risk. True risk management also means planning well for the possibility of success. To manage downside risk, you need to balance your most uncertain projects against other areas with steady income. To manage the upside risk, you need to restructure how you are paid to include an ownership stake.

In fact, the ways most industries structure ownership are outmoded. Apart from musicians and writers who are paid royalties and entrepreneurs who retain equity, many people do not own a portion of what they create. Owning shares makes it easier to assign value that is not yet known. Technology makes it simpler to manage networks of fractional shares more easily than ever before.

5. To Be in the Fray: Assign roles and adapt tools of conversation to set culture and manage projects.

For the mindsets of art thinking to thrive in an organizational setting you need to create a conducive environment for creative work. The manager becomes more like an art school teacher or a guide. As you see in especially successful companies like Pixar, you need what I will call colleague-friends, people who understand your expertise but also relate with the generosity of friendship.

In tandem, you can designate specific roles that help bridge the idealism of creation and the realities of execution. Generalizing from film production, a producer can engage in the parallel creative process of bringing an idea into the market. And, adapting project management tools used by computer programmers, you can designate roles, define milestones, and structure larger-scale working processes around open-ended lighthouse questions.

6. To Build a House: Build artistic business models working within the design constraints of capitalism itself.

Anything you produce—whether a house or a meal or a pair of glasses or a consulting report or a university education, whether for love or money—has a cost structure. Its production is made up of fixed and variable costs. Fixed costs are those like factory rent that don't change in the short term no matter how many pairs of glasses you produce. Variable costs are those like acetate frames or metal hinges that do. The combination of fixed and variable cost forms the internal skeleton of the business model. The money the business makes has to cover the cost structure or else the business will fail.

The particular combinations of fixed and variable costs tell you the species of the business—including some fascinating patterns of business models that are unique to our time. Designing business models is artistic in a way that extends beyond the mechanical truth of cost structure. The builders of business models become the artists of enterprise.

7. To See the Whole: Navigate the complexity of organizations and disciplines to tackle the big questions of the day.

In so many complex projects, the artist is really a team more than a single person. How do you orchestrate conversations

to create this kind of meta-generalist—a generalist built out of many people? Universities are laboratories for the kind of cross-disciplinary thinking that we need in order to engage with the largest questions—about the environment or student debt, about the structure of working life or the design of the economy itself. The role of the individual is to own your own metaphor and to build skills to be able to ask questions, if not answer them, in any field.

EVERYONE IS AN ARTIST, AND A BUSINESSPERSON

What is true for everyone—for artists *and* for business-people—is that there is no such thing as space outside the market, only the possibility of space within it.

For all of us, the market economy is the fabric of our lives. It is almost impossible for anyone to avoid participating in it. People work, get a paycheck, run businesses, pay taxes, buy things, invest, raise money, and sometimes secretly hope to become rich. Doctors master insurance claim forms. Teachers manage book budgets. Artists hold day jobs. Students hold debt. Anti-market activists own iPhones. Even homesteaders who live in yurts in Montana buy duct tape.

Every day people try to make things, to start things, to navigate the formless beginnings of putting anything new into the world. The traditional ideas of the economy map a single-vector system around making a profit. But the market is a broader and more flexible tool. It can still hold space for the early days of making things, putting them out there, and moving step by step into a future of your own design.

ART, DESIGN, AND CREATIVITY

Art thinking shares some similarities with design thinking, the framework for generalizing the process of designing a product into a creative problem-solving tool. The differences between art and design are somewhat academic, especially as fields of conceptual and speculative design flourish. But whereas a framework originating in product design starts with an external brief—"What is the best way to do this?"—art thinking emanates from the core of the individual and asks, "Is this even possible?"

Design thinking values empathy with users and rapid prototypes so that you can build a better airplane. Art thinking is there with the Wright brothers as they crash-land and still believe that flight is possible.

The definition of art is not about the size or magnitude of the point-B world, a pebble skipped across a lake, or a thunderous cannonball. The creativity guru Mihaly Csikszentmihalyi, author of *Flow* and *Creativity*, makes a distinction between "big-C" and "little-c" creativity—the great works of Michelangelo compared to the very excellent Halloween costumes of regular people.

That distinction does not apply here. The idea that big-C and little-c creativity are separate perpetuates the stereotype of artists as preordained geniuses. It grants people too much fortune-telling ability of the Monday-morning quarterback variety. The way that Csikszentmihalyi describes little-c creativity—as "the kind all of us share just because we have a mind and we can think"—describes the ground that all creative work comes from.

If you are truly reinventing something, you may not know at the outset that it will be a big-C kind of breakthrough. Even the Starbucks Corporation was a little-c coffee shop when it began—as a storefront near Pike Place Market in Seattle, Washington, in 1971. Trying for big-C creativity can crush the process of exploration. It can make you want to skip to the end. Creativity as a process only has traction with the present moment.

The people in this book—writers, thinkers, parents, teachers, entrepreneurs, scientists, filmmakers, and even working artists—have found ways to design creative lives and whole organizations in the market economy. Relative to the myth of artistic genius, their lives show patches of failure, talent in other fields, and years spent starting small. Their business models show the resourcefulness of starving artists and the belief that everyone has something to offer that is of value.

Throughout this book, "business" is a term I use to mean organizational form in the economy, whether a household or a nonprofit, a small company or a multinational. "Art" is a term I use to mean the human capacity for exploration and originality, for thinking and making in ways that are uniquely your own. I use the term "art" willfully instead of relying solely on something more general like "creativity" because I want to borrow it back from the art world as an old-fashioned part of all of our humanity. And I use the term "work" broadly to describe anyone engaged in labor of any kind, paid or unpaid, publicly or privately.

In my own life, I have written this book while working full-time, mostly as a professor teaching business to artists, designers, and arts administrators. I have worked in environments that are no more immune to politics and people complexities than anyone else's office. I have experienced love and loss, been unwell and then well, tried to install an air conditioner in a window, paid bills, binge-watched television on the Internet, and otherwise been a person in the world. I hope all of that makes me a more honest guide. The questions in this book aren't ones you necessarily answer so much as revisit as a practice.

The gift of art thinking is, paradoxically, in the idea that you cannot control the outcome of any endeavor and you might fail. That may sound like cold encouragement, but in so many situations, that permission to try and fail frees you to ask questions that really matter. It allows you, in the words of the designer Dror Benshetrit, "to discover your own integrity." What I find most heartening is that, at its best, creative work—the kind that merits the Latin phrase *ars longa, vita brevis*, or "art is long, life is short"—comes from a core that is human and particular. The more you are yourself, the better chance you have to make your own contribution and to create your own life and work.

The simple reality is that most of us need a paycheck, have a boss, and feel some weeks that Monday is like Tuesday and Tuesday is like Wednesday, and Friday is only different because Saturday comes next. Even in that world of routine and duty, the tools of artistic process are available to everyone, and we can use them to build anything from inventive business models and management structures to well-spent afternoons and meaningful lives. What starts with an everyday feeling of "Hey, I made this!"—whether that's dinner or a deal structure or a set of bookends—can expand into the largest of canvases. We create our lives, we build our workplaces, we design our society, we make our world. Art thinking is the process and business is the medium.

WHAT WOULD LEONARDO DO?

Leonardo da Vinci is considered one of the greatest artists of all time, someone for whom the label "genius" is not hyperbole. He was an artist but he was also a botanist, a defense engineer, an architect, and a scientist. He was a polymath. His brain was a university with all the departments. I have often wondered what Leonardo da Vinci would be doing if he were alive today. Would he have been standing outside an art school smoking a cigarette in three-quarter-top sneakers, or standing on a stage in a black mock turtleneck pitching the first iPhone?

The most satisfying answer I have heard lately came from Frank Vitale, a videographer and professor at the School of Visual Arts, who simply said that Leonardo would just be trying to figure something out. Being an artist is that process of exploring ideas, sometimes by means of producing objects, sometimes not. In that sense, being an artist is a part of all of us.

Yet it is especially difficult to imagine Leonardo in contemporary life for two main reasons, which have to do with education and economics.

It is harder to be a generalist now. Educational paths have become more specialized at the same time that information has proliferated. In his time, Leonardo could attempt to learn everything and wear his unique combination of botanist-defense-engineer hats.

Leonardo also had patrons. Now, you often have to invest in something yourself ahead of time to prove the concept. Countless organizations we now take for granted were self-invested in that way at the outset.

What Leonardo's story points out is that we now need to design into the creative process systems for coordinating across many fields of knowledge and new ways of managing the financial risks of creative work ahead of time.

Leonardo had advantages that few of us have but that we can all try to replicate: Instead of knowing everything, we can imagine being able to *ask* anything and to own our curiosity toward *everything*. We can pose questions and have conversations in any field.

We don't need to mimic creative genius. We need to find our own authenticity. Instead of slotting into preexisting categories and labels, we can describe ourselves in our own terms and fully own our particular cross sections of knowledge. We can be custom generalists, and design our own metaphors.

Instead of going hat in hand to the patron families of Italy or the king of France as Leonardo did, we can design more alternate funding arrangements like licenses, royalties, and equity stakes, to better support exploratory work before its full value is known.

We do not have to project the veneer of genius onto other people. Rather, we need to be honest and transparent about where we are. When you admire a finished project—a film, a song, or even a PowerPoint presentation—it is easy to feel distanced from the messiness of how it came to be. The finished work airbrushes out the realities of the perseverance and accident that brought it into being. That distancing does a disservice. It makes it so much harder to start.

No doubt, the world contains a few modern Leonardos who stand on that perch of genius with ease and elegance. But, just as often, the world moves forward propelled by the inelegant, the sincere, the awkward, the slow, the quiet, the local, the unexpected, the inefficient, and the downright surprising. As a body politic, that motley collective effort does more to push society forward and to create meaning for individual people and value for organizations than any one miraculous Leonardo ever could. Finding space for that process allows amazing projects or whole enterprises to appear in the world the way most of us do, slightly gangly or shy or adolescently a work in progress.

The British writer G. K. Chesterton once observed, "We are perishing for want of wonder, not for want of wonders." Leonard Read quotes Chesterton early on in his story of the market, "I, Pencil." The world is full of wonders within the market and far outside. That sense of possibility does not yield to focusing just on work, but on the vast ecosystem of your whole life—and then defining the questions that will propel you forward.

CHAPTER 1

From a Wide Angle

A human being should be able to change a diaper, plan an
invasion, butcher a hog, conn a ship, design a building, write
a sonnet, balance accounts, build a wall, set a bone, comfort
the dying, take orders, give orders, cooperate, act alone, solve
equations, analyze a new problem, pitch manure, program a
computer, cook a tasty meal, fight efficiently, die gallantly.
Specialization is for insects.

—Robert A. Heinlein, *Time Enough for Love*, 1973

When you meet Thomas Fogarty, the cardiovascular surgeon who
invented a medical device called the balloon catheter, he has a wry
twinkle and the affability of someone who has, since 1978, owned
a winery in Northern California. He is not one of those wiry surgeons who appear to run ten miles each morning—alienatingly
healthy and otherworldly in equal measure. He speaks in an

Ohioan accent with wide-open A's and a cadence as simple and percussive as a one-drum musician in the New York City subway. It makes much of what he says sound like a punch line.

This is fair—Dr. Fogarty is a pithy man. He possesses a childlike ability to see things as they are while also trying to make them better, as observant of the broad design challenges of modern medicine as of any single device. He speaks like a doctor, that subset of the population who can say, "He died of cancer of the rectum" the way someone else might say, "I'm going to the store to buy oranges." He's not unfeeling—it's his own father who died that way, when Fogarty was in grade school. He had already seen his father taken away to an asylum, straitjacketed, when Fogarty was about five.

Dr. Fogarty is part of that elite and dubious club of people who did something big in their youth—not the captain of the football team who threw the game-winning Hail Mary pass but a badly behaved, resourceful kid who invented a medical device that opened up the world of noninvasive cardiovascular surgery and that still saves three hundred thousand lives each year. Fogarty's story springs from what I call a "whole life" approach. His insight came not from separating his work life and his leisure time, but from a wide-angle view toward the combination of both.

Growing up in the 1940s and '50s, Fogarty was never in terrible trouble, but he was a self-proclaimed juvenile delinquent who had to be either busy or supervised. When the teacher wasn't looking, he would jump out of the window to go fly-fishing. Not knowing where he had gone, his teacher would call his mother at her job, where she supported three kids by working at a dry cleaners, what Fogarty called "a sweatshop in every sense of the word." So, in the eighth grade Fogarty got a job at the Good Samaritan Hospital in Cincinnati, Ohio. The sole reason he went to work there was that hospitals were exempt from child labor laws. He was only thirteen.

Fogarty started as a dishwasher in Central Supply, cleaning out stomach pumps for eighteen cents an hour. The cleanup job was so grim he invented a new dishwashing agent—made from green soap, ether, and baking soda—to cut the time in half. Much of the life of the hospital passed through Central Supply, providing Fogarty's Venn diagram brain a chance to build up a mental encyclopedia of usable forms—a certain shape of scissors used in gastric procedures that could, if scaled down in size and changed slightly in angles, be used for eye surgery. Fogarty was observant, and the doctors let him sit in on a lot of things. By the time he was fifteen he had seen two autopsies. "There were a lot of things you just learn without the intent of learning. You just make an observation and say *holy cow*."

Already, Fogarty had a synthesizing mind and an impatience with a lack of action. He wanted to *do* things. Around the age of fifteen, Fogarty became a scrub technician—an assistant inside the operating room—for a surgeon named Jack Cranley. Dr. Cranley had ten kids. Fogarty essentially became the eleventh. One of the main procedures in Dr. Cranley's surgical practice was the removal of blood clots. To retrieve a clot, a surgeon would have to make an incision the length of the blocked artery and open it up in its entirety. Sometimes patients died or had to have limbs amputated. Those who healed often bore long scars on their chests or legs. "[T]hey'd do an operation, which would take about eight hours, and then one or two days later, the patient would be back in the operating room, having his legs cut off. When you see that repetitively, you say, 'There has to be something better than this.'"

Fogarty had always been a tinkerer and entrepreneur. As a child, he built soapbox cars and model airplanes so good he sold them to neighbors. He bought the model airplane kits for eighteen cents and sold the finished planes to other kids for seven or eight dollars. He was his mother's personal handyman, fixing anything she asked him to.

Fogarty even worked part-time in a motorcycle repair shop that mainly serviced scooters. The manual clutch on a scooter had a problem when you dropped into a low gear: "[I]f you

were going up hill, you'd lurch forward and suddenly find a certain part of your anatomy on the street, with the scooter about ten yards ahead of you. My idea was to smooth that transition. . . ." Fogarty and his friend invented the predecessor to the centrifugal clutch that is still in widespread use today. They wouldn't profit financially from the invention because the garage owner had a claim on their intellectual property through "shop rights," something Fogarty would remember. (Later, when his mentor, Dr. Cranley, advised him to get an intellectual property attorney, he listened.)

Blood clots were a problem far worse than landing on the seat of your pants off the back of a scooter. Dr. Cranley challenged Fogarty to find a better solution, and so the scrub technician started experimenting. He was working with a urethral catheter—a piece of vinyl tubing like a tiny garden hose—and the single pinky finger of a number-five latex glove.

He wanted to build a device that could, in a compressed state, be threaded through an artery past a blood clot and then expanded to rake a clot back, pulling it out through a single, much smaller incision. "I think I tried two or three other things that didn't work, but the minute that idea came to me, it was pretty clear it was going to work."

By 1959, Fogarty was in his fourth year of medical school tinkering with the balloon catheter in his attic. He had just decided to become a heart surgeon. (As he explained it: "[Cardiologists] certainly do a lot now, but all they did then was read EKGs and pronounce people dead.")

He imagined what the balloon catheter would look like, but his key challenge was that no glue of the late 1950s and early 1960s would make latex and vinyl adhere. Fogarty's breakthrough was to tie the device together—with the fly-fishing knots he learned while cutting school. "I'd always tied flies and made lures so it was just a natural thing."

And so it turned out that a device that is still in use today—saving more than 20 million lives or limbs since it was introduced—came into being not from specialized expertise or a large pharmaceutical lab, but from a Huck Finn propensity for jumping out of windows to go fishing during school and an imaginative leap from the domain of fly lures to the design challenge of adhesion.

The idea of a whole-life approach—that your work and your leisure are not always separate, that necessity and luxury sometimes cross over, that the whole accounts for the success of the part—opens up broad questions about pathways to progress and habits of creative work. Thinking about your life as a whole ecosystem is the first step.

THE OBJECT AND THE ENVIRONMENT

In his 2005 commencement address at Kenyon College, the writer David Foster Wallace told the story of the fish:

> There are these two young fish swimming along, and they happen to meet an older fish swimming the other way, who nods at them and says, "Morning, boys, how's the water?" And the two young fish swim on for a bit, and then eventually one of them looks over at the other and goes, "What the hell is water?"

Economics assumes a world of profitable products. It is a world of fish, not water. Whole-life thinking models the world as the entire system—taking into account all of life underwater. The "fish" can be anything—a report, a number, a person, a product—seen in isolation, as if it is floating on the green screen of your life. This kind of object-based thinking can lead to an artificial separation of different spheres. It can lead you to judge what is important or unimportant prematurely and to miss out on the times a solution to a problem comes holistically from another area of life.

In his 2003 book, *The Geography of Thought*, the social psychologist Richard Nisbett recalls the origins of his graduate student Takahiko Masuda's research. Masuda, a six-foot-two football player, arrived at the University of Michigan, there straight from his native Japan and wildly excited to take in his first Big Ten game. In the colossal and electrifying stadium in Ann Arbor, Masuda was shocked by what he perceived as the rude behavior of the people around them. In Japan he had been taught to "watch his back"—to be mindful of how his location in space affected other people. There in Michigan, fellow fans were standing up right in front of him with no awareness that they were keeping him from seeing the game. Masuda designed an experiment to see if he could isolate this cultural difference.

Masuda hypothesized that Eastern and Western audiences simply perceived the world differently. The Eastern view held up a kind of wide-angle lens of looking out for others and noticing the context; the Western view focused a kind of tunnel vision from the point of view of the actors themselves, the context taken as given. To test the hypothesis, Masuda gathered two groups of students, one from the University of Michigan, the other from Kyoto University. He developed eight animated scenes, each about twenty seconds, of life underwater—replete with fish, plant life, rocks, and bubbles.

In each scene, at least one "focal" fish crossed the screen bigger, brighter, faster, and more colorful than the others. After showing the individual research subjects the animations twice, Masuda asked the students to describe what they had seen. Both American and Japanese students homed in on the focal fish, mentioning them a roughly equal number of

times. But the Japanese observers also made twice as many comments about the relationship of the focal fish to the background elements and, in fact, mentioned the background elements 60 percent more frequently than did their American counterparts. Americans were three times as likely to begin their description with the focal fish—"There was a big fish, maybe a trout, moving off to the left." The Japanese were more likely to begin by describing the overall environment— "It looked like a pond."

In an object-based world, if you were shown a picture of the ocean below the surface, you might name a fish or an anemone, or a shark. In an environment-based world, you might describe the whole ocean. Profitability of a single product looks for the single focal fish. Sustainability and overall health takes in the whole environment. Creativity often does too.

Taking in a wide-angle view of possibility can feel less analytically efficient than just watching the fish. Keeping in mind the whole picture takes energy. In fact, in management consultant parlance, "boiling the ocean" is a pejorative shorthand for taking an inefficient, unfocused approach. The water is vital; without it, the fish dies. Yet, looking away from the fish can feel risky and off point in an answer-driven and outcome-oriented culture that embraces the 80-20 rule as an article of faith.

The 80-20 rule comes from an observation Vilfredo Pareto made in 1906. He noticed that 80 percent of the land in Italy was owned by 20 percent of the population, and generalized the Pareto Principle—that 80 percent of the gains come from 20 percent of the effort. This idea that focusing on 20 percent of the work can yield 80 percent of the outcome creates pressure to stay focused. "Boiling the ocean" is a form of getting the 80-20 rule backward. Yet sometimes the important, world-changing work lives in what initially appears to be the inefficient part. The 80-20 rule helps you to execute well within the known world. But it also makes it harder to see enormous opportunities outside the frame of low-hanging-fruit efficiency, in the lake, not in the trout.

A life like Fogarty's, where his breakthrough in science came from idle patches of his youth, is a reminder of how much the whole of your life matters. That makes it hard to moralize work as more important than leisure and by extension science as more important than art, or short-term profit as more important than a long-term investment that might at first appear to be fruitless. They are all connected. As Nisbett points out, the word "school" comes from *schole*—the Greek word for "leisure." The merchant traders of ancient Athens valued school for cultivating their sons' curiosity.

The further you get into adult life, the less often you get to indulge your pure curiosity—to swim around in the water without having to get somewhere—and the less often you have to master something truly new—to remember how hard and clunky that process is but also how fast you can learn. Making art—in any area of life—can feel that way.

The question is how to start. How do you set up a process that eventually includes performance evaluation, collaboration with other departments or people, and coordination with structured goals? If you look at all the parts of your life as a landscape with hills and valleys and lakes and towns, the tools come from seeing how the pieces relate. Whole-life thinking begins with managing energy and time and then building in space—mental, physical, and managerial—for exploration, observation, and discovery. Ultimately what you are doing is arranging the artistic composition of your life.

MANAGING ENERGY AND TIME

In their 2003 book, *The Power of Full Engagement*, Jim Loehr and Tony Schwartz made the case for a much more personal view of whole-life thinking. They argued that your own life is a system in which you are constantly managing not just time but energy. They posited four general types of energy—mental, emotional, spiritual, and physical. According to Loehr and Schwartz, most of us play to two types. We lack a regulated personal ecosystem. We might play to our mental and physical energy if we mostly work, and work out. Parenting might draw more on emotional and physical energy. The desk-sitting office worker gets overweighted toward mental, underweighted toward physical, and so on.

Loehr and Schwartz's research originated in a study of elite tennis players. They asked why some players dominated world-class tournaments, while other players who weren't necessarily worse on a skills basis didn't win. What was it that separated the elite? Loehr and Schwartz hooked players up to EKGs that monitored their brain waves while they were playing. Tennis, with its possibilities for endless sets, offered a particularly deep case study in stamina. What Loehr and Schwartz found was surprising yet consistent. The elite players succeeded because they had developed ways to rest. Their ways of resting didn't mean stopping outright but switching. They were practicing rituals that pulled them into other forms of energy. One player would bounce the ball against his racquet in a very particular way each time he served. The players had developed activities that came together as a whole—the intense concentration of play and the ritualized reprieve of habit. Loehr and Schwartz believed that this pattern extended to all of us. We didn't need a complete rest. We needed a respite from one activity by changing to another.

Loehr and Schwartz began working as consultants helping people to redesign their lives toward balanced energy. One woman worked all day and neglected physical activity. Instead of telling her to go to the gym twice a week, they helped her find a specific class and helped her to ritualize going every Tuesday and Thursday. Her energy ecosystem existed as a set of microclimates, delineated by rituals and habits. She wouldn't have to push herself to the gym. The ritual would pull her.

You can take a moment to think about your own life and which forms of energy you play to most. In your mind's eye or actually, you can take a piece of paper and divide it into quadrants, labeling each quadrant with one of those four types—mental, emotional, spiritual, and physical. You can start to see the relationships of the different activities, connecting with arrows the activities that go well together, that provide forms of active recovery one to the other. You can even sketch in the activities that you never get to but that seem to promise a yin-yang opposition and renewal to what is there.

For Fogarty, the time in the operating room with blood clot victims had such an immersive kind of energy it created its own yin to the yang in Fogarty's personality that slingshotted him to the attic to tinker. For us, the trick is to design the overall composition of our ecosystem to be as energizing as possible by pairing and combining our activities well. Once we do that, we can then create a kind of black box of space in our schedule, a protected time or place or ritual in which no outcome is expected of us and we can explore.

FIGURE/GROUND

In the language of artistic composition, all of these forms of shifting from an object to an ecosystem are about *figure* and *ground.* To build the composition of your life and work projects you will need these tools.

When you draw a vase of flowers on a piece of paper, you can talk about figure and ground in the drawing. The figure is whatever object you have drawn, the vase.

The ground is the space around it, the background. The figure is the object. The figure and ground together create the whole composition. In a successful composition, your gaze tends to enter in one place and to travel around. The composition works because it has areas of focus and a harmony of parts. In contrast, if a painting is "samey all over"—if it tediously calls for your attention in a uniform way—the human eye fatigues and can't take it all in.

What is critical about the figure-ground distinction is that it allows you to do two important things. First, it allows you to balance the wide-angle view with the realities of needing to focus and prioritize. Second, it allows you to save patches of blank space in the composition of your own life—places that are intentionally left as ground.

Together, these tools of composition—prioritization and blank space—give you access to more elegant and imaginative forms of 80-20 thinking: You are aware of the power of efficiency but not limited by it. You can better make choices about where to focus now while reserving space for what is possible later.

One thing that made Leonardo da Vinci a master of the relationship between figure and ground was his interest in the ground itself. In many portrait paintings of the Renaissance, the background—the ground behind the portrait subject—is a

window onto some form of landscape. The patches of ground within Leonardo's paintings and in the background of his portraits reflect his detailed studies of nature.

Paying attention to the landscape is something more. It is an acknowledgment that the space around something—the space that, in daily life, many of us hardly register, or look past as if it were nothing—is as important as the thing itself. The ground is integral to the figure. In 1503 or 1504, as Leonardo was working on the *Mona Lisa*, he wrote, "Amid the vastness of the things among which we live, the existence of nothingness holds the first place."

Leonardo's observation hints at why it can be hard to take this kind of wide-angle view of one's life. The exercise may involve, as it does for me, admitting that the landscape of your life

is very crowded. Yet if you operate only from an object-based viewpoint, you can end up being in a space that is all figure and no ground. There is no unused space. The vase doesn't sit on a table; it sits chockablock in a field of vases.

New York City, with its skyscrapers and building-to-building construction, is all figure and no ground. If there is a seemingly empty plot of land, usually someone owns it, or the real reason that it is a park is that a governmental agency gave a commercial developer permission to build a taller and more profitable tower next door in exchange for leaving that patch of grass. In Manhattan, even the air rights above existing buildings are owned. The city invites a constant state of doing, of vertical assertion, of filled space. The Manhattan footprint is the equivalent of a schedule that has no downtime, a calendar in which meetings are bookended back to back and in-case-of-cancellation plans are already waiting. A walk to the subway is also a chance to check email. For many of us, our lives are all figure and in need of more ground.

The venture capitalist Will Rosenzweig, a cofounder of the Republic of Tea who taught some of the first classes in social entrepreneurship at the University of California, Berkeley, and now runs the Food Business School, has observed that many of his accomplished friends get so busy they have no space in their lives—little time for a spontaneous meeting, no room on the calendar for drinks with a new acquaintance. One of his own strategies in this area draws on the Hebraic tradition of setting an empty place at a Passover seder. The empty chair symbolically holds a space of honor and welcome for the prophet Elijah. Says Rosenzweig, "I always think about that, as how you create enough room in your life for the unexpected guest or unexpected stranger to actually play a significant enough role." The pressures of work and life can make it hard to leave the metaphorical empty seat for the passing serendipity of creative work.

Like Will's Elijah chair, you need some sort of protected space that is held intentionally open. Imagine being at an outdoor concert with general seating on a great open lawn. You take a picnic blanket to cordon off a patch of grass. The economy is like a giant amphitheater of assigned seats and a lawn full of other people's picnic blankets and if you don't pitch yours—to set and hold a blank space—the lawn will otherwise get filled up.

Creativity is about doing, but doing from a position of being. Instead of skyscrapers and vertical ascent, it is about pitching a picnic blanket, about carving out space for exploration.

Pitching the picnic blanket has both a spatial and an economic piece to it. You are holding space within your calendar. But doing so also means you need to pay for that space, or to know that you will not be doing gainful work in that time. That space is your personal R&D department. It is where you explore ideas without the pressure of producing something.

I see this all the time teaching business to artists and designers, and it applies to everyone. The artists or designers struggle with a business model to describe what they do, and then realize that what they ultimately need is not to be paid to make the things they already know how to make, but to somehow find space inside their financials to play and take risks to develop the next thing. This sense of spaciousness—this slight give, this productive slack, this momentary pause—is the basis of what I call "studio time."

STUDIO TIME

Studio time is a patch within the composition of your life that is protected as ground. It can be a physical space you go to or a psychic space held by a ritual or habit that allows you to explore a project. It can take on as many individual incarnations as actual art studio space does for working artists. The hallmark of studio space is that—physically and temporally and economically and mentally—it is open. Two examples of studio space concern the invention of versatile materials: masking tape and email.

In the early days of the 3M Corporation one of their workers, a man named Richard Drew, went to see a client, an auto body shop. While there, Drew noticed a worker having a really hard time painting two-tone stripes onto the curved body of a car. If only the worker had an adhesive tape he could use to "mask" one color while he painted the other so that they didn't bleed, his job would be much easier.

Drew got the go-ahead from his manager to look into developing some tape. When he went back to the auto body shop he found that the tape he made was too rigid to work on the curved form of a car. 3M decided to sell the product anyway. But Drew kept thinking about it. He wanted to be able to make a tape that would be useful. He kept working on it even though it wasn't really his job.

His manager decided to look the other way and go with it for a while—to practice the managerial equivalent of the 1970s school of parenting called benevolent neglect—leaving children relatively unsupervised in a way that let them invent their own forms of play. One day, walking around the 3M offices, Drew happened to see some of the backing they used on their sandpaper and thought it would make a good flexible tape. Masking tape was born, as was the entire adhesives department of 3M, later to become the home of the storied Post-it note.

Drew's manager looked the other way and gave him the slack—the space, the time, the container—to explore. That act of looking the other way gave Drew a little patch of ground of studio time.

You can also look at the whole idea of 20 percent time—the corporate policy made famous by Google and embraced in various forms earlier by stalwarts of innovation like 3M and Hewlett-Packard—as a form of studio time. Those policies give employees a fraction of their working time to investigate projects of their own choosing—a significant picnic blanket in their time and energy landscape. The freedom that 20 percent time gives people to focus on process and not outcomes has led to a number of now-iconic breakthroughs. Those successes drive home the idea that anyone, not just a working artist, benefits from designated space and time to explore.

In one of the most famous examples of 20 percent time, Paul Buchheit, a Google engineer, designed Gmail and then created AdSense to pay for it. Buchheit had wanted to bring email fully onto the Internet since he was a student at Case Western in the 1990s. Taking advantage of Google's 20 percent time policy, Buchheit set to work. One of his previous programming jobs at Google had been to build a porn filter that would recognize certain forms of Google keyword search and conclude that they were pornographic.

In the same way that Fogarty would observe a pair of scissors that could be modified only slightly and used for eye surgery, Buchheit realized that his porn filter could be modified to recognize any kind of search term and match that term to targeted advertising. The adapted porn filter became AdSense, the program that pairs search terms to customized advertising messages, otherwise known as the backbone of Google's business model. AdSense made it possible for basic Gmail to be free for users by supporting itself on advertising. Buchheit's 20 percent time project led to a radically different and more generative business model for web-based mail than previous plans to charge for levels of storage space.

Buchheit never knew ahead of time that he would succeed. He only knew that he had some space and time to try. When he went to work for Google in 1999, no one could have accused him of having unrealistically high expectations. As he said, "I expected that [Google] would likely get squashed by the much larger Alta Vista, but the people were really smart, so I believed that I could learn a lot in the process."

There is no guarantee that some interesting project will come out of your studio time. You just show up to that patch of ground.

STARTING WITH CATEGORIES OF CREATIVITY

One way to get started on studio time is to choose an area of creative activity to focus on. Like Loehr and Schwartz's idea that we are all managing many forms of energy—mental, emotional, spiritual, and physical—we are all drawing on many forms of creative activity, playing more to some than others, finding a combination of them that works for us.

See if any of these categories prompt something that you're interested in exploring, or that you are deep into doing already.

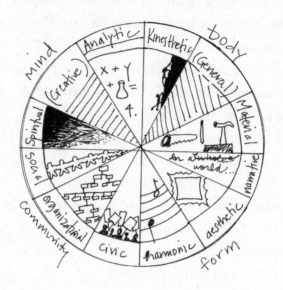

SOCIAL

The practice of friendship and the invention of play

The baseline of social creativity is just *showing up*, gathering people together in places, in conversation. My friend Sabrina—who originally proposed adding a list of categories to this book—hosts a craft night. My friend Jesse hosts Tinkerer's Club with his daughter and other father-daughter pairs. My friend Jennifer hosts a Ladies Drinking Club. Do you love to cook and have people over? Do you organize sports teams? Do you start a neighborhood garden?

ORGANIZATIONAL

Managing people, designing systems, running processes

In his 1962 book, *Strategy and Structure*, Alfred Chandler first described the M-form of corporation, a canonical structure of large firms. General David Petraeus reimagined the structure of military offensives. How can a task be better assigned or managed? How do all the pieces fit together? What is the best way to coordinate the parts? Are you extremely resourceful even designing the system by which you make a meal or schedule errands? Are you inventive in managing projects and figuring out how teams of people can work together to realize them?

CIVIC
The domain of civic involvement and social change

Occupy Wall Street reimagined activism as a process- and not agenda-based form. Bob Geldof worked with Midge Ure to found Band Aid in 1984 for famine relief, and later worked with Bono and others on the ONE Campaign. Then presidential candidate Barack Obama mobilized volunteers in 2008. How do you create change? How do you participate well? Does your everyday creative practice have an activist bent?

ANALYTIC
The domain of problem solving within constraints, the intersection of logic and ingenuity

Analytic creativity includes precision engineering, the scientific method, and many other means of designing experiments and making sense of the results. Many forms of academic research—whether in history or English, mathematics or chemistry—fall here, depending on the methodology. It may seem logical rather than creative to work under the scientific method but those methods also provide ways of knowing how to move forward in unexpected directions, for instance, to treat autoimmune diseases with steroids instead of antibiotics. There can be a great deal of creative resourcefulness in figuring out how to prove something within the constraints of a required method of research.

SPIRITUAL
The domain of religion and the cultivation of the self

Spiritual creativity involves the exploration of existential questions and forms of curiosity toward what the writer Milan Kundera called "the infinitude of the interior world." Practicing could include meditation, reading, being in nature, personal development, or organized religion.

Spiritual creativity easily overlaps with social and storytelling forms, but at its heart it entails the practice of balancing knowledge and belief, fact and trust, hope and despair, intention and acceptance, belonging and solitude, adherence and tolerance. That creative practice manifests in the pedicab driver in New York's Central Park who has paused from the fracas to place a rug down and pray toward Mecca. It shows up in the talk-show host Stephen Colbert's Sunday school teaching when he used to teach the sacraments using a *Jeopardy*-style tournament. It shows up in the interior life of the agnostic person wrestling with an idea of faith, or a faithful person wrestling with fact.

KINESTHETIC
The exploration of the body, in sports or dance or movement of any kind

When Tommy Caldwell and Kevin Jorgeson became the first freeclimbers to scale the Dawn Wall route up Yosemite National

Park's El Capitan in 2015, they found a pathway up an almost sheer rock face, choice by choice. Many forms of sports and outdoor exploration involve kinesthetic creativity. For many people the greatest creative space of the body is the intimate creative collaboration of sex. As Roger von Oech, the self-styled "Creativity Consultant of Silicon Valley," wrote in his 1983 self-help volume, *A Whack on the Side of the Head*, creativity is like sex for the brain. Relatedly, sex is like creativity for the body; dance too.

AESTHETIC

The purview of design, art, and other arrangements of form

Although associated with fine art, aesthetic creativity includes interior design, personal style, the formal arrangement of objects on a desk, or any other visual design task. Part of aesthetic creativity is spatial reasoning, and the compositional tools of line, shape, color, and form. Aesthetic creativity can seem like art for art's sake. But for two months around Valentine's Day in 2014, a postoperative nurse at New York Presbyterian Hospital cut all of the white gauze bandages for tiny laparoscopic incisions into the shape of hearts. Patients would wake up from surgery vulnerable, scared, and tired, and look at bellies or legs covered in tiny white hearts. Aesthetic creativity includes designing for joy, as in the case of the bandages, or for simplicity, as in the case of train timetables and elegant clocks.

PHYSICAL (MATERIAL)

The resourceful manipulation of materials

Material creativity is the domain of artists like Jackson Pollock flinging paint or Michelangelo extracting a figure from a block of marble, and also the domain of repairmen, plumbers, electricians, product designers, and seamstresses. Material resourcefulness allowed the Mars Curiosity Rover to land successfully on the surface of the planet in 2012. It invented the nearly indestructible Tyvek envelope. It extends to cooking onions with salt in a way that extracts their flavor. Do you have an obsession with understanding or realizing the raw capacity of materials—whether the nature of copper pipes, the give of fabric cut on the bias, or the properties of building materials made out of mushrooms?

NARRATIVE
The construction of stories about the past or future,
reality or fiction
Entertainment media—National Public Radio or the British Broadcasting Corporation or films and other television programs—as well as friends over dinner and the world of books all pull us through stories, but most of us are storytellers in some form. We make sense of past events, and tell stories of the future, through words or movement, writing or acting. As Harper Lee said of southerners generally in a 1962 interview with Roy Newquist, "I think we are a region of natural storytellers. . . . We simply entertained each other by talking."

HARMONIC
The domain of rhythm and cadence
Harmony governs music and dance, the patterns of spoken or written word and song. It is the part of language that pulls you along poetically, and the entire register of music.

IN PRAISE OF WORK IN PROGRESS

To work within any of these categories, how do you decide how much studio time to start with? Ask yourself in your life right now, how much time can you afford to lose? Look at the time you are already spending—say, on your commute. Or look at the parts of your life that constitute passive recovery, like watching television. Look at your work calendar and ask if a meeting that is weekly could be biweekly. Whatever that amount of time is—five minutes daily, two hours every other week—designate it as a studio time budget. Give yourself a "20 percent time project" for that period of time (regardless of whether the time is 0.001 percent or 20 percent of your week). You can delve into one of the creativity buckets above or simply invent some fun. You can learn a new recipe, host an event, devise a research project among your friends. How does it go? What do you learn from it? Does it make you want to keep going or to experiment with a different area?

The idea here is not to fix your calendar or to optimize it, but to borrow that time temporarily in the spirit of an experiment. Creative process is about the power of delving into uncharted territory, but working open-endedly may feel uncomfortable at first. You may feel silly or grip tightly to wanting the studio time to lead somewhere specific. While it would be great to invent the next Gmail or to immediately solve your most vexing problem in your studio time, you will need to park those visions of success in order to actually work toward them.

It can help to start with something you like for its own sake, and to take the attitude of experimentation.

During the time I was finishing this book, I took on a video class as a studio time project. I got to spend Monday evenings filming absurd but simple scenes with nice people I didn't know well, while learning to use a camera. I think we all felt exposed screening our films to the group. That is just a human experience of the vulnerability of work in progress. The spirit is to lean in and play through.

Studio time doesn't need to be exotic and foreign, the limited domain of the professional artist or the Silicon Valley tech worker. Whether it's a small DIY project or a grand research plan, the studio time mentality means choosing a project that interests you, large or small, and then giving yourself ritualized time and space to work on it. The time you spend is not a test but an experiment, a chance to learn and to do, not to succeed or to fail.

THE MYTH OF ARTISTIC GENIUS

Being an artist is not a rare earth element. Yet it's easy to hesitate because you think that you must start with a blank page and immediately create a masterpiece. Art exists on more of a continuum. That range may culminate in blank canvas masterpieces, if you are so inclined, but it also includes the recent phenomenon of adult coloring books. (A Scottish illustrator named Johanna Basford's 2013 adult coloring book, *The Secret Garden*, sold well over a million copies in its first two years. Some fans host "coloring circle" get-togethers with their friends.)

In the same way that you might walk your way into any other category governed by a platonic ideal, you can approach creative activity by ramping into the mythic category of the artist. Consider that even for professional artists there are many ways they spend their time—including filing, administration, scheduling, grant applications, stretching canvases, and otherwise preparing to make work.

In 1943 the social psychologist Abraham Maslow introduced a Hierarchy of Need to offer a theory of human motivation. Maslow's pyramid rises from basic needs for food and shelter through affiliation and achievement to the pinnacle of self-actualization. Creative activity can be mapped similarly, from the baseline work of copying through adaptation and synthesis, to the apex of whole-cloth creation of something from nothing.

Copying is a way of understanding and seeing, and a staple in the training of professional artists. From the mid-1600s to the mid-1800s, European men of means took the Grand Tour, traveling a circuit of important cities and landmarks to form a cultural awareness. Most of them learned by copying what they saw in museums. Copying is a form of looking closely to see how something was made, and understanding what cannot be copied easily, or only with great care.

Emulating is a form of copying not the letter but the spirit of something. It is a form of taking a pattern and adapting it. Laszlo Bock, the head of people operations at Google, specifically encourages people to emulate résumés that they admire.

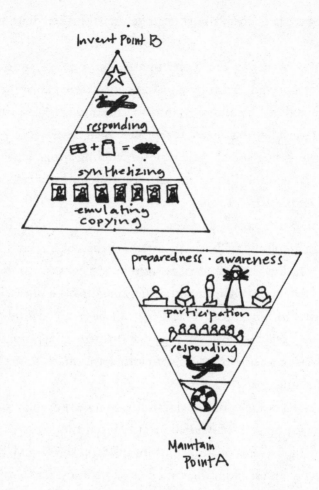

If imitation is the sincerest form of flattery, emulation is the sincerest form of praise—taking on board the pattern enough to make it your own, extending it from one use to another.

Synthesizing is a form of putting things from two different fields together. I always loved the 1980s television commercials for Reese's Peanut Butter Cups, with their Count-Chocula-meets-*Goonies* level of fright and comfort, and the punch-line moment when the baritone voice accuses, "Who put their chocolate in my peanut butter?" only to realize what a good combination it is. That is an act of synthesis. Whereas emulation involves taking an observation and adapting it to another use, synthesis involves combining two or more different things to form a unique third thing, a metaphorical Reese's Cup.

Responding means coming up with a new or novel solution—*in response to a situation that immediately calls out for it*. I have had countless conversations with people at all levels of organizations who say that it actually feels like an even bigger success to find a creative solution within deep constraints, than in a vacuum—to do something when you feel straitjacketed and in a bind, not from a moment of rest and Zen, blank-space equanimity. As we will see, sometimes the market is the constraint against which you are responding.

Blank-canvas creativity is whole-cloth creativity that is not in response to a given environment but in response to a question you set yourself. Working from the question or brief of your own making, is a form of, back to Maslow, creative self-actualization. Many creative acts will hit notes up and down this register of hierarchy.

What lands in blank-canvas creativity usually begins elsewhere. The Beatles got their start not with an original song but a 1961 rock adaptation of "My Bonnie Lies Over the Ocean." That version led their future manager, Brian Epstein, to discover them, which in turn led to job titles ending in "–mania."

If in doubt you can start with small, everyday acts of love—meals or gifts or ephemeral gestures. If you watch a road race like the New York City Half Marathon, the course is peppered with creative gestures of care. People have made things to cheer others on. One sign will say, "No Time for Walken," with a picture of the actor Christopher Walken. Ten feet down, a man will be standing nonchalantly waiting for his runner with a metal broomstick casually stuck down the back of his shirt at the top of which is affixed a letter-size, laminated photo of their bichon frise dog, a white furball of family pride. Whether you are prone to Christopher Walken puns or not, you can experiment with creative gestures of affection. In doing that, you raise the level of everyday life.

Or, as Buchheit did when creating Gmail, you can start to notice what bothers you and work on it:

> Start to notice every time you have to wait for something or every time you get slightly confused or aggravated with the product, every small annoyance . . . most of the things we put into Gmail were just, like, I was annoyed with something, and we would try to think of a solution for it.

Either way, you can think about different categories of creative activity as a brainstorming list for studio-time habits, and feel invited to ease your way in.

NOTHING IS WASTED

The secret to studio time is to realize that all of the parts come together as something greater than themselves. They contribute

to the whole, even if it's hard to see their contribution immediately. In 2014, Brené Brown, the shame and vulnerability researcher and author of *The Gifts of Imperfection* and *Daring
Greatly*, wrote a public letter to a student who was worried
about taking a job for the sake of working instead of following
her passion. Brown said:

> I live by the saying "Nothing is wasted." Your studies
> and that internship—combined with your passion—will
> serve you if you squeeze every ounce of learning from
> them. I may be a researcher, but I attribute a lot of my
> success to my years of bartending, waiting tables, and
> working the night shift in customer service, and to stints
> as a social worker and a teacher. These jobs taught me
> about empathy and human behavior.

For studio time, the time is never wasted because it is spent
learning and because it is a practice.

Whether that learning is immediately useful does not
mean that it will not be vital one day. Fogarty jumped out the
window to go fly-fishing long before he knew that his rules-
breaking hobby would produce the breakthrough in his medical invention. Doing what you love—following hobby interests
and passions—is never wasted. And following through on what
you have said you will do—finishing a difficult task or a long
slog well—is never wasted either.

The annals of invention are littered with stories of what appears to be wasted time. The Wright brothers were passionate
about inventing a "flying machine," but many of the tools that

let them do that came from their jobs running a bicycle shop in Dayton, Ohio. Had they not had that shop, or had they not read so much about the mechanics of flight while Orville was convalescing from typhoid fever, they might never have invented the flying machine.

On February 14, 1884, Theodore Roosevelt, who became the twenty-sixth president of the United States in 1901, learned that his wife and mother had both died that same day. Bereft, he took to nature and spent three years living on a ranch in what is now North Dakota. Compared to the current era, in which anyone with presidential ambitions seems loath to leave the Washington, D.C., beltway for more than three weeks unless actively governing a state or courting a donor, it is refreshing to see Roosevelt simply live his life, not plan his future ambition. When you consider that it was Roosevelt who, during his presidency, set aside 230 million acres of land for national parks, that time in the Dakotas was hardly wasted. (Nor was his time as a sickly child taxidermizing animals in New York City.)

It's easy for the same thing to happen in your own life. You do something for someone as a favor and years later that person helps you more than you could have imagined. It's not a transaction. It's not that you did the favor expecting it would come back in kind. It's that everything is part of the same ecosystem. Things appear in the periphery of your hopes and current projects like the seminal clue in a good murder mystery: All of a sudden the throwaway detail is central to unlocking the plot and what was almost unnoticed in the corner of your eye moves to center stage. Your view widens to take in a broader and more varied landscape of passions and pastimes, obligations and sore spots, and mistakes and false starts, any of which might actually turn out to be important.

While you are figuring out what you want to do, or how best to solve a particular problem, you can take solace in the fact that the sheer act of work is the engine of meaning. As Pope Francis says, "[W]ork has not only the economic objective of profit, but above all a purpose that regards man and his dignity." Work—whether literal employment or showing up presently in any area of your life—has dignity. Pope Francis himself worked as both a chemical lab technician and a nightclub bouncer before going to seminary in 1957.

Although work always has dignity, not every problem yields to direct effort. Writing about creative process in his "Ten Bullets for the WSJ," the artist Tom Sachs acknowledges that creative projects don't always bend to sheer acts of effort. They require direct work but also sometimes get solved unexpectedly. Here is his Bullet # 9:

> Procrastinate: If at first you don't succeed, give up immediately, move on to some other task until that becomes unbearable then move on again circling back around to the first problem. By now, your subconscious will have worked on it, sort of like sleep, only cheaper.

Countless creative projects get solved after you take a break. The work and the break are not morally separate. They are parts of a whole. Disrupting those boundaries between work and play is, as in the case of Fogarty, not just the means of moving from invention to invention but being curious and present in the exact moment in which you find yourself.

Research from fields as far apart as education, business, and neuroscience bears this out. The German neurologist Hans Berger was the first person, in 1929, to show that the brain is in a considerable state of activity even when the person appears to be resting. As brain imaging technology developed in the 1990s, fMRI (functional magnetic resonance imaging) studies were able to show pictures of this active brain at rest, by mapping blood flow through neural networks. These observations developed into a theory that the brain has a "default mode network," a constellation of activities that occur when the brain otherwise appears to be at rest. Those activities allow the brain to synthesize, settle, and corral what it has learned.

THE ANXIETY OF DOING NOTHING

Even when science proves that appearing to do nothing can actually be productive, there is still a considerable amount of anxiety to looking like you're not hard at work. There is comfort in being productive. You are moving things off your to-do list, which can also make you feel in control. Yet counterintuitively what your creative self really needs is rest and pause. It needs that empty space to stitch together all of the isolated parts of your experience into a meaningful whole.

In a 2012 paper called "Rest Is Not Idleness," by Mary Helen Immordino-Yang, Joanna A. Christodoulou, and Vanessa Singh in *Perspectives on Psychological Science*, the authors found that this default mode of settling and reflecting was actually foundational to the formation of the self. If you are too focused on having to accomplish tasks in the external world, you don't have time for the kind of "wakeful rest" and introspection needed to maintain the boundaries of being a person.

Translating the importance of rest into a workplace setting, Harvard Business School professor Leslie A. Perlow and a research assistant, Jessica L. Porter, conducted a multiyear initiative with workers at the Boston Consulting Group and published their results in 2009. The experiments were designed to give management consultants not just rest but predictably scheduled rest. In one group of consultants each team member would take a day off in the middle of the workweek. On another team, each person would agree not to check email or otherwise engage with work after six o'clock on a designated evening. After the initial anxiety—one of the teams had been intentionally chosen because they were in the middle of a high-stress, postmerger reorganization—the employees reported back feeling refreshed and better able to perform. The experiment also led to enhanced communication and trust. As of 2014, BCG had implemented "predictable time off" across thousands of project teams in more than seventy-five of BCG's offices around the world.

Many modern office settings spiral into 24/7 commitments in which workers are not needed all the time, but the possibility that you might be needed on short notice some of the time keeps you plugged in to checking email and generally being on call. Perlow's experiment showed the importance of the ritualized, predictable break. In 2014, Perlow followed up her study concerning the effect of breaks on individual performance and happiness with another study concerning the effect of coordinated breaks on the productivity and well-being of whole teams.

In global corporations where the sun never sets on an operating company, and in day-to-day cultures full of meetings and interruptions, she found that people were taking work home with them, even in cultures that only expected them to keep 9-to-6 hours. If the teams could sync up and take time off at the same time—in what Perlow called "enhanced productivity days"—the chance for coordinated rest improved the team's overall productivity significantly. The fact that these initiatives led to happier teams and employee retention indicates that taking a break nurtures and perhaps even repairs something fundamental to the humming engine of the brain.

THE BENEFITS OF NOT KNOWING

Not too far down the highway from the world headquarters of Google, in Mountain View, California, Dr. Fogarty now runs an innovation institute housed at the El Camino Hospital. He intentionally set up shop in a community hospital instead of a rarified academic research center because he wanted to stay grounded in what patients really need. As he says, "Patient first. Patient first. Patient first." The problems he works on now concern whole systems like the way doctors are trained as much as single devices like the balloon catheter. Fogarty says that when he and his team are discussing a complicated problem, he will ask someone who doesn't know anything about it to join them. It improves their conversation. Gathering people from many fields is an intellectual form of whole-life thinking. Inviting someone from another field is like holding the Elijah chair within the space of the conversation.

It's easy to forget how unsure the balloon catheter's success was when it first came into being, how brave the first surgeons who used it had to be, and how close the device came to not getting made. The creative work of getting the catheter manufactured and popularized in use wasn't just figuring out the device but putting it into the world through the channels of Fogarty's field: medical journals, device manufacturers, and surgeons.

It was Dr. Cranley, Fogarty's mentor, who first used the catheter in several successful procedures. Even still, Fogarty could not find a major medical journal that would publish their results or a company that would manufacture the device. Twenty firms turned him down before he found one that would.

There is something in Fogarty's path that is, as in any original and authentic story, not directly replicable. It is not a pattern to copy but a reminder of where to start. The starting point is to cultivate space for curiosity and observation, to let go of constantly needing a 1:1 work-to-solution ratio and to set aside space in which to explore. As Fogarty said of his early forays, "The fact is, I didn't know enough to know if it would or wouldn't work—that's one of the benefits of not knowing: you're not deterred and I think that's often how a lot of new things are tried." That was a long time ago for him now, his life a landscape of much older trees. Or as Fogarty himself put it, "The balloon catheter was so long ago, people think I'm dead. They think I'm Tom Fogarty's son."

The lesson is that art often comes less from a siloed sense of goal completion and more from the sum total of all of the areas of your life. The larger landscape of hills and valleys of working life needs to include pockets of space in which to tinker. What connects those parts of the landscape, latex to vinyl, is how attentively you show up to any given afternoon or set of years.

CHAPTER 2

In the Weeds

[A]ny life when viewed from the inside
is simply a series of defeats.

—George Orwell

In 1949, an unassuming twenty-three-year-old woman from Alabama dropped out of school and moved to New York. She found a cold-water flat on the Upper East Side and started working at a bookstore. The next year she found a job that paid double as a reservations agent for the airlines. She worked for several years for Eastern Airlines and then moved over to BOAC, which became British Airways. By most accounts she was shy and ordinary. She wore broken-in blue jeans and had a tomboy haircut. Said a friend, "We didn't think she was up to much. She said she was writing a book, and that was that."

After working for the airlines for ten years, that woman published the novel she had been working on. Her editor warned her not to expect much—maybe two thousand copies, which was how most debut novels performed. But then positive signs trickled in. In March, *Readers Digest* asked to publish a condensed version. And when the full book was officially released on July 11, 1960, it received a "summer storm" of high praise. Three weeks after its publication, the novel, *To Kill a Mockingbird,* joined the bestseller lists of the *Chicago Tribune* and the *New York Times.* In 1961, its author, Harper Lee, received the Pulitzer Prize.

In 1964, the radio announcer Roy Newquist interviewed Lee for his program *Counterpoint* on WQXR, New York.

Customarily conducting his interviews at the Plaza hotel, Newquist asked Lee variations on the questions he had asked 250 other writers about their career aspirations and "working philosophies." When he asked Lee what she had imagined would happen when her book was published, she replied, in what would become a famous quotation about her process:

> I never expected any sort of success with *Mockingbird*. I didn't expect the book to sell in the first place. I was hoping for a quick and merciful death at the hands of the reviewers, but at the same time I sort of hoped that maybe someone would like it enough to give me encouragement. Public encouragement. I hoped for a little, as I said, but I got rather a whole lot, and in some ways this was just about as frightening as the quick, merciful death I'd expected.

From the vantage point of 1964—and even more so now—it is possible to see how Harper Lee got from point A to point B, like pins on a map. But while she was working day in and day out in the 1950s, point B didn't yet exist. She did not have an aerial view of the path her life would take. She was in the weeds.

The second mindset of art thinking follows from this difference between the weeds and the aerial view. To inhabit the weeds of making something, you have to make friends with the creative vulnerability of not being done yet. If you are trying to do anything for the first time—bravely trying to switch jobs, find a spouse, start a company, pivot an idea, or even write a book—your experience is much more aligned with "sit[ting] down before a typewriter with [your] feet fixed firmly on the floor," as Harper Lee once joked when asked to describe her writing process, than with winning awards, as she did after the fact.

Reorienting your perspective to being comfortable and ultimately productive in the weeds requires three tools that all focus on process instead of outcome. First, you have to change how you think about judgment. You have to trade the judgment of a critic for the discernment of a maker. To embrace discernment, you will need to consciously defer judgment for periods of time as to whether the work is good or bad and instead ask yourself what is working and what could be better.

Second, you need to become slightly philosophical and skeptical about your own sense of what is good or bad. In actual fact, our judgments shape-shift over longer periods of time. What looks like success or failure now may seem like the opposite later, or turn out to have been a step along a path. Third, you have to build out a very immediate attentiveness to the present moment, a process that has similarities to mindfulness meditation. That focus on attentiveness will help you to stay in the headspace of simply making the work.

These tools will build your ability to inhabit the studio time of the last chapter, by making it easier to stay rooted in the process. If you succeed, your finished work may have a way of making itself look easier to do than it was. From the inside, you will, like Lee, have to discover the work step by step.

Being in the weeds is the essence of what it is to be an artist in any field. It is a process of trusting yourself absolutely, believing that if you can connect to your own authentic self and can show up wholeheartedly, you will create something of value—whether it fails or succeeds at different points along the way. The sheer act of trying is triumphant, and the success you ultimately find is often much greater than if you had tamped down your process with judgment along the way.

The vulnerability of not knowing is in fact the only portal through which breakthroughs occur. As Harper Lee wrote, in the character of Scout's father, Atticus, in *To Kill a Mockingbird*: "[R]eal courage is . . . when you know you're licked before you begin but you begin anyway and you see it through no matter what. You rarely win, but sometimes you do." Being in the weeds asks you to be a bit brave and optimistic, and also unwavering in choosing the questions you care to risk working on.

CREATIVE PROCESS VS. CREATIVE OUTCOME

In 1971, social psychologists Edward Jones and Richard Nisbett described a phenomenon they called the actor-observer bias. It illuminates the discrepancy between the weeds and the aerial view.

According to Jones and Nisbett, we tend to see our own behavior as circumstantial and other people's behavior as fixed. We are having a bad day, but you are a jerk. We are hurrying to pick up our child from school and must make a left-hand turn now. If you do the same thing, you are an awful driver. Our own behavior arises from the situation, and yours reflects your basic character. We are ourselves in flux and you are a fixed point. The actor-observer bias describes the mental gap between considering ourselves works in progress and considering everything else as a fully baked outcome.

It's easy to confuse beginnings and endings and to forget the false starts and mistakes along the way. When you see someone else's finished work, it is easy to want to compare it to your own work in progress. When you do that, it is almost impossible to start. You compare the song you are trying to write with the Beatles' finished album, not with the moment they too were scrawling lyrics on the back of a napkin. Recognizing the gap—between process and outcome, between the weeds of working on something and the aerial view of seeing its completion—helps you remember that the beginnings of most things are more likely to be clunky, scrappy, or seemingly unimportant. You can often tell a coherent story after the fact but that story is usually a construction.

I was once at a wedding that was so beautiful, the bride and groom so happy and in love, the toasts so sincere and effusive, that I told my friend I couldn't imagine anyone else falling more deeply in love than those two. He turned to me and said, "You know, she didn't go out with him the first time he asked." Creative process is similar.

In Harper Lee's case it would be very easy to arrange her biography on a preordained, linear path: Born April 28, 1926, Lee grew up in Monroeville, Alabama, a county seat with a striking resemblance to the town of Maycomb, in which *To Kill a Mockingbird* is set. Her father bore an uncanny similarity to the character of Atticus. Her high school English teacher mentored her. Truman Capote was her summertime next-door neighbor and close friend when she first moved to New York. Although Lee had never written anything besides student newspaper pieces before *To Kill a Mockingbird*, she had always loved language enough that her father had bought her and Capote a black typewriter they used to cart around everywhere.

When Lee transferred from a women's finishing school called Huntingdon College to the University of Alabama and started writing for *Rammer Jammer*, the campus humor magazine, her essays showed what in hindsight seemed a sophisticated handling of race relations. Lee also exhibited an original personality. She was a unique combination of sorority pledge and chain smoker who liked to wear men's pajamas and had a penchant for cursing. She was her own person, even in the land of the husband-hunting "Mrs. Degree." She was a witty, Tina Fey–like character of her time. It is possible to write that story, but only from the outside.

The plot of Lee's life turned on a curious event that arose from a disappointment. In 1956 Lee was not able to get enough time off from work to go home for the winter holidays, as was her habit, so she stayed in New York and celebrated Christmas with her friends Joy and Michael Brown. Joy was a ballerina and Michael was a composer of industrial musicals—large Broadway-level productions funded by companies like Electrolux in order to advertise their products.

The Browns had had a banner year financially. They and Lee didn't normally exchange more than token gifts. But after the Brown children finished unwrapping their presents, Joy and Michael pointed to an envelope that they had tucked into the evergreen tree. In it was a note telling Lee that they wanted to give her a year's salary so that she could work on her book.

As Lee wrote to a friend a few weeks later, "[T]hey don't care whether anything I write makes a nickel. They want to lick me into some kind of seriousness toward my talents, which of course will destroy anything amiable in my character, but will set me on the road to a career of sorts. . . . Aside from the *et ceteras* of gratefulness and astonishment I feel about this proposition, I have a horrible feeling this will be the making of me. . . ."

Even then, Lee still had to get an agent and an editor and then completely rewrite an earlier manuscript that we now know became part of a separate book, *Go Set a Watchman*. Writing *To Kill a Mockingbird* had so many ups and downs that there was one day when Lee threw the manuscript out of the window in frustration. She called her editor, Tay Hohoff, who coaxed her into putting on her galoshes, going outside in the snow, and retrieving the pages.

At any point in the story, Lee was busy making the work itself. She was not privy to her future mythology.

JUDGING VS. DISCERNING

When you are engaged in early-stage creative work, there are two different forms of evaluating the work—judgment and discernment. At its best, judgment is an act of understanding and making sense of the work. But it is also a form of reducing the work to "good" or "bad." Judgment turns you from an actor into an observer. To move forward as the creator of the work yourself, you need the subtler tools of discernment. Where judgment is a fixed, moment-in-time evaluation of success, discernment is a process of figuring out what is working or not working. If judging is a process of labeling, discernment is a process of learning.

One place you can see this role of discernment in very early-stage work is at Google X, the research incubator within Google. Ricardo Prada, a Ph.D. psychologist, leads the central design team for Google X on the Mountain View campus of Google's world headquarters. Ricardo is a mild-mannered and thoughtful researcher who radiates humility and kindness and whose job requires him to make sense of the viability of seemingly sci-fi projects years before they come to market. When a news outlet first unveils a project like a self-driving car that seems mind-bendingly futuristic, Ricardo's team first saw the idea years before. His team of designers, developers, and researchers has the responsibility for what are both potentially world-changing and also commercial products. They are asked to consider whether to take those projects on at such an early stage that the possibility of their point-B success feels genuinely abstract.

To bring those ideas into the world as actual products, they need a high degree of conversational discernment. Their job necessarily involves evaluation. Because they can't work on everything, they do have to say "no" to some. Yet they are also not static critics, simply labeling things as good or bad. As Ricardo said, "It's better than nothing but it's not very helpful to tell people if an idea is good or bad. It's better to say, it's bad here, and here's how you fix it. Or, you know, it's great here, and this is what would make it even better." This process of discernment can be terribly analytic, the product of research, but it is also fundamentally human. Ricardo may parse spreadsheets or rely on social science methods, but ultimately, his team is a group of human beings navigating the weeds.

A core piece of this difference between judgment and discernment mirrors the research Carol Dweck, the Stanford University social psychologist, has done on the difference between a "learning" mindset and a "fixed" one. Dweck found that those with a learning mindset were not frustrated by failure, because they saw failure as a process of teaching themselves something. In contrast, people with fixed mindsets saw failure as a referendum on their intelligence. Those with a fixed mindset believed that by arranging their lives like a lily-pad jump from success to success, never tarnished by failure, they would constantly reinforce their self-concept as smart. The learners were not labeling something as good or bad, but taking it in as information and synthesizing the experience.

Whatever creative project you are working on, it isn't a test of your intelligence or fundamental goodness. It's an exploratory process of making something, and then making it better. The average working environment makes it hard to cultivate that learning mindset, especially if you feel like your intelligence or fundamental ability is being constantly evaluated. If you are continually asked to account for your work, it is easy to get defensive or paralyzed. Judgment certainly has a role in the workplace but ideally foremost at points of entry—when you decide to hire someone, to take on a project, or to agree to a merger.

In the short term, the engine that will take you out of the tire spin of defensiveness or paralysis is curiosity. As long as you are working hard, try to give yourself permission to be more curious than absolutely correct at any point in time. How to set up that kind of culture is a theme we will return to later in this book.

One way to ask yourself if you are judging or discerning is to picture yourself as a painter. If you are at an easel, you can either stand close enough to put a brush on the canvas or back up far enough away to see what the whole picture looks like. There is usually no way to do both at the same time. Most artists' studios have an ancient armchair somewhere. You can sit there and take in the work, or you can be making it. Both are important. Sitting in the armchair helps you discern what is working. But if you sit in the chair too much you won't get anything done.

Leonardo da Vinci included in his famous notebooks his advice to other painters on this practice of toggling between

discernment and making. In one passage, Leonardo wrote, "If you stay doggedly at the work you will deceive yourself." What he meant by that was that if you keep working without stepping back you will not be able to know what you have made. He recommended that painters keep a flat mirror nearby so that they could stop working periodically and hold up the mirror to see their composition in reverse. By seeing it flipped left to right, they would be shocked out of familiarity and be able to perceive the strengths and weaknesses in the work. What Leonardo is conveying is the necessary balance of standing at the easel and sitting in the armchair, of making the work and seeing how it is going.

Notice that he is not saying you should stand back to know immediately if the work is good or bad. His primary counsel

is toward awareness. In the case of making a painting, or met-
aphorically in the case of another project, you simply need to
be able to see what you have made. Observation is the crux of
discernment. Wanting to skip past observation to judgment is a
form of racing to the end instead of staying in the weeds.

Art is already intimately linked to observation: To draw
something is to really see it. Kenneth Clark—the British art
historian perhaps best known for the BBC *Civilisation* series
but also the author of particularly influential books about
Leonardo da Vinci in the 1930s—wrote of Leonardo, "It is
often said that Leonardo drew so well because he knew about
things; it is truer to say he knew about things because he drew
so well." The artist draws in order to see, and sees in order
to draw. Discernment connects the act of observation—true,

detailed, insatiably curious observation—with the act of making work. As Clark also wrote of Leonardo, he was "undoubtedly the most curious man who ever lived." Again, that curiosity becomes the engine of discernment that drives the process forward.

At any moment in your workday, interacting with a group of people or working on a solo project, are you sitting in the armchair or standing at the easel with a brush? Can you identify moments of feeling glued to the chair, or can you picture people who put a brush to other people's canvases? Are you able to stand at the canvas, figuratively speaking, without feeling like someone is staring over your shoulder evaluating as you go? The most ideal state of being in the weeds is to simply be in the work itself, and to back up often enough to see what that work is. What have I really made? How can I make it better?

One of the most important reasons to avoid judgment is that it is too blunt-nosed a tool for early-stage work that needs protection. As Ed Catmull, one of the founders of Pixar, writes:

Originality is fragile. And, in its first moments, it's often far from pretty. This is why I call early mock-ups of our films "ugly babies." They are not beautiful, miniature versions of the adults they will grow up to be. They are truly ugly: awkward and unformed, vulnerable and incomplete.

But the natural impulse is to compare the early reels of our films to finished films—by which I mean to hold the new to standards only the mature can meet. Our job is to protect our babies from being judged too quickly. Our job is to protect the new.

Protecting the new doesn't mean championing mediocre work but practicing discernment with rigor and generosity. The rigor is in holding high standards no matter how far the early work is from meeting them. The generosity is in holding on to optimism toward what is possible, and skepticism that what you see now is all there is.

The idea of generosity is worth meditating on. Generosity is not usually part of the corporate strategy lexicon, to say the least. When I teach business to artists, I often tell them that they are asked to be generous, to put something out there before they get something back. Creative work in any field asks you to risk offering something first.

The generosity required to put something out there is not just toward the market or the audience. It is also toward yourself and your colleagues. You will mess something up and so will they. Wesley ter Haar, the founder of Media-Monks, a global digital production studio started in Amsterdam, said that he notices that the managers who work under him are often less forgiving of mistakes than he, the CEO, is. He said he reminds the managers that when they started years before, they were not any better than the person who may have made a mistake. Paradoxically, being generous and maintaining optimism about what is possible can actually be signs of being at the top of one's field. Excellence is the steady base of humanizing patience that comes from having trekked through weeds from the front of the pack.

You can also absorb a lot about the learning mindset from watching people who have received prizes and awards as they begin work on new projects. When I spoke to the writer Anthony Doerr for another part of this book, he had just received the Pulitzer Prize for his novel *All the Light We Cannot See*. Gracious and honored, he was also philosophical. He said he doesn't necessarily love that book any more than the four he wrote before it and that his job is always to sit down at his desk and start the next one. Every time, he has to risk that the story might crash in halfway through, and he doesn't know at the start whether that will happen or not. He also doesn't know at the end of writing how the work will be received. Anyone launching a product or a company is in the same position.

We all have our tools for managing the chaos and unpredictability of the human experience. Doerr's is to come up with an outlandish storyline. He tries to start with something ridiculous to take the pressure off. Of *All the Light We Cannot See*, he said, "It's about a blind girl and a Nazi boy. They don't even meet until page [redacted—spoiler alert]!"

In your own life, you want to be able to notice the inflection points—awards, raises, promotions, smaller successes—when you could easily camp out in the rest stop of the fixed mindset, sitting on your laurels, paralyzed by judgments, however positive. In those moments, you still want to choose a discerning mindset. You want to choose the next thing. Your ongoing success depends on it.

DEFINING A GRACE PERIOD

One of the best ways to embrace discernment is to actively decide to defer judgment to the future. You can acknowledge that at some point you will want to know if something is good or bad, but you can allow yourself to do it later. Procrastinate on judging. Stretch out the making by defining a grace period.

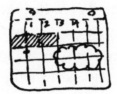

Think of the big looming task that you feel you must fix or complete or solve perfectly. What amount of time could you bracket before you have to do any of that? It could be thirty minutes or a year. Let's say I have a graduate student who feels she must figure out her career path all at once. The questions and decisions are absorbing and feel urgent. But the truth is, she probably doesn't really need to know anything for the next two weeks—or even the next few months—and definitely not in the next two hours. If she can give herself that time to be in the weeds, she can temporarily untether from the need for an outcome and use that time to set up a process of learning.

Once she figures out her grace period, she can design a research plan for herself. Instead of staying in the judgmental space of thinking, "Do I know yet? What is the answer?" she can ask herself what she needs to know in order to make a decision and then how she can go about getting that information.

In that particular case, there are conversations she needs to have, questions she needs to ask herself, and research she can do. Most likely, her career will arise from that process of inquiry itself. By not trying to jump to the end, she is giving herself ways of staying at the easel of her own decision instead of sitting in the armchair hoping it will all come together.

What happens when you start any kind of project with a grace period before any goals? In 1901, Wilbur Wright said, "Man will not fly for fifty years." Then he and his brother flew four trials, from 120 to 852 feet—on December 17, 1903, only two years later. Believing the end point is far out into the future can be freeing. It can give you space to explore. While it's true that deadlines create a crucible in which work gets done, it is also true that deadline pressure for open-ended work can sometimes cause you to deliver just to the minimum acceptable standard. If someone had told the Wright brothers that they had to fly by 1905, they might have made a glider instead.

The strategy of defining a grace period can be complementary to the "minimum viable product" approach popularized by the lean start-up movement. Described by Eric Ries in his book *The Lean Startup*, the minimum viable product is the scrappiest version of a product possible. Building an MVP can be a tremendous tool for testing and refining an idea. But you want to exercise care that in building an MVP, you don't make something of a different type all together—a glider and not a plane. To be sure, the Wright brothers prototyped and tested flying craft. But they allowed themselves to fail in service of trying for their bigger objective of building a plane. In rounds of testing and prototyping you may still need to consciously protect the space of exploration and invention, not just staged execution.

An artist friend Corinna once told me that when she has been away from the studio for a while, all of the things she wants to work on appear in her mind like grand plans. But, when she is actually working, the sensation of being in the studio feels more like pottering around. Moving the deadline is a way of giving yourself productive space to experiment and to learn. Deferring judgment lets you potter.

BASE CAMP VS. EVEREST

Over longer periods of time, it is easy to find that our judgment is actually pretty fallible and that what we thought was good or bad turns out to be the opposite.

Elvis Presley failed music class and also got fired from the Grand Ole Opry after one performance. Oprah Winfrey got fired from an early job as a television anchor. Fred Smith got a C on the term paper at Yale that laid out the ideas for what would become Federal Express. Michael Jordan got cut from his high school's varsity basketball team. Dr. Seuss's first book got rejected twenty-seven times. In response to his first screen test, Fred Astaire received the note, "Can't sing. Can't act. Slightly balding. Can dance a little."

Stephen King's first book, *Carrie*, got rejected by thirty different publishers. To the extent that receiving external judgment makes it easy to judge yourself too, it's not surprising that King got discouraged and threw the *Carrie* manuscript away. His wife fished it out of the trash. Similarly, when publishers were evaluating Dr. Seuss's first manuscript, for *To Think That I Saw It on Mulberry Street*, a future with *The Cat and the Hat* or *Green Eggs and Ham* may have been hard to see. Like Harper Lee's life story, it is easier to connect the dots later. Art thinking requires an acceptance of failure or rejection but also a realization that what feels like a win or loss can be part of a much longer process.

When you are in the weeds of building something, it is especially easy to mistake success and failure, or to misestimate the degree of each. When Paul Buchheit, the originator of Gmail, recalled his early days at Google, he said, "I remember when it was a tiny startup that nobody had heard of, and I had to explain to people that it was like Yahoo minus all of the features other than search. People would just give me this sad look that seemed to say, 'I'm sorry you can't get a real job.'"

In 1915, Winston Churchill was forced to step down from his post as the First Lord of the Admiralty. That is when he took up painting as a hobby, writing the essay *Painting as a Pastime*. Although he held various governmental posts, he had no idea that he would become First Lord of the Admiralty again in 1939 and the next year become prime minister and unofficial savior of the free world during World War II. It would have been easy for Churchill to have felt like he failed, or to have catastrophized and assumed that the failure was permanent. In Churchill's own words, you never know what will be your "finest hour." What might seem an Everest peak is really a base camp. Or, as in Churchill's case, what seems like a sudden fall down a sheer face is a minor loss of footing on a much larger path.

Even when the moments later become enshrined as Everest ascents, there is no memo identifying when they will occur in anyone's life: Alexander Graham Bell invented the telephone at age twenty-nine. Ruth Handler designed the first Barbie doll at age forty-three. Louise Bourgeois received her first major museum exhibition as a sculptor in her seventies. Before he became a brilliant screenwriter, Aaron Sorkin was a failed actor. Babe Ruth was a failed actor too. Raymond Chandler only started writing crime novels in his forties, after he was fired as an oil company executive. When David Seidler won an Oscar for *The King's Speech* at age sixty he said, "My father always said to me I would be a late bloomer."

Whole companies can be in the weeds too. If you had evaluated the success or failure of the 3M Corporation shortly after it was founded, you would have seen a group of people who realized that they had bought an entire mine in Minnesota containing the wrong mineral and that they would have to find another way to make sandpaper. When the company's stock was first offered to the public in April 1901, it was priced at $10 per share. By late 1904, its price on the "barroom exchange" was "two shares for a shot, and cheap whiskey at that." You would not have known then that the company would still exist more than a hundred years later, let alone that it would be trading on the New York Stock Exchange at an $80 billion market cap.

In October 2008, U.S. credit markets tightened suffocatingly in the wake of the demise of Lehman Brothers and the onset of a global financial crisis. To search for financial transactions would make you a surfer on a waveless sea. Thomas L. Friedman wrote an editorial in the *New York Times* encouraging banks to take some risks so that credit markets would not dry up completely. Banks had a responsibility to respond to the capital-raising needs of companies that had good fundamentals but that had not yet succeeded.

Friedman asked what would happen if two guys in T-shirts walked into a bank, circa 1998, to ask for a loan for something called a "search engine" that they had named "Google." "They tell you to type any word in this box on a computer screen and—get this—hit a button labeled 'I'm Feeling Lucky.' Up comes a bunch of Web sites related to that word." Friedman tried to persuade bankers not to unfairly compare every early-stage company asking for a loan to its late-stage equivalent—not, as Catmull said of Pixar films, to hold the fledgling Google to the standards that only the adult Google could meet.

The weeds are universal. Everything we see now had an earlier incarnation in which it was in the weeds. Every person you know almost wasn't. Every couple had to meet sometime. With some exception, every person had a job interview for what they do currently. What was the first job of the CEO of the largest firms internationally? What was the first job of the person you most admire? The world itself has only had longitude, latitude, and a common clock set off the prime meridian for about 150 years. All the things we can take for granted were once invented—the phone, the Internet, Coca-Cola. Even technologies we have moved beyond—the eight-track, the cassette tape, the Walkman—were once in the weeds too.

You could spend a day or an entire lifetime picturing all of the adults you encounter now as they might have been as children, or imagining what was on the land you inhabit three hundred or fifty or five years ago. The majestic island of Manhattan is, in significant part, a landfill. Boston is as much a history of landfill projects as rebellion by the colonies. London used to have six tons of soot per square mile of fog cover, along a river that was an open sewer. Wherever you live, was the shopping center a meadow or a landfill? What layers of life have happened in the places you spend time?

Teaching business, I am always stunned and heartened at how for every casual spreadsheet tool in use today, there is a paper or a book from tens or hundreds of years ago, laying it out as a brand-new idea. Remembering that those ideas were once invented gives you more space for creative maneuverability in your own thinking.

Half of the battle is remembering that other people are in

the weeds too. The other half is cultivating a meditative aware-ness toward the impermanence of the process and an ability to keep going. The key to being in the weeds is not necessarily to do anything differently but to think about it differently. No matter how together other people look from the outside, they are there too. And if they aren't in the weeds they are probably stuck. Being in the weeds is being alive.

GOOD NOTICING!

The poet Mary Oliver once wrote: "This is the first, the wildest and the wisest thing I know: that the soul exists and is built entirely out of attentiveness." Poetically speaking, attentiveness is the composition of the soul; economically it is the scarcest resource we have.

Attentiveness is the engine of productivity when inhabiting the weeds. It is what anchors your ability to stay in the work itself and not want to skip immediately to the end. Being in the weeds can make you feel antsy. It is hard to stay with the work when you are not positive where it is going. Yet staying at the easel is the only way the work can possibly get made. Atten-tiveness is what keeps you there.

In 1974, the Buddhist monk Thich Nhat Hanh was asked in a letter from a staff member at a Vietnamese school to ex-plain what meditation was. Thich Nhat Hanh had founded the school—the School of Youth for Social Service—in the 1960s to teach "engaged Buddhism." The graduates would go into the field and attempt to reconcile warring factions using practices of compassion. Their methods were misunderstood, and some of the Buddhists were kidnapped and killed. Thich Nhat Hanh was in exile in France when he received the letter. His long letter back, simple and warm, was translated by Mobi Ho and published as a book called *The Miracle of Mindfulness*.

In one particularly relevant passage, Thích Nhât Hạnh writes, "There are two ways to wash dishes. The first is to wash the dishes in order to have clean dishes and the second is to wash the dishes in order to wash the dishes." Attentiveness is the practice of washing the dishes to wash the dishes—to commit with wholeheartedness and curiosity to the part where you stand at the sink with soapy hands instead of driving single-mindedly toward the future in which the dishes are clean.

The term "mindfulness" itself can put some people off. In the words of Dan Harris, the ABC reporter who chronicled his own forays into meditation in *10% Happier*, the field has "a towering PR problem, largely because its most prominent proponents talk as if they have a perpetual pan flute accompaniment." For some people, "meditation" can sound like its own orthodoxy—that there is a right way to do it and that if you do it the right way, it will lead to definite and earnest benefits—all of which is antithetical to the actual ideas of mindfulness itself.

I think of mindfulness in terms of some old-fashioned advice on manners. In 1926, Lady Troubridge wrote in *The Book of Etiquette*, "[A] true knowledge and understanding of social laws will indicate when they can be put aside with impunity in obedience to some greater law, such as the law of kindness, should a special occasion indicate that politeness will be better honoured in the breach than in the observance." If you are sitting next to someone and they accidentally drink out of their finger bowl, the correct response is not to tell them what they have done but to drink out of your finger bowl too, because the purpose of manners is not to enforce rules but to put people at ease. Similarly, the purpose of mindfulness is not to enforce the rigidity of meditating well—itself an oxymoron—but to create a habit of intention that you can return to. The spirit of the practice is more important than the rules.

What I will call attentiveness, but you could call mindfulness, is a form of being awake and being yourself at the same time. In that way, it is a helpful tool for staying rooted despite the vulnerabilities of being in the weeds.

Attentiveness can be a porous practice, a form of play and showing up. Like the Elijah chair from the last chapter, it is a way of holding space. Your meditative practice may be taking a break to play sports, or taking a short moment to clear your head. A primary care physician, Christopher Schultz, said that his meditation is rowing. But then he pointed to a bottle of medical-grade hand sanitizer and said if he spent thirty seconds staring at that bottle, he would feel focused and calmer too. That moment of pause represents the act of being and not doing. It represents seeing and accepting things as they are, even if the reality isn't great. That pause creates a stability and openness from which creative flexibility can develop, helping you to access your fuller capacity while not yet knowing exactly where you are going.

In the past decade, mindfulness practice has sprung up all over corporate America. Companies that promote meditation by offering classes or whole programs include Apple, Nike, Google, Target, McKinsey, Deutsche Bank, General Mills, Goldman Sachs, and HBO. Mark Bertolini, the chairman and chief executive of the health insurance company Aetna—one of the hundred largest companies in America—started offering mindfulness meditation classes as one of a number of changes he made after surviving a near-death skiing accident in 2004.

In the past several years, thirteen thousand of Aetna's employees have participated in yoga and meditation classes. Because Aetna is in the health-care business, the company started studying the effects of meditation experimentally. They divided 239 volunteers from the Aetna workforce into three groups: one doing yoga, one taking mindfulness class, and one a control group. After three months, the workers who had stuck with either yoga or mindfulness meditation showed marked decreases in their perceived stress levels.

In January 2015, Bertolini decided to increase the company's minimum wage from $12 to $16 per hour. He credited his decision to Thomas Piketty's *Capital in the 21st Century*. He also attributed his ability to take the creative managerial risk to his own experience of meditation.

In the late 1980s, a psychologist named Marsha Linehan adopted mindfulness to the framework of cognitive behavioral therapy (CBT) in a way that supports attentiveness and also loops back to your relationship with judgment. Linehan's framework, dialectical behavioral therapy (DBT), engages mindfulness to uncover distortions in patterns of thought—for instance, generalizing from one event to predict pervasive doom—and then uses tools of cognitive behavioral therapy to retrain the mind.

One starting point of the mindfulness side of this practice is a habit called "good noticing," in which you take whatever is happening—in your life, in your work, in your studio time, in your weedy explorations—and validate it by commending yourself for noticing it. No matter how disappointing the news, "good noticing!" orients you toward intimacy with your own experience. Instead of resisting things by wishing they were otherwise or getting fidgety with process and wanting to skip to the outcome, it is a way of giving yourself positive reinforcement simply for being engaged attentively in the work itself. In the language of mindfulness guru Tara Brach, "good noticing" is a practice of "radical acceptance" of whatever is happening.

The truth is that most creative process is steeped in failure, and that's okay. You are likely to work on something for a long time and then realize one day—good noticing!—that it is not working and you need to scrap it and start over. Not enough people talk about how important it is to be able to do that. Leaving things on the cutting room floor is as important as putting them in the movie. Being in the weeds requires you to be able to go all in on whatever you are working on, and then, if you need to, to change direction and keep going.

You can start to notice these threads of attentiveness and

playing through in the practice of many leading creative think-ers. Norman Lear, the legendary television writer and pro-ducer, describes his mental habit of work as "over and next." From the outside—we know that Lear created phenomenally successful shows, like *All in the Family* and *The Jeffersons*, that changed the larger culture, and television itself. On the aerial view of television history, Lear is like the incandescent city you can see from the window of the airplane. But Lear the person, like any of us, had to work through the weeds. He has pro-duced megahits and also shows that were canceled after sev-eral episodes. He will tell you what he loved about the shows that got canceled. One of his daughters, Kate, described him as someone who "walks through life's peaks and valleys with equal wonder."

Lear describes his own internal compass like this:

When something, however great it was, is over, it wants to be OVER without regret, because immediately avail-able is NEXT. Reflecting on this later, I imagined a bulg-ing hammock between Over and Next, and realized: that is where the struggle to live in the moment resides.

That bulging hammock is the space in which the work actually happens. It is the place you try to find to just explore and make.

The key takeaway to being in the weeds is to make friends with your own thoughts. "Good noticing!" helps you make friends with your thoughts by validating them. The improv comedy habit of saying "yes, and" and never "no" in the middle of a scene can also help. By agreeing to stay with whatever your thoughts are—by validating them with "good noticing" or building on them with "yes, and"—you treat your thoughts like that tricky relative who becomes easier to deal with the less you judge and the more you let them be. Trying to avoid a thought just makes it sticky. And sticky thoughts—even positive ones—can clog your ability to move forward.

Ultimately, making friends with your thoughts means directing a discerning mindset, instead of a judging one, toward your thoughts themselves—to see your thoughts as opportunities to learn, not observations set in stone. Over time, the internal soundtrack that says this is terrible or this is great gets parked on a bench so that you can simply keep going.

THE LONG ARC

A last tool for being in the weeds is to reverse-engineer your perspective on them by taking a successful event and unfurling it over its longer arc of creation. You see the successful outcome—like Paul Buchheit's process of building the Gmail platform discussed in the last chapter—and unwind it to see the everyday, weedy moments on the way there. As Buchheit's Google colleague Chris Wetherell described it, "Can you imagine working on it for two years?" . . . "No daylight. Very little feedback. Many [interface] iterations, many. Some so bad that people thought, 'This will never launch, this is the worst thing ever.'"

A large and complex event like the New York City Marathon similarly unfurls back to its early weedy days. In 2015, the New York City Marathon hosted almost 50,000 runners, along with more than 1 million spectators, 10,000 volunteers, and 175 New York Road Runners staff. The event used more than 60,000 gallons of water and 30,000 gallons of sports drink, and donated 207,000 pounds of discarded clothing to Goodwill.

If you rolled the race back to 1976, the first year the marathon was run through all five boroughs of New York City, it would look something like this: There were 2,000 runners including the actor James Earl Jones's father, Robert, age seventy-one, and Diana Nyad, who would go on to swim from Cuba to Florida in 2013.

You would have seen Bill Rodgers, then three-time winner of the Boston Marathon, cross the finish line wearing borrowed soccer shorts because he had left his racing kit at home. You would also see Rodgers borrow a hundred dollars from Fred Lebow, the marathon founder, to get his car out of the impound lot because it had been towed during the race. You would have seen all the runners complete new registration forms, because the original forms were kept hostage after the man handling a then newfangled computer registration system got kicked out by his girlfriend and she refused to return them. You would have seen Lebow pick up Frank Shorter, the Olympian, at the airport, personally, in Lebow's Fiat X19.

If you rolled the event back even further, to the first marathon in 1970, when it was just laps of Central Park, you would have seen a firefighter named Gary Muhrcke win a ten-dollar wristwatch and an old bowling trophy. And rolling it back even further, you would have seen Lebow run his own first marathon—Cherry Hill in the Bronx in 1970—kitted out like everyone else "in some crazy looking Long Johns and a turtleneck," getting handed not water by race organizers but a cup of bourbon by a random spectator on almost every lap.

The snapshot moments of being in the weeds come together to form a movie of a developing idea—one foot in front of the other over a very long arc.

FAILING ON THE WAY TO SOMEWHERE ELSE

Along the way, you may technically fail at what you set out to do and succeed at something else. When I was researching Harper Lee's story for this book, I traveled to her hometown of Monroeville, Alabama. It was the May weekend when the town was, as it does every year, staging a production of *To Kill a Mockingbird* on the lawn next to the courthouse that anchors the town square. The trip was to be a life adventure I fondly referred to as "stalking Harper Lee"—until I learned that to do that even jokingly required serious A game: The last person to do it had moved in next door. In contrast, my level of investment was calling ahead and talking to a woman named Dawn at the local historical society, losing her phone number, realizing this town of 6,400 was home to three Dawns, and lucking into meeting her again because she ran the lemonade stand outside the courthouse.

If the goal of the trip was to meet Harper Lee, I failed. But what happened instead is that I had an unexpected experience of the town. They gave me the gift of participation.

Instead of meeting Harper Lee, say, in the cereal aisle of the Piggly Wiggly, I got to hang out with "Doc," the local veterinarian who played the character of Mr. Cunningham in the play of *To Kill a Mockingbird* in the town square. I got to stand with him and his fellow actors as they congregated "backstage" around a dark green trash can—a lattice-covered wood square—that doubled as a bar. We shared a tipple of Southern Comfort before they went onstage. The second night of the play, I got to be an extra, wearing a bonnet and riding through a scene in the back of a Model-A Ford pickup. I also got to attend the Methodist church picnic, to take a nap on the sofa of Dawn of the lemonade stand who became my friend, to have lunch in a farmhouse and stroll through pastureland with one of Truman Capote's cousins, and to meet the bank manager who played Atticus, the policeman who played Boo Radley, and two girls who played Scout.

Like any life adventure or creative process, this was all happening within the rhythms of everyday routines—from driving from my motel past the Wal-Mart they called Wally World, to watching Dawn run out of ice and have her wry, aspiringly gallant friend joke, "The worst thing about losing the city council election was giving up the key to the ice machine." All that is to say, I failed at what I set out to do but what actually happened was so much more interesting.

Any sincere attempt may stay in obscurity and never lead to a significant outcome. As is true for the lifelong lab scientist, it is noble simply to confirm that an area of exploration is a dead end. That entire career doesn't look very different from the sloggy, pre-breakthrough years of the person who does discover something new. To boot, if the breakthrough moment does happen, it easily starts to look like a foregone conclusion. The brain's dislike for cognitive dissonance, the human struggle for coherence, makes it tempting to think that whatever happened was always going to. Of course Harper Lee the obscure person in 1955 would become Harper Lee the famous author in 1961.

Taking the risk of working on a project that does not have a proven solution is a frontier in the business world. It is tempting to go for incremental improvement instead. The sure small win can be the enemy of the big gain. Asking big questions entails risk but can also lead to somewhere unexpected. Buckminster Fuller once said, "How often I found where I should be going only by setting out for somewhere else."

Only by changing our relationship to judgment and process can we open up that space of possibility—not all of the time but some of the time. For each of us as a metaphorical athlete, it is that capacity for openness and flexibility that makes our strength powerful.

Once you accept the advantages of being in the weeds—or the simpler reality that that's just where we happen to be no matter what—the next choice becomes how to navigate. In the weeds, your greatest navigational tool is the lighthouse of a question that pulls you forward.

CHAPTER 3

To the Lighthouse

Failure is as exciting to watch as success,
provided the effort is absolutely genuine and complete.

—Sir Roger Bannister, *The First Four Minutes*

The art thinking framework has so far begun with zooming out to see the whole. Within that larger landscape, patches of studio time have given you space to work on open-ended creative projects. That kind of work can feel weedy from the inside, vulnerable and uncertain and hard to parse within the structured, performance-driven cultures of working life. Even if you make peace with that uncertainty and manage to cultivate deep Cirque du Soleil–level flexibility about the fallibility of your own ability to judge work in progress, how do you decide what to work on? How do you make your way into the starting blocks for a process of inventing point B?

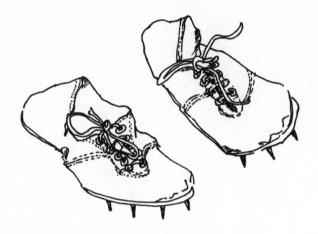

Art thinking by its nature is question oriented, not solution based. It is about raking possibility forward. It moves like a wave, not like an arrow. (If you pause to consider it, a wave is far more powerful than an arrow.) Leading from questions is the crux of art as a process. Business optimizes; art asks. Business hits the target; art invents the world in which the target exists.

In that context, a story of athletic achievement can actually fall on the art side. The feat can come from a question of possibility and opens up a world, only to be bested shortly thereafter.

On May 6, 1954, at Iffley Road track at Oxford University, Roger Bannister became the first person in modern recorded history to run a mile in under four minutes. Bannister was not a professional athlete but a trainee neurologist who ran his workouts on his lunch breaks. At the time, people believed that it was physically impossible to run a mile that fast.

In the 1860s the gold standard for "an almost superhuman performance" was four and a half minutes. By the 1940s, the four-minute mile had taken on a mythic status. The barrier seemed like a law of nature—backed up by the nine-year tenure of a world record at four minutes and 1.4 seconds. In the early 1950s, three runners started vying to break the mile barrier—Bannister, the American Wes Santee, and the Australian John Landy. That 1.4 seconds budged as easily as a cement wall. Then came Bannister—with his "chest like an engine block" and his "space-eating stride"—and the sense of what was possible changed.

On that day in May 1954, Bannister's friend Norris McWhirter announced the race results with a comically long preamble:

> Ladies and gentlemen, here is the result of Event Number Nine, the One Mile. First, Number Forty-One, R. G. Bannister of the Amateur Athletic Association and formerly of Exeter and Merton Colleges, with a time which is a new meeting and track record, and which subject to ratification will be a new English Native, British National, British All-Comers, European, British Empire and World's Record. The time is three—

The roar of cheers overwhelmed him, and the point-B world was created. Bannister had run a mile in three minutes and 59.4 seconds.

Overnight, Bannister became an international sporting sensation and he remains to this day one of Britain's most celebrated athletes. What is curious about his accomplishment is that Bannister only held the record for *forty-five days*. He stepped through the wall, finally achieving the seemingly impossible, and then someone else—the Australian John Landy—ran a 3:58 flat.

Bannister believed that something was possible and did it. He moved into the unknown and made it known. He took something seemingly inhuman and put it on the board of actual fact. It is always possible that someone else would have done it instead of Bannister, whether Landy or Santee, or even Louis Zamperini, had his running career in the 1930s not been curtailed by war. We are all beholden to circumstances and made better by competition.

Yet, this story brings up the larger question: What is the difference between believing something is possible and doing it, as Bannister did, and, as Landy did, knowing that it is possible and doing it a little better? Both men won races and set world records. Only Bannister invented a point-B world.

NAVIGATING WITHOUT A MAP

If you are, as Bannister was, trying to do something that has never been done before, there is no template. Without a map, how do you navigate? The way forward is by defining an animating question that pulls you toward possibility. These questions are like lighthouses. They take the most basic forms of "Wouldn't it be cool if?" or "Is it possible?" and help you rake progress forward through much broader possibility. When a breakthrough happens, your success may look like a foregone conclusion but it wasn't. Your lighthouse question holds

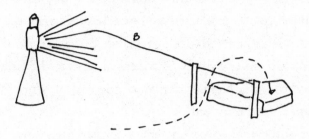

the space of belief absent proof. Even asking it takes everyday courage.

From where we sit now, it looks like Bannister had a training goal and met it. In some ways, the story is that simple, except that in early 1954, the ability to run that fast was an article of faith, not a demonstration of fact. As far as running a sub-four-minute mile went, the world was flat. If anything, the *impossibility* had been proven. From 1942 to 1945, two Swedes, Gunder Hägg and Arne Andersson, raced each other repeatedly, vying for the title. In 1942 they had tied at 4 minutes, 6.2 seconds. By 1945 Hägg had whittled that time down to 4 minutes, 1.4 seconds—a record that stood from 1945 until Bannister's historic run in 1954.

Bannister had grown up as a shy kid. At age eight he ran to avoid neighborhood bullies on his way home from school. At age ten he ran for cover when air-raid sirens blared during World War II. His family had moved to Bath to escape the bombings of London, and he ran another time because a shell fell on their house and they had to flee as the roof crashed in. When Bannister was eleven, he ran in the school's annual cross-country race and came in eighteenth. The next year, at age twelve, he won and then kept winning all through school.

In 1945, Bannister's father took him to White City Stadium in London to see an electrifying matchup between the Swede Arne Andersson, "a six-foot giant," and the "gutsy, diminutive" British miler Sydney Wooderson. It was the first international running competition since the end of World War II. Bannister was captivated.

Bannister applied to university a year early and went to Oxford in the fall of 1946. When he arrived on campus, the first thing he did was drop his bags and head for the track. He had never run on a track and, not finding an attendant there, he left. A few days later, he convinced a classmate who was built like a stocky rower to come back with him. As they were finishing their run, the groundskeeper came over and complimented Bannister's companion on his powerful stride. The famous miler Jack Lovelock, a New Zealander who had studied at Oxford in the 1930s, had this same compact physique. The groundsman turned to Bannister and said, "I'm afraid that you'll never be any good. You just haven't got the strength or the build for it."

Despite Bannister's love of running, it was also a relatively unformed time for sport. In 1954 there were only eleven running tracks in all of the United Kingdom. In comparison, Finland had six hundred. Bannister ran in what looked like extremely lightweight wing tips. When Bannister was invited to join the third-string team at Oxford, the team leader, an ex-military captain—90 percent of 1946 undergraduates were ex-servicemen—named Eric Mackay, was a chain smoker. In fact, Mackay had a reputation for stationing a friend at the two-and-a-half-mile point of a three-mile course to hand him a lit cigarette midrace.

At the time Bannister was trying for the sub-four-minute mile he was also carrying on a regular life, much more Clark Kent than Superman. It is now easy to tell Bannister's story with a mythologizing breathlessness. I have wondered if it felt that way at the time. And actually, my mother—who lived in Arkansas in the 1950s and who is allergic to hyperbole—said that in fact Bannister's run did have a mythologizing greatness at the time. She remembered following it in the news and being amazed when it happened. It represented the frontier of human endeavor.

What is so interesting about that frontier is the human part. Bannister lived as a mere mortal near Earls Court in a small basement apartment. He struggled to find time to do laundry. He cooked for himself, usually a stew, with a side of pickled herring for extra protein. His work life was consuming. He was studying at St. Mary's Hospital in Paddington on a scholarship. Cutting corners at the hospital in any way would have seemed inconceivable.

Bannister was part of the British tradition of the "gentleman amateur," someone participating in sport for the love of it. As Bannister said, "The university athlete is first and foremost a human being who runs his sport and does not allow it to run him. He drinks beer and he listens to coaches when he feels inclined." Bannister felt that that ethos "produced men whose personality and determination were sufficient to enable them to achieve balanced lives . . . and to stand the strain of first class competition." From the hospital where Bannister was completing his medical training, he had it timed exactly to get to the track, run his workout, return, and have a sandwich, all on his lunch break.

By 1953, Bannister was seriously considering giving up running. He had suffered disappointment competing in the 1952 Olympics. He was well into his hospital work, and running was taking up a lot of his time. Over the course of two months, Bannister debated stopping. In the end, he decided he would give himself two more years. (Note the tool from the last chapter of defining a grace period.)

That year, 1953, Sir Edmund Hillary summited Everest. News of his ascent reached England on the eve of Queen Elizabeth's coronation. For runners, the four-minute mile seemed at the time like it was their Everest. As Bannister would write in his 1954 book, *The First Four Minutes*, the mile barrier was "a challenge to the human spirit. It was a barrier that seemed to defy all attempts to break it—an irksome reminder that man's striving might be in vain." The four-minute mile was a barrier that required imagination as well as effort.

Bannister was not attempting to break the mile barrier alone. He trained with two friends, Chris Brasher and Chris Chataway. The plan was that Brasher would pace Bannister in the first and second lap, then Chataway would pace him in the third lap, and then Bannister would finish the fourth and final lap on his own. Bannister was known for his finishing kick. The pacing would keep him from going out too fast and keep him steady until the final lap. As Bannister the doctor would later explain, the art of racing a mile is in the uniformity of speed: The more variable the pace, the more effort a runner expends. The aim is to run at a constant speed and have nothing left at the end.

By April 1954, Bannister, Brasher, and Chataway had

whittled the time down to the equivalent of a 4:04 mile, but they couldn't get any faster, so they took a break. Brasher and Bannister drove to Scotland to go climbing with their friend Dr. More, who drove a repurposed Aston Martin racecar. Bannister, six foot one, rode all the way to the Scottish Highlands in the luggage space behind the seats. While they were hiking, Brasher fell and, although his rope caught him, it spooked them to realize their luck. The break had served them, and when they got home, their time had dropped to the four-minute range.

As the race day grew nearer, the gap between everyday life and such a large hope grew wider. On May 5, the day before Bannister broke the mile barrier, he slipped on a newly polished floor at the hospital. On May 6, the day of the attempt, the weather was abysmal even by British standards. Bannister went to the hospital to sharpen his new running spikes. Eustace Thomas, an alpine climber, had advised Bannister on how to get a pair of running shoes that weighed four ounces instead of the usual six after Bannister had told him he only needed the shoes to work once.

By sheer luck, Bannister ran into his friends' coach, a man named Franz Stampfl, on the train to Oxford that day. Stampfl was an epic man. He had fled Austria to England as Hitler rose to power, and then was interned to Australia as an "enemy alien" and survived a shipwreck en route by swimming in the North Sea for eight hours. On the train, Bannister told Stampfl that the weather was so bad he was considering abandoning the attempt in order to save his strength for another day. Stampfl convinced him to try, by lodging the crystallizing question in Bannister's brain: "In any case, what if this were your only chance?"

The race was scheduled for 6 p.m. and Bannister, Brasher, and Chataway agreed that they would not decide until after 5 p.m. Bannister spent the afternoon with his university friend Charles Wenden, who met Bannister at the train station that day and enveloped him in a protective cocoon of family routines with his wife, Eileen, and small children, Felicity and Sally.

Arriving at the track to warm up, Bannister still didn't know that he would run. A rainstorm came through and a rainbow even appeared, but up until a few minutes before the race Bannister still thought he would not try. Then, as they were getting into the starting blocks, Bannister saw the flag on a nearby church go slack in a break in the wind. He signaled them that they would try. There was a false start but the break in the wind held and they were off.

A newsreel of the entire race exists. It shows Chataway, Brasher, and Bannister starting out with the three other competitors. Brasher and Chataway flank Bannister. In their white singlets and racing shorts, they are going so fast that they seem to loop a static background of gray trench coats and trouser legs. Taken from the center of the track, the film is almost dizzying. Their form has the kind of ease and economical speed that looks misleadingly unlike exertion. Bannister keeps his arms folded high. His stride is gigantic and churning.

I didn't discover the reel until well into writing about Bannister. Then I watched it every day for a week. It is beautiful like a painting and beautiful as a portrait of the arc of human endeavor. It shows people starting out in ordinary circumstances and giving everything they have to attempt something larger than themselves. In their formation, you can almost see their accumulated years of practice and their present bonds of friendship.

In the first lap, Brasher ignored Bannister's shouts of "faster" and kept to what turned out to be a 57.5-second lap. "[H]e had made success possible," Bannister later wrote gratefully of Brasher's insistent pacing. When Chataway passes Bannister and Brasher to take the pacer's lead in the second lap, you sense the clarity of duty. Bannister trusts them and relies on them completely. Then Bannister steps out in front of Chataway at the start of the last lap, and you see someone who has already been working at capacity fully empty everything he has.

Looking back on the last hundred yards of that mile, Bannister said, "The only reality was . . . the track under my feet. The tape meant finality—extinction perhaps. I felt at that moment that it was my chance to do one thing supremely well." Bannister broke the tape and then almost collapsed and blacked out. His parents had come to see the race, unbeknownst to him, and they came to the track, where Stampfl was physically holding him up.

One of the most beautiful parts of the story—in addition to the fact Bannister was a generalist doctor-runner—is how much, counter to the myth of the lone artistic genius, he got by with the help of his friends. The "first four minutes" was a collaborative and resourceful act on the part of many people. Bannister's most visible collaborators were Brasher and Chataway, his pacers and training partners, but there were many others. In that moment of having just broken the mile barrier, Bannister—even on the weakest of legs and the most partial of mental faculties—immediately looked for Brasher and Chataway to run their victory lap. He could not have done it without them.

FROM SMART TARGETS TO
MAJOR DRAMATIC QUESTIONS

In retrospect, breaking the mile barrier looks like a goal and not a question, and the distinction is subtle but important. Much of management is based on goals—quantifiable metrics and outcome-oriented deliverables. Often credited to the management guru Peter Drucker, SMART targets are those that are "specific, measurable, achievable, realistic, and timebound."

A SMART target looks like a simple tool but it also reflects a belief system that the future responds to specific, knowable plans. The problem with SMART targets is that they limit what you are able to ask of the future. They leave little room for messy questions, or big hairy audacious goals. SMART targets can be helpful for getting things done, like filing your taxes. But art thinking needs a different kind of engine. You might set a *process*-based SMART target—setting a goal of showing up to a daily practice of research or training. A SMART target can structure "studio time" from chapter 1. It can help you commit to a habit.

Yet you can't set a SMART target for something like the four-minute barrier. Trying to break what many people perceive as a law of nature is not, to say the least, realistic. To explore the possibility of point B, you need a question to pull you forward, because where you are going is harder to imagine. The engine of the question is not necessarily its surface-level specifics but the deeper motivation underlying it.

In this regard, a lighthouse question is similar to the MDQ, or "major dramatic question" in a movie. The screenplay of a film has two guiding questions: a plot question and, underneath it, an MDQ. In *When Harry Met Sally . . .*, the plot question is, what will happen between Harry and Sally? The MDQ is, can men and women really be friends? In the Harry Potter films, the plot question is, will Harry vanquish Lord Voldemort? The MDQ is about whether good can triumph over both the celebrity and the quiet banality of evil, and whether Harry can be ordinary and extraordinary at the same time.

For Bannister, the plot question was, "Will he round the field at Iffley Road Track fast enough?" The MDQ was, "Can a man run that fast?"—or even, "Is the frontier of human capability bigger than we know?" Like a lighthouse, an MDQ is the orienting point on a horizon. When it gets answered, a whole new world opens up.

A lighthouse in the physical world is an aboveground beacon visible over a long distance. An MDQ in a movie is a powerful current under the surface of the story. Sometimes your lighthouse question may be buried in this way. It may be so fundamental to who you are that its current pulls you around without being acknowledged. Bringing that sense of purpose into intentional awareness can give it more power. However acknowledged or unacknowledged, these questions can determine the story structure of your life and the path of your organization.

That Bannister had a lighthouse question does not mean that he or anyone else was guaranteed a success. We know his story because he didn't fail. His lunchtime runs in the early 1950s might have otherwise fallen into the obscurity of personal history. The artistry in his story is that he went wholly and completely all in, while also being a person in the world who worked and had friends and went on dates and endured setbacks and got lucky breaks like everyone else. Like Fogarty with his balloon catheter in chapter 1 and Lee with her reservations agent job in chapter 2, Bannister's accomplishment came from his whole life. In fact, Bannister has always said that his proudest contributions in life have been to neurology and to his family.

THE ORIGIN STORIES
OF LIGHTHOUSE QUESTIONS

In the years following art school, I started to see friends who had achieved something in their field grapple with the realization that their lives were answers to questions they hadn't meant to ask. When I was first starting to teach economics, I called one friend, let's call him Ben, to help me understand transfer pricing. (Transfer pricing is the construction of internal markets within any organization and also the tool that multinational firms sometimes use to realize profits in countries with low tax rates.) After a dizzying tour of international tax strategy, he said to me, "You know, I've always wanted to be an interior designer," and then broke out in peals of mischievous laughter.

The answer to the dilemma is not as simple as saying Ben should stop being a tax strategist and become an interior designer. There are very real differences in those two fields, compensation being only one. What is more interesting is trying to uncover the underlying principle that draws him to both fields so that he can articulate a lighthouse question and better navigate the gray area between them.

Even among artists I talk to, it is not uncommon to see people with half-buried interests. They make amazing creative work, but if you talk to them in an honest and open way for more than twenty minutes, they will say "You know, I've always secretly wanted to make this *other* project that I haven't done." Even for people who have, by professional category and often deep financial sacrifice, dedicated themselves to the title of "artist," it can be hard to focus on what you care about most. In some respects, all of us can be journalists who bury the lede in the stories of our own lives.

Knowing your lighthouse is a way of uncovering your buried interest—not choosing a concrete path like banker or yoga teacher, interior designer or transfer pricing specialist, but understanding at a level deeper than that what you believe in and what work agrees with you. The lighthouse question is a touchstone for how your authenticity manifests itself in the world.

For whatever reason of Bannister's personal psychology—whether his early runs to avoid bullies or the experience of seeing Andersson and Wooderson compete at White City in 1945—he chose to commit to wrestling with the four-minute barrier. His lighthouse question had the story structure of

"Is it possible?" Many lighthouse questions boil down to that common denominator of proving something possible or asking, "Wouldn't it be cool if . . ."

Yet lighthouse questions—for people and organizations and whole social movements—can take more specific forms. They can be discipline specific, meaning they stem from the domain in which you work—science, security, trade, teaching, childrearing, and so on. Or they can come about authentically in reaction to circumstance—a kind of bloom-where-you-are-planted version of creativity.

As we are about to see, the story of pioneering computer programmer Whitfield Diffie embodies the discipline-specific lighthouse, and the story of an attorney named Louise Florencourt illustrates the bloom-where-you're-planted kind of lighthouse path that grows from duty, ability, and circumstance.

Whitfield Diffie invented public-key encryption in the 1970s, radically reimagining computer code-breaking by sepa-rating the code into two keys, one public and one private, that have to act in combination. The technology, which he devel-oped with Martin Hellman, is a strong foundation of privacy on the Internet. In the words of Steven Levy, who wrote about Diffie in *Wired* magazine and in his book *Crypto*, "splitting the key" was "the most revolutionary concept in encryption since the Renaissance."

Like Bannister's, Diffie's contribution began in his own particular story. He didn't read until the age of ten, when he plowed through an entire book called *The Space Cat*. His light-house question began to take root around this time when his

fifth-grade teacher, one Miss Collins, gave a lesson on code-breaking. Diffie was fascinated and asked his father, who worked at City College of New York, to check out all of the library's books on cryptography. Diffie read all of the books, the ones for children and for adults.

We probably all know someone kind of like Diffie—unstoppable where their innate interests are concerned but lacking in patience for what is merely assigned. Diffie was a disinterested student but scored exceedingly well on standardized tests and was admitted to the Massachusetts Institute of Technology (MIT). There his guiding interest in cryptography started to evolve in a specific context.

When Diffie graduated from MIT in 1965, computer programming was still considered something of a tacky upstart compared to the pure pursuit of math itself. Stanford University had only just created a computer science department in 1965. Yet at the same time, the nascent development of the Internet and the U.S. government's privacy policies were bringing into sharp relief the importance of protecting privacy.

Diffie originally took on a computer programming and research job for the government-affiliated MITRE Corporation in order to avoid the draft for the Vietnam War. The U.S. Department of Defense's Advanced Research Projects Agency (ARPA, later DARPA) was just laying the groundwork for the Internet. The experimental ARPANET used packet-switching to connect a consortium of research universities via an electronic network. This predecessor to the Internet was envisioned and beta-tested in the 1960s, and built out in the early 1970s.

Research in computer science and cryptography in the United States was at the time bifurcated along the fault line of whether the researchers themselves had decided to cooperate with the National Security Administration (NSA) or not. The NSA offered companies like IBM a Faustian bargain: Cooperate with us and we will share all our top-secret research but you will never be allowed to publish anything you discover subsequently on your own, or work independently without knowledge of what we have already figured out.

Diffie didn't take the deal. As he later said, "I have always believed that one's politics and the character of his particular work are inseparable." Diffie's lighthouse question surfaced out of the particularities of his interests, talents, and context. His MDQ, in the words of his wife, Mary Fischer, was, "How do you deal with a trustworthy person in the midst of a world full of untrustworthy people?" That question pulled him forward.

Carving a distinctly original path, Diffie became a renegade researcher, crisscrossing the country in a few different versions of a Datsun 510, reading all the books he could find on cryptography, and meeting with mysterious characters, what Diffie's then wife-to-be Fischer called "really cloak and dagger— . . . people who put coats over their faces, . . . who wanted to know how . . . he'd found out their names."

He eventually met the man who would become his collaborator, Martin Hellman, through a happenstance introduction. One man whom Diffie had visited at IBM, Alan Konheim, couldn't share his research with Diffie on NSA grounds, but Konheim decided to tell Diffie the name of the other researcher asking the same questions. That man was Hellman. The two met and Hellman hired Diffie so they could keep talking.

Like Harper Lee and Roger Bannister, Diffie found himself in the weeds in this phase of his life. He was thirty and living in California, nominally a research assistant for Hellman. He and Mary were house-sitting for John McCarthy, an artificial intelligence pioneer, and looking after McCarthy's daughter. One night, Diffie hit a low point. He wanted to give up. Mary said, "He was telling me that he should do something else, that he was a broken-down researcher."

By chance the next day Diffie experienced something of an epiphany. As was his routine, he made breakfast for Mary—an Egyptologist then working for British Petroleum—and started pottering around. Here's how Diffie described his breakthrough moment:

The thing I remember distinctly is that I was sitting in the living room when I thought of it the first time and then I went downstairs to get a Coke and I almost lost it. I mean, there was this moment when—I was thinking about something. What was it? And then I got it back and didn't forget it.

That idea was a way of "splitting the key" that unlocks a code. Developing the technology would take Diffie and Hellman longer, but the insight came to the original and prepared mind of a man who had walked around for years with a lighthouse question about privacy and trust, and spent his life exploring it.

Diffie's story shows how your lighthouse can surface from your most idiosyncratic experiences and your most taken-for-granted foundational beliefs. These stories of experience can be grand or small—as public-facing as solving for privacy or at the scale of a duty-bound sense of family.

What you will also notice in Diffie's story is the push and the pull. His lighthouse question guided his inquiry, but he also responded to the urgencies of his historical moment.

This mix of drive and receptivity is important to pause on. A creative process that happens in response to circumstance can be just as important as one that grows from maniacal and single-minded focus. Remembering back to John Coward, the pilot described in the introduction who landed the British Airways plane in the grass after the engines failed, his resourcefulness was responsive. He was in the creative space of a wholly unscripted moment.

In slightly more everyday circumstances, a woman named Louise Florencourt embodies the ways in which your authenticity and sense of duty can come together to form your lighthouse. Louise—Miss Florencourt—is the first cousin of the southern writer Flannery O'Connor. I met her when I gave a talk on creativity in everyday life at Andalusia, Flannery O'Connor's home, in Milledgeville, Georgia. After the talk Miss Florencourt, in a cowboy hat and jeans—a vision of elegance and gumption well into the age where it is impolite to ask—came up to me and said, "You know, I always wanted to be an artist but I became a lawyer instead."

I didn't understand until later that, when she said she was a lawyer, she was in the very first class of women at Harvard Law School. I would consider that an art project in the point-B sense.

Corresponding later, Miss Florencourt told me she had majored in political science in college but taken many art history and studio art classes. One summer not long after she graduated, she took a painting class at Columbia University in New York. As she wrote, "The apex of my career as an artist was the professor's choosing of my watercolor painting as part of an exhibit in the lobby of the Seagram building." She loved making art but also took the LSAT. "My thought was that a law degree offered the opportunity to earn a living. As an 'artist' I envisioned myself starving in an attic. As an art historian I envisioned myself dusting paintings and artifacts in storage in the basement of a museum."

In a way, Miss Florencourt's story calls to mind what could have happened if Harper Lee had followed her father's advice, not dropped out of law school, and become an attorney.

Miss Florencourt's great creative adventure unfolded in her retirement. Flannery O'Connor's mother asked her to move to Milledgeville to help maintain O'Connor's legacy. Looking back, Miss Florencourt said that her choice to go to law school was practical. Her decision to come to Milledgeville in her retirement was to fill a need. And what came after that was a different form of art—of vocation and reinvention. Miss Florencourt's lighthouse came from her equally authentic belief in duty and service, a desire to support herself, and an ability to apply her talents where they were needed.

Limiting lighthouse questions to pie-in-the-sky artistic impossibility engages some of the bias that art is a leisure pursuit and not a workaday necessity—and that artists are impractical geniuses who, in the words of John Maynard Keynes, the famous economist and also the first chairman of the Arts Council of England, "[walk] where the breath of the spirit blows [them]."

For professional artists and anyone else, your lighthouse can grow out of the ground of what is necessary. It can change over time. It evolves out of your integrity and wholeness as a person in whatever circumstances you find yourself—in a stalled plane, holding a law school acceptance letter, receiving a call from family to come help, or staring down the lane of the track about to spring forward at the sound of a starting gun.

When the palliative care nurse Bonnie Ware wrote about the regrets people voice on their deathbeds, the most common was not living a life true to themselves. Living a life that is true to yourself is a simple practice of staying present with the questions that matter to you, whether born of duty or possibility, whether seemingly large or small. Believing there is an original contribution that is yours to make, you can anchor your starting point to a question.

FINDING YOUR OWN LIGHTHOUSE

If you want to think through your own lighthouse question, there are a number of routes you can take. See if one of these works for you:

- Choose something you did recently that was a big success, something you felt really proud of. What was the underlying value at stake? Now take something that felt like a failure, a real blow, and look at the question underneath it. Write these down if you can. Put them away for a day and come back to them. What is the hope or the problem underneath those events?

- If you won the lottery so that money was no object but you had to work, what would you do? Imagine this next chapter as a movie that you star in. What is the storyline? What happens? What does that answer tell you about what your underlying question is?

- Looking back at your life, what were the questions that characterized different phases? Whether you divide it by decade or year or other marker—job, school, family, where you lived—make a map or a timeline of your life.

What were you exploring in different chapters? Did you find an answer, or multiple answers, to your question? You might see questions of personal passion or of duty and financial necessity. Without thinking of it as success or failure, explore how a question in one phase led to and opened up the next.

- If you had a magic wand within your life, your organization, or the larger world, what would you do with it? What is the value underneath that hope, and how can you design that value into a question that is at a scale you can manage?

- Your lighthouse question might exist best in the near future or in the far future. What would you like to see happen in the next month or year? What do you think is important to think about in the next thirty years? Let your mind roam freely in a sci-fi brainstorming mode, and then ask yourself why you care. Does that translate into what you care about now too?

THE FRIENDS-AND-FAMILY PLAN

The key difficulty of lighthouse questions is that asking them makes you a first mover. They make you risk being out in front unprotected by the entrenched patterns of past events. As in business theory, there is a first mover advantage. You might overtake a new market, design a new product first, or just get a jump start on anything. But just as easily, being a first mover takes extra energy. It makes you the front rider in a pack of cyclists, so to speak, with the extra exertion of having to drive into the wind without drafting off of your teammates.

As with Bannister and Diffie, asking an MDQ takes the extra effort of courage. A big part of the headwind you are cycling into is that you don't know if you're crazy to even try. From a business standpoint, if you succeed others may copy you quickly at less cost to them. The risks and vulnerabilities of being a first mover are great, but the potential gains are greater.

Along the way, these lighthouse questions—thrown toward the future like a beacon—need structural supports. At a personal level, that means friends and collaborators. At a business strategy level, that means barriers to entry—ways of protecting your success in the point-B world you create.

Of Bannister's collaborators in his Iffley Road triumph, his friend and pacer Chris Chataway was working as an under brewer at Guinness. His other friend and pacer, Chris Brasher, was a management trainee at Mobil Oil. Brasher and Chataway were both gifted runners in their own right. On the day they helped Bannister break the mile barrier, Chataway finished second in an impressive 4:07.2. Chataway would go on to set world records in the 3-mile and 5,000-meter distances in 1954 and 1955. After watching Chataway in a 1953 track meet, Joseph Mallalieu, later a Labour politician, wrote in his "Sporting Days" column for the *Spectator* magazine, "Running a record mile is less effort to Chataway than running for a bus is to us."

Bannister's loose and larger constellation of collaborators included others, such as the twins Ross and Norris McWhirter. For years they had timed his races, shuttled him to meets, and kept him apprised of the performance of his overseas competitors. Of them, Bannister wrote:

> The energy of the twins, Norris and Ross McWhirter, was boundless. For them nothing was too much trouble, and they accepted any challenge joyfully. After running together in Oxford as sprinters they carried their partnership into journalism, keeping me posted of the performances of my overseas rivals. They often drove me to athletics meetings, so that I arrived with no fuss, never a minute too soon or too late. Sometimes I was not sure whether it was Norris or Ross who held the watch or drove the car, but I knew that either could be relied upon.

Norris—who had been announcing the race on May 6, 1954—had single-handedly convinced the only journalists in attendance that they should be there. Norris had also hired a local electrician to wire up the speakers so that Norris could helpfully announce split times at the half-lap point too. For years they had kept Bannister informed about how John Landy and Wes Santee, the Australian and the American, respectively, who were also vying to break the mile barrier, were doing. They also told Bannister that the mile barrier was becoming such "an almost uninsurable risk" that newspapers had begun to prepare obituary notices for Bannister and his competitors.

The McWhirters shared Bannister's belief in what was possible. In contrast to the original Oxford groundsman who had told Bannister he should probably give up running, Norris had been on a train with Bannister in Italy once on a trip for the

Achilles Club—a combination of the Oxford and Cambridge athletic clubs—and looked at a napping Bannister and said, "There lies the body that perhaps one day will prove itself to possess a known physical ability beyond that of any of the one billion other men on earth."

The idea of accomplishment growing out of friendship disrupts the idea of the lone-wolf genius. It also, however subtly, flies utterly in the face of more modern notions of cooperation and empowerment that have at their core the idea of each of us as a highly individual, achievement-oriented worker. Sheryl Sandberg's idea of "leaning in" is important and potentially an engine of a point-B world. But it is also true that in some of the ways that "leaning in" at work gets framed, you are acting out of individual professional ambition, as supported by other individual actors, many of whom are edited out of the final story. Here the achievement may in name go to Bannister when it was a team effort. The accomplishment arose out of the ground of friendship and an amateur sporting tradition.

As to the pathways of Bannister's friends, Brasher went on to cofound the London Marathon. Chataway, while a trainee at Guinness, introduced the company to Norris and Ross McWhirter, who both had a near photographic and encyclopedic memory for sporting records. In 1954 the brothers became founding editors and publishers of *The Guinness Book of World Records*—which itself set a world record as the best-selling copyrighted book in the world, only surpassed by uncopyrightable books like the Bible and the Koran. Of the McWhirter brothers, Ross was killed by the IRA in 1975 and Norris continued editing the books alone until 1986, and then stayed on as an advisory editor to Guinness for another decade.

THE FRENEMY WORLD OF SUCCEEDING FIRST

At a business level, the friends-and-family plan still holds true; individual leaders are surrounded by important teams. Yet being a first mover holds particular risks for businesses. If you prove something is possible, you may have had to invest substantially to get there. If you do succeed wildly and invent a point-B world, what is to stop others from copying you and profiting without having had to take on those risks and investments? The second mover advantage is powerful.

When uncovering a lighthouse question in the business world, you need to think particularly about how you will erect barriers to entry to prevent a second mover from copying your success in the event that you have it. The most common of these structural supports are patents and other forms of intellectual property rights, designed to reward inventors for their outsize risk. In cases where patents are not available, you still need to design other ways of stopping people from taking advantage of your own discovery. Softsoap, the unassuming and now-ubiquitous—and ubiquitously copied—hand soap, was born of such a story.

Softsoap was the brainchild of the 1970s and '80s wunderkind company Minnetonka, located fifteen miles to the west of Minneapolis, Minnesota, in the town of Chaska (1986 population: 8,643). The company's founder, Robert Taylor, started Minnetonka Corporation in 1964 with three thousand dollars and a dream. He was a Maryland native with a Stanford MBA in his pocket and Johnson & Johnson on his résumé.

Up until the mid to late 1970s, Minnetonka operated in an unusual hippie-luxury crossover market, making hand soaps that looked like lemons or green apples or Hershey bars. Then Taylor had a breakthrough idea while driving to work: liquid soap.

The first patent for any kind of liquid soap was issued in 1865, but the product never really caught on outside of its use in public lavatories. Minnetonka started making liquid soap as a luxury product, in ceramic pumps and with wonderful names of the 1970s like "Crème Soap on Tap."

Taylor wanted to create liquid soap for a mass market. But he was a minnow in an industry of giant fish. He was worried—rightly so—that his success could be his demise: If he could prove that a market existed for liquid soap, other manufacturers would join in. And those bigger companies with enormous marketing and distribution machinery might be able to outcompete him.

He needed an advantage but struggled to find one. There was no patent available on the soap itself, but looking at all of the component parts, he discovered one limitation: There *was* a patent on the unique pump mechanism needed to dispense liquid soap. Two companies in the entire United States manufactured these pumps. Taylor bought up the entire capacity of those firms for roughly two years, equating to 100 million pumps. Although each pump cost only 12 cents, he had to invest $12 million, more than the company was worth. They were betting the farm.

It worked. From 1979 to 1981, Minnetonka's revenue quadrupled to $96 million. The product, Softsoap, took 38 percent of a then $120 million market. Because Minnetonka had locked in all of the productive capacity of the pump manufacturers, Softsoap got a one- to two-year head start over larger companies like Colgate-Palmolive and Unilever. That lead sputtered after other companies entered the market, but it proved the strategy of erecting roadblocks for competitors. Without the barriers to entry, Minnetonka would not have benefited from the point-B world it created.

Buying up all of the pumps was a small but effective blocking mechanism. The larger business strategy followed from a clear and bold question, about something as simple as soap.

WHEN THE SMALL THINGS HAVE BEEN DONE
AND THE BIG THINGS SEEM TOO HARD

Challenges take different forms in different eras. Bannister approached a frontier question of whether something was possible. We often face more incremental questions of whether something can be improved. Questions of improvement and incrementalism somehow suit current capitalism more. They are parts of the creative process that have been so far subsumed into a profit motive that they are acceptable to the mindset of hitting quarterly numbers, of driving to the win. But whether you can get a little better is only one kind of question.

When Bannister added a new afterword to his original 1954 book, *The First Four Minutes*, in 2004, he wrote, "It is . . . increasingly difficult to find legitimate challenges." The days of amateur athletics—of training on one's lunch break—seem harder and harder to reconjure. The word "amateur" itself hasn't appeared in the official Olympic Charter since 1974. Bannister may be right that we have already addressed many of civilization's great problems, from penicillin to steel to the Internet.

Maybe the new "legitimate challenges" feel so far out of comfort—global warming, the structure of education, the design of working life, the need to repair, not just to build— that only a few have undertaken them, and none of these people has yet, figuratively speaking, broken the tape in under four minutes. They may currently be failing. When the challenges seem so big, it is tempting to just move the pieces around on the board or to nervously reach for a buzzword instead of acting from a first principle. Limiting yourself to what you can answer successfully tethers you to the known world, to the current ordinary, not the new ordinary that your work could create.

Certainly there is a time and place in business to operate from what you know and to continue to serve a well-known market. And there is also a time and place in which you may know your MDQ but not yet be able to work on it. Following lighthouse questions is inherently risky because they concern the unknown and unknowable future, but trusting a pattern that worked in the past is risky too. The world is always changing regardless.

There are habits to make asking lighthouse questions easier. You can start an MDQ club to mull over and explore your questions in conversation with friends or colleagues. Like Bannister or Diffie or Minnetonka, you can simply practice asking yourself if the things you are trying to get done reflect the questions you mean to ask. If you take a "good noticing" attitude from chapter 2, it is easier to observe the distance between your calendar and your higher objectives in a kindly way, with more curiosity than criticism.

What is possible is not always a leap forward. The new ordinary can include war and famine, or business failure, or lasting environmental damage—for which incremental improvement may not be possible. Some of the great MDQs of our time are political questions. And they are not necessarily the questions put in front of us by the news, in reaction to events. They are questions that come from our own imaginations, from our own attempts to make sense of the world, to consider what is possible not just to meditate on what just happened.

CREATING THE NEW NORMAL

When Bannister broke the mile barrier, he pulled all of us through the membrane between the ordinary and extraordinary, creating a vacuum. And then the greatest change agent of them all—normality—rushed to fill it. In the new point-B world, the accomplishment became ordinary again. Some 1,300 runners have achieved the sub-four-minute mile, and the current world record (as of January 2016) in the mile is 3 minutes, 43.13 seconds, run by the Moroccan Hicham El Guerrouj in Rome in 1999. Running a four-minute mile is still a gold standard, impressive but not impossible, the same way that it seems still impressive but increasingly possible to have female CEOs and board members, or vegetables at dinner that did not come out of a can, or wider-spread civil and human rights, or any number of advances that have come to seem, or are still coming to seem, ordinary in the space of our lives. In his book *The Perfect Mile*, Neal Bascomb writes of Bannister:

> [I]t is initially difficult to see the heroes around whom events unfolded as true flesh-and-blood individuals. Myth tends to wrap its arms around fact, and memory finds a comfortable groove and stays the course. What makes these individuals so interesting—their doubts, vulnerabilities, and failures—is often airbrushed out, and their victories characterized as *faits accomplis*. But true heroes are never as unalloyed as they first appear (thank goodness). We should admire them all the more for this fact.

For anyone, lighthouse questions exist as part of a larger portfolio of other projects and activities, and they more often than not get explored in the midst of some sort of whole-life thinking. Bannister did not quit his medical training to run. He survived on his medical pay and sacrificed to find time to train. His training schedule was a studio-time practice, at a scale at which he could afford to fail without disrupting the larger portfolio of his life, a topic we will explore more in the next chapter. The other crucial context for his MDQ is that he pursued it not in a vacuum of heroic individualism but along-side his friends. The lighthouse has a human dimension.

Even if you fail to answer your question, even if asking it in the first place is quixotic and more than likely doomed, there is great power simply in naming the question and giving it space to unfurl. Clear MDQs guide people to great things that grow out of ordinary life. Sometimes you have to hold the question mindfully for a long time before you are able to move toward it, your lighthouse a small pinprick on an otherwise dark horizon.

At some level it is just as extraordinary that we all breathe in and out, day in and day out, as it is that one person among us can run the first sub-four-minute mile. The sheer fact of belief requires energy but also sustains dignity. Lee and Bannister and Diffie's accomplishments grew from a bed of vulnerability, from a weedy present, one foot in front of the other, until each of them had done the thing.

A few months after Edmund Hillary and Tenzing Norgay first summited Mount Everest, Bannister, wearing his doctor hat, was in the position to give Hillary a treadmill test. In their feats of athletic heroism, it is easy for Bannister and Hillary to seem apart from us, men who have never skipped a run or gone for the second slice of cake. But when Bannister read Hillary's tests, he simply said, "I don't know how you did it." That's not to say Hillary was out of shape, just that he was, like Bannister, not superhuman.

Before Bannister broke the mile barrier, a French journalist asked how he knew he wouldn't die trying. The answer was, he didn't know. He didn't know that he could do it and he didn't know that he would not die. His success doesn't diminish the vulnerability of holding the lighthouse question beforehand. To think that on some random Thursday it was entirely possible for the lanky doctor, in a brief lull late in the afternoon of a windy day, in front of his friends and parents but without the world noticing, to convert the impossible into the proven. He had to believe it was possible before he did it as surely as any of us have to leap before we can land.

Your moment of insight might be sliver thin like Bannister's fraction of a second, or an accident of timing like Diffie's walk into the kitchen to get a Coke, or a response to circumstance like Miss Florencourt's return to Milledgeville. The breakthrough may never happen, and when it does, it is unlikely to be the first thing you tried.

But in navigating that space, you have the lighthouse of knowing and revisiting the question that guides you—and the artistic permission to ask a big enough question that you don't know whether you might fail. The next tool is figuring out how to manage the risk of the question by applying investment thinking to your lighthouse, placing your question in a larger portfolio of your life and work.

CHAPTER 4

To Make a Boat

[T]he beginnings of all things are small.

—Cicero

When you accept that you are in the weeds and navigating from a question, how do you frame and manage risks—not just of failure but also success? Do you start small and pilot? Do you self-invest to get something off the ground? To effectively manage the risk of early-stage creative work, you need two tools: what I will call portfolio thinking and ownership stakes. Portfolio thinking helps you protect against the downside, staying in balance if your project fails, so you can keep a roof over your head and eat more than lentil soup. Ownership stakes help you claim the upside, having exposure to a piece of the value you create. Together they make it possible to be generous, to try to put something out there and to share in the

rewards if it succeeds. In order to explain how and why, we need to first look at the ways in which scale happens differently in business and art.

THE WRAPPED REICHSTAG VS. TWITTER

In 1995, the artistic duo and married collaborators Christo and Jeanne-Claude wrapped the Reichstag—the German parliament building in Berlin—completely, in one million square feet of fabric. Ten years later, in 2005, they created *The Gates* in New York's Central Park—7,503 pumpkin-orange metal frames each with a swath of same-colored parachute fabric that hung from the top like a sheet on a laundry line. Christo and Jeanne-Claude never accepted government or private money to sponsor these works. Although they didn't judge others for taking funding, they felt that, for them, accepting outside money would compromise the integrity of their work. Instead, they self-funded the projects on the sale of related drawings—preparatory sketches and editions of prints that they made.

I once explained Christo and Jeanne-Claude's strategy to a group of students and one asked me: How did people know to start buying their drawings in the first place? I didn't know the answer.

It turned out that Christo and Jeanne-Claude started small and scaled up over decades. In 1958, Christo wrapped a soup can. In 1962, they wrapped a motorcycle, in 1963 a Volkswagen. They worked at that scale day in, day out for more than ten years before they started thinking about their bigger projects. The *Wrapped Reichstag* and *The Gates* list starting dates in the 1970s. It took them from 1971 to 1995 and from 1979 to 2005, respectively, to build up to those monumental works.

They started at a scale that was close to them, using quantities of fabric they could buy themselves, covering objects they could reach around and wrap with their own hands. Then over time they eked out a surplus in reputation and cash that enabled them to scale up while self-investing.

Consider how different that story is in structure from the growth of Twitter. On November 7, 2013, Twitter listed on the New York Stock Exchange at $26 per share. It closed at $44.90 on that first day of trading. The company had been founded in 2006 out of a pivot from an earlier venture called Odeo. One of the Twitter founders, Evan Williams, bought out the Odeo investors using proceeds from the sale of his Blogger platform. In that sense he, like Christo and Jeanne-Claude, funded the project himself as it scaled up, but that is where the stories diverge.

For the first six months of 2013, Twitter made $21 million through the "eyes of management." Through the eyes of generally accepted accounting principles, the company posted a loss of $69 million. Part of that discrepancy was of course that Twitter had issued stock options in advance of its initial public offering and that those options had to be accounted for as an expense. Even still, Twitter was able to list on the stock exchange arguably without having any earnings.

Theoretically, the value of a company is based on its cumulative future earnings (discounted back to the present). That means that Twitter sold on imagination, not proof—on the belief that they would have earnings just not yet.

If Christo and Jeanne-Claude had been like Twitter, they might have in 1979 written a business plan, received funding, and made the project in 1980. The ability to sell Twitter before it had earnings lets those founders reap huge financial rewards in advance of actual profits. The difference between Christo and Jeanne-Claude and Twitter tells a contrarian story about what it is to manage the risk of investing—in time and money—in early-stage projects whose value is not yet known.

If you are self-funding your work as Christo and Jeanne-Claude were, gearing up for momentum takes time. You have to make enough money to cover your moment-to-moment expenses while also setting aside enough surplus to invest and grow. Over a long arc, the wooden roller coaster can make the creaky ascent up the first hill and then still tip over the top and take off. To harness that power, you will need design tools to manage risk and claim value, so that you can plan for the good or bad future while staying balanced in the present. You need to think in terms of what I will call an "income portfolio" to keep your production economics in balance while you work, and also in terms of a traditional investment portfolio to manage the risk and return of what you create. As we will see momentarily, the income portfolio has the characteristics of a "cross-subsidy" in which one area supports another. Through the lens of both income and investment, you get the advantages of a diversified portfolio.

PORTFOLIO THINKING

Harry Markowitz, who won the Nobel Prize in 1990 for modern portfolio theory, was born in Chicago in 1927. His parents owned a grocery store. All of the Nobel Prize winners are asked to write an autobiography. His reads, toward the beginning, "We lived in a nice apartment, always had enough to eat, and I had my own room. I never was aware of the Great Depression." Markowitz's accompanying photograph exudes warm, salt-of-the-earth kindness.

The research Markowitz began in the 1950s is a mathematical proof for the benefits of a diversified portfolio. Typically, you should never be able to get a return that is disproportionate to the level of risk you take on. Risk big, win big; venture small, win small. What Markowitz proved was that, by assembling a diversified portfolio—owning lots of different things instead of putting all your eggs in one basket—you could actually get a higher return for a given level of risk. If all of your holdings move independently—some up, some down—they have the effect of insuring each other. As long as they do not move perfectly together or exactly in opposition—as long as the stocks are more like tipsy walkers loosely tracking each other than synchronized swimmers in tight formation—your overall return will be higher for any given level of risk. That risk-return adjustment protects the downside and supports the upside. Companies like Vanguard stem from this logic.

The portfolio approach is incredibly common among working artists, investment advisors, and venture capitalists. It is also useful for other workers and whole companies. The artistic variation on general portfolio thinking is the day job. You have some areas of your life that are steady and low risk. You may not enjoy them as much as working on your art, but they pay for your life. The other parts of your portfolio are projects that may be successful artistically or financially, or neither or both. The day job covers the research-and-development budget of the other projects. That structure is called a cross-subsidy—one area of income that you use to cover another area of expense. It also diversifies your portfolio into a mix of risky and less risky income.

Matthew Deleget is an artist who lives in Brooklyn, New York. Along with his wife, Rossana Martinez, he is also the founder of Minus Space, a gallery that was housed solely on the Internet until they opened a brick-and-mortar space in 2014. Every year, Matthew does an audit of how he spends his time and how he makes money. For a few years, he has presented these pie charts in a workshop I teach for artists every summer at the Lower Manhattan Cultural Council. A few years ago, he spent 12 percent of his time on consulting projects that accounted for 48 percent of his income. Over time the percentage has shifted, with a larger share coming from his gallery. His goal is to have all of his income from his gallery or from the sales of his own art. While he is getting there, he self-invests by working in other, more lucrative areas that cross-subsidize his art and his gallery.

As we will see shortly, larger corporations often have this cross-subsidy structure too. Most firms are portfolios of projects and departments that operate a little like Christo and Jeanne-Claude. Some divisions grow and scale. Others spin off cash in the short term. Companies use that cash from one area to cross-subsidize others, to be able to invest in what is new.

For your life or for your organization, you can take an audit of how you spend your time and how you make your money. Are time and money aligned, or are you earning money in one area to support work in another? You can actually draw it on paper as two pie charts—one for time and one for money—or you can map it in your head for a moment. Are there areas that are vitally important to you that are not income generating? (I am reminded of Mrs. Moneypenny, the *Financial Times* columnist who referred to her children as Cost Centres 1, 2, and 3. There are many worthwhile things that are not income generating; the purpose here is just to ask and to notice.)

Looking at the areas that do not make money, identify the ones that are research and development, or studio-time practice, and consider exactly which other activities are supporting them. This structure of uneven time and money is a signal that you are self-investing—that you are paying from your income in one area to support start-up work in another, and that that crossover financial support is an act of investment.

SELF-INVESTMENT

Almost all of the people in this book so far had to self-invest in their projects in order to get them off the ground. Like Christo and Jeanne-Claude, they had to see their potential projects within the larger ecosystems of their working lives, supporting themselves through other jobs, or earning money in one area to support another.

Thomas Fogarty invented the balloon catheter by having a part-time job and still having the lucky economic container of childhood and enrollment in school. Bannister was paid as a trainee doctor and did his track workouts on his lunch break. He gave himself two years to try to make the mile attempt before giving up. Whitfield Diffie, the inventor of public-private-key encryption, took a low-paying research position and subsidized his living expenses by house-sitting. Fred Lebow, the founder of the New York City Marathon, worked as an executive for a company that made women's double-knit polyester suits. Harper Lee supported her writing with her day job as an airlines reservations agent, until she received the gift of a year's salary from her friends and after that a book advance from her publisher.

It is interesting in this context to read the note that Harper Lee's friends gave her to announce their gift. Lee recounted the events—finding a note hidden in the Christmas tree promising her a year off from work to write her book—in a 1961 essay she wrote for *McCall's* magazine called "Christmas to Me." She wrote:

> [The Browns] wanted to give me a full, fair chance to learn my craft, free from the harassments of a regular job. Would I accept their gift? There were no strings at all. Please accept, with their love.
>
> It took some time to find my voice. When I did, I asked if they were out of their minds. What made them think anything would come of this? They didn't have that kind of money to throw away. A year was a long time. What if the children came down with something horrible? As objection crowded upon objection, each was overruled. "We're all young," they said. "We can cope with whatever happens. If disaster strikes, you can always find a job of some kind. Okay, consider it a loan, then, if you wish. We just want you to accept. Just permit us to believe in you. You must."

At this point, Lee said to them, "It's a fantastic gamble. It's such a great risk." And Michael Brown said back to her, "No, honey. It's not a risk. It's a sure thing." Despite Brown's charming assuredness, any form of investment entails risk, and the "harassments of a regular job" are often part of the bargain.

In all these cases, these people took real risks and made sacrifices to commit to their projects. To drive cross-country learning about encryption, Diffie saved $12,000 and then vowed to "live low on the hog." The job he took at Stanford to be able to work closely with his collaborator Martin Hellman paid, according to Hellman, only about half of the going rate. Rolling that back a step further, even the author of *The Codebreakers* whose work was so important foundationally to Diffie's thinking, David Kahn, quit a job and moved in with his parents to finish writing the book. Snapchat, the $3 billion start-up, is based in Los Angeles because the founders had to move back home financially to start the company and—despite advice that they had to be in Silicon Valley—they stayed and built the firm in Los Angeles. Lebow personally paid for the New York City Marathon the first two years, and then guaranteed it financially in the third.

The process of self-investment can be especially hard because the market economy is designed to take away that surplus that inches you along, like Christo and Jeanne-Claude from wrapping a soup can to a car to a building. Another actor or just a competitive marketplace can easily take that extra bit of buffer in money or time that you need to scale up or just to maneuver. If you have ever rented an apartment in New York, the annual raise you receive in your job is usually swiftly followed by a letter from your landlord raising your rent by, if you're lucky, only a comparable amount. When you are on the profit harvesting side, that can feel great, but on the long-term value creation side it can prove difficult unless you have deep reserves of savings or a means of passive income at the outset. The market, like nature, abhors a vacuum. To preserve the surplus to be able to self-invest, you have to counter the inertia of the market toward profit maximization. Going back to chapter 1, you are essentially providing financial cover to keep a patch of ground for your studio-time practice. The way around this dilemma is first to think in terms of constructing your income and investment portfolios and then to own shares in your own projects.

Imagine that the economy is a vast body of water. To stay afloat in it, you will need a boat. To consider whether to invest in an early-stage lighthouse project, you have to ask if your boat can stay in balance. The balance question is one of portfolio thinking. Portfolio thinking will govern whether and how you can afford to invest in your lighthouse questions. You will need a balanced income portfolio in the short term and investment portfolio in the longer term.

The investment portfolio depends on ownership stakes. If indeed you can afford to work on a creative project without capsizing the boat, then that means you are protected against risk that the project won't go well. Your income portfolio has kept you in balance while you have been working. If it fails, your boat will not sink. But what if your project succeeds? If your project does well, you will need a bigger boat. Here you need the tools of ownership. If you can own a part of what you are making—if as an investor of time and effort you are an owner of a financial stake in it—then the boat will grow with you.

Building the creative project for balance and growth is a creative design task that takes some of the most free-market parts of free-market capitalism and pulls them out of theory and into the actual world. You may be surprised how much— even for people who swear by the tenets of the market—we actually don't get this right, but at the same time how much technology is now primed to make it easier to do. Too often the tools of the market ask people to work for free to prove something is possible but then not own any of the value they create. The concept of ownership stakes is really about assigning property rights. Only by owning shares or other exposure to the upside can you accurately reflect the risk and effort that go into creative work and the value that may get created.

What I am going to show you is how to more accurately calibrate the risk-reward space of creative work. You could say that this change is a form of putting the free—as in liberty—into free-market capitalism, instead of putting the free—as in unpaid—into freelancer.

The missing link in talking about ownership rights around investment is the idea of generosity and the reality that much creative work, from Harper Lee to Kickstarter, takes root within a gift economy. The gesture of Harper Lee's friends giving her a year's salary to write her book or of Fred Lebow's funding the marathon are gifts that hopefully set off chain reactions that lead to sustainable economic and social value.

Consider for a moment any people who have given you gifts like that, people to whom you have given those kinds of gifts, and the possibility that you have given those gifts to yourself—funding your education, for instance. In that context, the very idea of studio time or of research and development of any kind is an act of protecting space around the generosity of creation.

Assigning property rights, meaning thinking in terms of ownership, is not just a means to wealth. It is also a prerequisite to generosity. To give something away you must own it first. That kind of ownership does not immediately sound urgent, because there is usually a long gap between the moment you take a flyer to create something and the time when you reap what you sow—or get sued by someone else claiming they own it. But these tools could not be more urgent. They are the basis of how you claim the value that you contribute—so that you can profit from it or share it or reinvest it in more work.

ALL THROW PILLOWS AND NO COUCH

In the first several years after art school, I experimented with different working arrangements to support my own creative projects. I worked full-time for two years in an investment management firm, and then entered a freelancer phase of juggling a few different projects. At some stage I realized that I had interesting work but not enough structure and stability for my own comfort. It was a period of my life that I would call "all throw pillows and no couch." I had great individual projects but no larger structure underneath them. The couch is the economic scaffolding on which the pilot projects—the throw pillows—are safe and secure.

This phenomenon of how the small projects and the structural supports come together is the underlying question when you build the boat that supports your life. As a person, or manager, or company, do you have enough stability and balance? Any one of the throw pillows might eventually grow into the next big couch, but in the meantime, you need some degree of comfort that you haven't bet the farm on that happening. Otherwise put, the more you want to explore creatively, the more

you need to know that you are safe economically. Or, the crazier the throw pillows, the more beige the couch.

In a typical investment portfolio, the alternative investments—hedge funds, private equity, art—are important smaller portions of a larger whole. They are the throw pillows—or, in investment management language, the "correlation busters" that balance out the beige couch. A creative project often has the characteristics of an alternative investment—high risk, high return; uncorrelated to the market; based on absolute value and not larger trends, or what hedge fund managers call "alpha"— and so it is important to build a stable structure that those riskier ventures sit on. Your lighthouse questions from chapter 3 exist within the structure of your financial ecosystem.

Years after the throw-pillows phase, I adopted more of a couch strategy. I took a larger job that gave me health insurance and a steady baseline income. I traded some income for flexibility. I could invest on the side in creative projects, some paying and some not, and some paying in equity, of which more later. Those choices likely ebb and flow over the course of anyone's life, sometimes more toward the pillow-fort direction, and sometimes more toward the single structured couch.

Some people's working lives look more obviously like portfolios. In fact working life has this portfolio nature for most people. It's just that sometimes all of the tasks and projects are bundled together into one job. If you have a single job, you probably wear many different hats within it. Your job is likely a collection of activities, grouped under one title. For freelancers, those activities are often unbundled into many different projects. Whether yours are bundled or à la carte, it is useful to think about them as separable.

Even Leonardo da Vinci had this kind of portfolio life. You could actually argue that the *Mona Lisa* itself was—at the time he was making it—the throw pillow. Maybe not, but follow me for a second. Leonardo had more than one project at the time, and one of the others was a large public commission.

Historians believe that Leonardo worked on the *Mona Lisa* between 1503 and 1507, perhaps even continuing to work on it for another decade. He had made it for an Italian nobleman, Francesco del Giocondo, as a portrait of his wife. According to his own standards—and Leonardo was famous for not finishing work—the *Mona Lisa* was still unfinished in 1507 when he first seemed to stop working on it.

In the same time frame, Leonardo was at work on a much larger public commission for a mural. Depicting the Battle of Anghiari, the painting was to adorn one of the walls of the New Council Chamber in the Palazzo Vecchio in Florence. Leonardo received the commission sometime before October 1503. An amended contract for *The Battle of Anghiari* dates to May 4, 1504, and states that Leonardo had already been paid 35 florins and that he would be paid a further 15 florins each month from April 1504 until February 1505, to create all of the preparatory sketches for the mural. (A florin *larghi d'oro in oro*—a larger gold as opposed to silver type of florin—as he was paid, was worth about 140 soldis at the time. For comparison, according to Leonardo's *Notebooks* the price of a haircut was 11 soldis, the price of a salad 1 soldi.) As part of the arrangement Leonardo was also given a studio and a place to live. If Leonardo didn't produce a "cartoon"—a special drawing used to transfer an image to the wall—by February 1505, then the "Magnifici Signori" on the other end of the contract could demand that Leonardo return the advance. If Leonardo did make it to the cartoon stage then they would agree on an appropriate salary while he executed the full mural.

The Battle of Anghiari was a high-stakes project. Michelangelo—arguably Leonardo's artistic rival—had been commissioned to depict the Battle of Cascina on another wall in the same location. By June 1505, Leonardo did complete at least portions of the cartoon and he started transferring it onto the wall. He never finished the mural itself. He was experimenting technically with different painting materials, and the experiment failed. More than fifty years later Leonardo's biographer Giorgio Vasari, himself a painter, covered over the failed *Battle of Anghiari* with another mural.

Consider the *Mona Lisa* and *The Battle of Anghiari* to be two parts of Leonardo's work portfolio over the time from 1503 to 1507. The *Mona Lisa* survives as one of the most prized artworks in the world. *The Battle of Anghiari* does not, except in a few sketches—Leonardo's preparatory ones and later artists' imaginings of what it might have looked like. The large-scale commission from the city of Florence is couch-like in its scale. The steady income contributed meaningfully to his day-to-day expenses. Yet now the throw pillow is the more valuable object. (It is also the object that exists.)

All that is to say that Leonardo was balancing a portfolio lifestyle that included multiple paid projects as well as his personal explorations into science and invention. The structure by which he was paid also varied—sometimes as a stipend contingent on producing a specific work (*The Battle of Anghiari*), sometimes as a commission (*Mona Lisa*), and sometimes as a general form of patronage, as during his time as an artist in the court of the duke of Milan and later the king of France.

As a postscript to what happened economically to Leonardo's work-life portfolio from 1503 to 1507, Leonardo never delivered the *Mona Lisa* to the nobleman who commissioned it. He took the "unfinished" painting to France, where it became part of the collection of the king, François I, and then entered the Louvre. Curiously, the contract for *The Battle of Anghiari* seems to have let Leonardo keep all of the money he had been paid because he did get to the cartoon stage. If that seems particularly strategic or opportunistic on Leonardo's part to get exactly that far or to find it easier to stop after that point, it is also curious that the witness to the contract for *The Battle of Anghiari* was none other than Niccolò Machiavelli, then chancellor of Florence and, in 1513, author of *The Prince*, who argued that the ends justify the means.

Take a moment to consider what in your life is the throw pillow and what is the couch. What would it look like if your side project—your throw pillow—became the next couch? Even if it is completely unlikely, imagine what that would look like and how you might get there.

The takeaway is that anytime you have a portfolio, you don't know ahead of time which area will perform. You are trying to balance risk and stability. That means that in the short term, you are designing so that you cover the expenses of your life or your company. In the long term, projects that start off as throw pillows—*Mona Lisa* and otherwise—may have real payoffs. Whether you do well when they do well will depend on ownership stakes.

Before delving into those, it is worth expanding on how portfolio thinking—which we have been applying to individual people—applies to whole companies as well. When Bruce Henderson, the founder of the Boston Consulting Group, introduced the classic management-consulting framework of the growth-share matrix in 1970, he actually intended it as a tool to help companies maintain a healthy portfolio of "products with different growth rates and different market shares." As

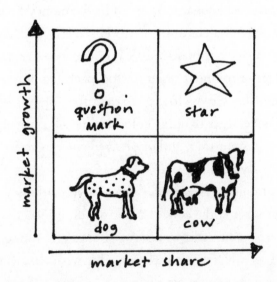

Henderson wrote, "The portfolio composition is a function of the balance between cash flows. . . . Margins and cash generated are a function of market share."

Henderson's 2x2 growth-share matrix crosses market share with market growth. If you have a huge market share and the market is growing, your product is a "star." If you own a huge share of the market but the market is not growing, it is a "cow" or cash cow, spinning off proceeds to fund other areas of your business. The art-thinking box on this chart is the "question mark"—the area where you do not yet own the market but it is growing, where there is possibility but not yet a payout. The last box, the "dog," is the one to avoid—low prospects and low preexisting success.

Although the chart was invented to describe business, it can pose helpful questions in the design of your life too. You can start by asking the general question: Which skills have I already built and which are new and growing? Of your new skills, if they are well received, you are a star. If you don't know yet if they will be, you have a question mark. Of your older skills, if some support you, they are the cash cow. If they have stopped being of service to you, they are the dog.

To generalize the questions of the growth-share matrix:

- Which project is your cash cow—spinning out money that supports your life but in a relatively established and staid way?
- Which project is a dog—taking all your energy and effort with very little to show for it? (There may be personal and noneconomic reasons to keep doing some of these things.)

- Which project is a question mark—something you are working on that might go very well but that is not yet known?
- Which project is a star—growing and succeeding at the same time? Whenever you see an opportunity to turn a question mark into a star you create your point-B world.

Portfolio thinking is a general tool to decide what to invest time and money in doing, and how to support yourself while you do. You want to be able to identify what you care about—even at the stage where you can only wrap a soup can or a Volkswagen so far. Identifying your MDQ from chapter 3, even if it can only be a throw pillow now, helps you structure support for yourself or your organization. That level of support becomes the couch you need to keep your working life in balance. As with studio time in chapter 1, money you invest in the throw pillow is not ever a loss so much as a tuition payment for what you are learning.

The diversified-portfolio approach allows projects to develop over time and at different rates. As unfashionable as slower growth is in a current climate of instant returns on technology, it can sometimes allow your ideas to bake in more interesting and lasting ways.

What complexifies the portfolio approach is that you are not just trying to manage the economics at a point in time—to get your income to cover all your expenses. You are also trying to build things that may grow to have greater value later. Thus you are caught in the middle of both production economics—cross-subsidizing—and investment management of risk and return. As noted before, it is especially hard by definition to know the value of creative work ahead of time because the value is only known in the point-B world you are creating, not in the point-A world in which you start. The value and even the character of early-stage work shifts over time. As we will see, that makes ownership stakes that much more important.

THE BRICK

In one perennial brainstorming exercise, the facilitator asks people to think of everything they can possibly do with a brick. It is a standard-issue brick, dark red, with several holes inside. In brainstorming—and take a minute here to do this if you like—you can build up quite a list: bake a chicken under it, pulverize it to make exfoliating powder, plant flowers in it, use it as a weapon, use it to weight down a body in the East River, make a chair, have a paperweight, the list goes on. If you—as I have done—do this exercise in a room full of professional artists or designers, it will take ages before someone mentions anything as obvious as building a wall or a house.

The reason I am so taken with the brick as a brainstorming exercise is that the brick is a metaphor for why it is so hard to know the value of something in its early days. In many cases, the companies we now take for granted started out with a brick that they were intending to use to make a wall or a house. Then circumstances conspired to tell them that the wall or the house wasn't going to be possible. They had to do something else.

Google started with a search algorithm that Larry Page and Sergey Brin tried to sell, but which no one would buy. Everyone that they met with told them search was dead. So they started a company instead.

DuPont started when Irénée du Pont, having arrived in America from France in 1800, wanted to go hunting but thought American gunpowder was very poorly made. The French chemist Antoine Lavoisier—a heavy hitter in the history of chemistry, contributing such helpful basics as discovering the necessity of oxygen to fire—happened to have taught Du Pont to make gunpowder. So Du Pont started a gunpowder business. The company grew into a munitions supplier, selling so many weapons to the U.S. government in wartime that they became known as the "merchants of death." Then the company very nearly went bankrupt. After recovering through a restructuring, they defined their mission more broadly and became stewards and trailblazers working under the trademark "the miracles of science." If you own clothing that stretches or cookware that is nonstick, chances are you have experienced their broader remit.

The next time you are in a store in your neighborhood, ask how long the store has been there and how it came to be. Maybe it is a deli that a family owns. In the same way you would study a toddler learning to walk, marveling at the subtle gain of skills and balance, notice the lives of companies—when they walk, when they run, when they reframe the stories they project about themselves.

Businesses must constantly change, explore, evolve, discard, and move forward to stay alive. The brick represents cultivating a present-minded mental elasticity to move forward with utter commitment and acceptance of uncertainty. None of us has a crystal ball, and seeing how much businesses change over longer time periods is a reminder to stay nimble in our thinking. It also solidifies the other core tool of risk management: planning for the possibility of success by owning some piece of what you create.

OWNING THE UPSIDE

If you have made creative work and it succeeds, what happens? If you picture the boat—the structure that protects your creative space within the ocean of the market—whether the boat grows with you or not when you succeed depends entirely on whether you own a part of what you make.

Ownership is such a basic concept it is easy not to think about its consequences fully. I spend a lot of time thinking about ownership because it is the single most broken part of the economy with regard to creative work. Ownership is required for value to circulate correctly within the market. What I want to show you is the difference between renting and owning anything, including your time or your work. That difference is one of the most profound levers in the economy, and therefore one

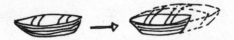

of the most ripe tools for better managing the ways in which creative work comes into the world.

Let me lay a foundation by looking at ownership—property—in the developing world, where it is easier to see what might get taken for granted. What is property? You might think of real estate as property in the sense of land, or the stuff in your home as falling under the heading of personal property. A broader definition of property has two parts—its nature as "stuff" and its legal nature as a tradable, salable, and investible store of value. For instance, you own a house that you live in, but that house also exists as a financial instrument to which you have legal title and for which you can get a mortgage. It is a house and a financial instrument. In his 2000 book, *The Mystery of Capital: Why Capitalism Triumphs in the West and Fails Everywhere Else*, Hernando de Soto argued that the collective poor in the developing world own trillions of dollars' worth of stuff—including real estate—but without owning the title. Without the legal ownership that title would give them, their belongings are what De Soto calls "dead capital." Their stuff cannot participate in markets. As De Soto writes, "They have houses but not titles; crops but not deeds; businesses but not statutes of incorporation."

The consequence is that the economy itself cannot develop in a modernized, Western capitalistic way. If your house appreciates in value, you cannot easily sell it to realize that profit unless you have legal title. If you wanted to buy a house but could only afford it with a mortgage, that wouldn't be possible. Without a robust legal system of financial ownership, the channels of trade get shut down, the economy stops circulating, and it becomes very hard for people to build wealth.

To make their case, De Soto's teams of researchers started in the 1980s and '90s to try to incorporate small businesses or to buy property in the developing world. They would adhere to the letter of the law and see how long it took. Their theory was that people had not previously pursued formal legal ownership because it was such a hassle—a high transaction cost. It turned out they were right. One research team attempted to open a small clothing factory outside Lima, Peru. They worked six hours each day—filling out paperwork, waiting in registry offices, taking bus trips into the center of town. Getting the business officially registered took 289 days. The process cost them $1,231, which was roughly thirty times the monthly minimum wage at the time. The researchers found similar difficulty obtaining legal ownership in many other countries.

Although we might not think of ourselves this way, entrepreneurs aside, most of us rent and do not own our own output as workers. We are employees of companies and those companies own what we make. We may have significant advantages in innumerable regards over the people De Soto and his researchers studied, but we also lack the full power of property rights.

If you make a movie and then sell it outright for $100,000, you are no longer a property owner in that film. If you had taken a 10 percent stake instead and the film grossed $1,000,000, you would make $100,000 but by a different mechanism and risk decision. With the 10 percent stake, you could get paid zero or infinity. A hybrid between the two examples is a healthy structure—perhaps a $50,000 salary and a 5 percent stake, or something else in between.

Anyone who is paid a salary or a flat project fee is essentially renting out their time and brainpower. Sometimes taking a salary is an excellent personal risk-management decision if steady income is the highest priority, but in the case of creative work it makes sense to own at least a small fraction of what you contribute.

The most common ways in which people own a fraction of what they create include royalties and equity shares (or stock options). What happens when you have ownership shares is that you share the risk and you may lose, but as you succeed, the boat grows with you.

The trajectory of the investor and technologist Andreas "Andy" von Bechtolsheim illustrates this point. Perhaps best known as the cofounder of Sun Microsystems, Bechtolsheim actually started receiving royalties when he was a teenager. Still in Germany, in 1973 at the age of fifteen, Bechtolsheim came up with a novel microprocessor system for the Intel 8080. He was in high school and too young to take a formal job, so the company offered to pay him a royalty instead of a salary. He was taking on both a general and a cash-flow risk— only being paid when a unit sold and receiving that payment well after he had done the work. Because the device sold well, he earned enough money to come study in the United States two years later. That financial base established by the royalty then led indirectly—for instance, in the absence of student debt—to his being able to found Sun Microsystems. That led in turn to his being able to write a $100,000 check to "Google Inc." in 1998—the check that caused Larry Page and Sergey Brin to incorporate the business so that they could cash it. By taking the royalty, he placed a bet on his own success and it paid off.

Royalties were also central in the life of Thomas Fogarty, the inventor of the balloon catheter, from chapter 1. Despite his breakthrough inventing the device, Fogarty could not find a company to manufacture it. After being turned down twenty times, by chance Fogarty met Albert "Al" Starr. Starr was a celebrity in Fogarty's field because, on September 21, 1960, he had become the first cardiac surgeon to implant an artificial mitral valve in a human heart. Starr had also invented the heart valve he implanted. He had worked closely with a retired hydraulics engineer named Miles "Lowell" Edwards. In order to manufacture the device, Edwards had founded a company called Edwards Lifesciences. When Fogarty met Starr, Starr in turn called Edwards and said, "You've got to make this catheter for this kid because he can't get anybody to make it."

Edwards did. And when Edwards Lifesciences went to write Fogarty's contract, they simply copied the terms from the contract Starr had. That gave Fogarty the exact same percentage royalty as the much more senior surgeon. That royalty became generative in Fogarty's life, paving the way for the more than 165 other patents he would come to hold.

When you make a creative work—something that was inefficient to produce and which you had to invest time and resources in before the value was known—owning all or part of it allows you to have exposure to an upside of your own making. Let's say someone offers you $1,000 for a project because they believe your work will lead to $2,000 in profit and they want to pay you half. If you take $500 instead and own a proportionate fraction of their projected revenue, if you exceed those expectations then you get more than the additional $500. If you can get the flat-fee portion to cover your living expenses, then you have kept the boat in balance and lined up an interesting ownership stake in your own work.

The lack of systematic ownership stakes in the visual arts is instructive in explaining the potential for owning shares in creative work of any kind. At the famous Scull sale in 1973 at the auction house then known as Sotheby Parke Bernet, the taxi magnate Robert Scull sold a Robert Rauschenberg painting for $85,000 that he had bought in 1958 for only $900. Rauschenberg attended the auction and confronted Scull at the end, allegedly punching or shoving him. The price Scull received was based on value Rauschenberg had helped to create through his subsequent career. But Rauschenberg didn't own any exposure to that upside. He no longer held ownership stakes in that work.

In that context, consider how differently artists and writers are paid. In 1973, the same year as the Scull sale, Rauschenberg's longtime romantic partner, Jasper Johns, gave or sold one of his paintings, *Flag*, to his close friend the writer Michael Crichton. In 2010 that painting sold from Crichton's estate for $28.6 million. Johns and Crichton, both enormously success-ful, were paid by different mechanisms. Crichton in his lifetime sold 200 million books. He was paid a royalty each time, even if a book he wrote in the 1970s sold a copy in the 2000s. Johns was paid only the first time each work was sold.

Since 1973, the art world has grappled with the idea of resale royalties, a structure that would let artists own a percentage of the increased value of their art each time it was resold. Califor-nia passed legislation in 1976 but it was later contested under the U.S. Constitution's interstate commerce clause and, by most ac-counts, was not well enforced. In the first thirty years of the law, only $325,000 total was collected, a paltry sum relative to the likely size of the art trade in California over that time. Critics also cited the fact that artists benefited from resale royalties later in their careers after they had already achieved some success.

But what critics failed to notice—and which applies far outside the arts—is the basic nature of a resale royalty as a property right. Once assigned, it can trade anytime. An artist who owns a resale royalty can sell that royalty to another person as an investment, many years before the royalty would ever be collected. An entire market for shares can follow—creating patronage for the artists who sell shares into it and a vehicle for diversified art investment for the buyers of those shares.

The same kind of scheme works for people in any field. Once you own equity or royalties in projects you create—whether working solo or under the umbrella of a company—your ability to make risk and investment decisions around your own work radically shifts. That logic of the tradable royalty or share can reframe many forms of ownership and pay, starting with a more general focus on value itself.

Think of the way in which you get paid. Do you receive a salary? Do you own equity—stock, stock options—or other forms of exposure to reward when you create value—bonus pay, dividends, royalties? Do you work in a culture where systems of bonuses, equity, or royalties would be conceivable? For instance, I have a friend, let's call her Jessica, who is a teacher. Her class size was increased by 30 percent but her salary did not change. Her workload increased, and the revenue the school brought in through tuition went up. Whether you feel like you will have the ability to negotiate for better terms immediately, try to notice how your compensation is related to your value. What total percentage of your organization's budget goes to your pay? What portion of your organization's value do you generate?

You can look up any U.S. nonprofit's financials on the website Guidestar, or the financial statement of any publicly traded U.S. company on the Securities and Exchange Commission website through their EDGAR database. You can also look up a study of salaries by job title on the U.S. government's Bureau of Labor Statistics. Can you come up with a mix of salary and upside that covers your expenses and accounts for your value?

If you are trying to assign a royalty percentage or amount of equity, the way to think about it is in terms of "added value." If you subtracted yourself out of a situation, how would the picture change? The answer to that question defines your added value. If nothing changes, you have no added value. Your ownership should be proportional to your added value, a fraction and not a dollar amount.

Sometimes added value is hard to quantify. I was once told the story of an unassuming city government employee who retired. A few months later, her team called and asked if they could pay her to come sit in on their meetings. They found that simply her presence elevated their conversations. Your value may be similarly ephemeral, or clearly quantifiable. If you cannot be given shares, you can make a case for nonmonetary forms of ownership like authorship or for options—for the promise of shares later if they come to exist. (It is increasingly common for start-ups to be funded by convertible debt—loans that can be converted to shares later. In cases where you donate your time, you may wish to give your time freely. But if you are giving your time because there is no money to pay you, convertible debt could be a potentially helpful structure. The value of your time would be agreed upon as a loan to the start-up and that debt would be convertible to equity later.)

When you try to align your ownership with your value, you want to keep in mind the support you are receiving—financial and otherwise—from other people. In some cases you will need to give up substantial ownership because someone else is taking on so much risk of funding a project. For instance, an employer who pays you a fixed salary is actually taking on a lot of risk that you will actually perform. Even if you own only a very small fraction of shares in your work, you have some exposure to the returns that you have created.

Ultimately, it matters more that you own something than that you get the amount exactly right. There is not a precise answer. There is a number that probably feels too high and another that probably feels too low, and you want to hit between those two posts. A serial entrepreneur I used to work for once said, either a number is big enough that it doesn't matter or small enough that it doesn't matter either. You either own a fraction of Facebook early on, or a fraction of a failed company. The outcome is either so huge that everyone shares in the wealth or so small that no one really does.

Either way, you will see financial decisions around creative work shift toward ownership. In the field of television, Matthew Blank, the CEO of Showtime Networks, said that over time he unequivocally chooses for the company to own its own productions—a vote of confidence in the quality of its programming and a risk-return investment decision to own the upside that they create.

Owning shares solves a few distinct and important purposes. First, it aligns your interest with the value that is contributed. Second, it clarifies the boundaries of property rights, which can make it easier to collaborate or trade or be able to give things away in the course of accomplishing a project. Third, it allows you to represent more accurately how collective so many acts of creative work really are by more easily having fractional ownership.

WHEN THE WHOLE IS LESS THAN THE SUM OF THE PARTS

Building a framework for fractional ownership requires us to consider both law and technology. Technology makes it possible to head toward a world not just where you own shares in your work but where many people can easily manage ownership of tiny fractions of many different projects. With the easily managed fractional ownership that technology enables, over time you could own an entire portfolio of shares in all the projects you have worked on in the past. That possibility leads to a potential future in which, instead of having a single salary, you have a pixelated investment portfolio of microshares. Instead of having the single large, beige couch, you have many different pieces that come together, like dots in a pointillist painting, into a steady enough base of support.

But to do that, shared economic ownership needs to be designed around existing law. Legal frameworks that grow out of intellectual property law tend to assign ownership wholly to one party or another. Instead licensing and royalty schemes need to be built around existing intellectual property law, or the law itself needs to be updated to reflect the realities of collaborative creation beyond simple joint copyright.

In some creative fields like writing, film, and music, these royalty schemes exist to let creators easily own a portion of the profits from their work. Sometimes, as in the case of music, the artists make a case that they need to own a greater share—that their fraction is below the low end of the comfort range.

In others, like visual art, the systems don't fully exist or, where they do, they have brought significant litigation.

The lack of schemes for fractional ownership has had a significant downside. What I am about to describe is like the story of an action film where the hero goes off for an unassuming hike in the woods but does not bring a raincoat or a water bottle. Storms strike, drought happens, the hero must fight. Fighting for survival after the storms has a sense of urgency. What is *important* though is taking the raincoat and water bottle in the first place. Taking a jacket is a boring habit, but far preferable to having to survive in the wilderness without one. In this case, the boring but vital habit is always maintaining clarity around economic and legal forms of ownership, so that you can avoid situations like this next one where a system of ownership around creative work is broken.

In 2000, a man named Carter Bryant decided to leave his job at the toy company Mattel Inc. to go work for their competitor, MGA Entertainment—about thirty miles north of Mattel's Los Angeles headquarters.

The largest product category for Mattel is Barbie, the leggy blonde first invented in 1959 by Ruth Handler. Since then, Barbie has become the marquee product for a company that was previously known for plastic ukuleles and miniature pianos.

Bryant had the idea to create a new kind of doll for MGA Entertainment. Part Spice Girls, part Benetton advertisement, part pouty-lipped Kardashian, the dolls would be called Bratz. With bigger heads and more exaggerated features, they took Barbie's surfer-blonde aesthetic to a much more parent-worrying level of sassiness. Bratz were also more multiethnic than Barbie. One darker-skinned doll, Yasmin, was named after the daughter of MGA founder Isaac Larian, an Iranian immigrant and entrepreneur.

The Bratz dolls debuted in 2001. In 2004, Mattel sued MGA Entertainment. Mattel claimed that Bryant had developed the Bratz dolls at Mattel and therefore, Mattel owned the doll. Since 2004, the courts have been volleying a verdict from one side of the argument to the other. With legal action still in play more than a decade later, the clearest winners have seemed to be anyone collecting fees. (By 2014, Mattel alone had paid an estimated $138 million in legal fees.) Whoever owns the intellectual property, Bryant's reward for inventing the doll has been a form of incarceration in a legal process.

Legal ownership is black-and-white, where the shades of gray of fractional ownership could more flexibly assign value. Binary legal ownership may sound simple and innocuous, in a frog-in-boiling-water way, because that is the system we have all become accustomed to operating in. Working on creative projects is risky. It is also collaborative. A legal system that assigns intellectual property in a winner-take-all way hits up against design constraints around supporting creative work.

In copyright, you either have "fair use" or not. In patent law, you either own the patent or you don't. In trademark law, you are either infringing or you are not. Particularly in the case of copyright, a key reason that legal frameworks tend toward binary ownership is that they originate in free speech. For speech to truly be protected, it needs to be owned outright: Yes, you can speak or, no, you may not. Free speech is one of the most central and important tenets of a democracy. Even so, some of our legal frameworks around the economic side of intellectual property may need to be updated to more robustly take into account the realities of collaboration and the need for joint financial ownership of creative work.

In the case of Mattel and MGA Entertainment, it may be that one side feels sufficiently wronged to merit the case, but anytime a verdict shifts back and forth that many times, the likelihood increases that both sides have a point. And the point may be that work-for-hire contracts—in which Mattel could even claim complete ownership of their employees' work in the first place—are themselves seriously outmoded.

With fractional ownership, companies could negotiate and settle on a percentage royalty instead of battling out for the whole stake. Intellectual property cases routinely settle by means of a negotiated licensing fee, but the system could be much more intentionally constructed. As the keeper of your own contracts, you need to develop ways of carving out shared ownership—of devising licenses, and of modifying work-for-hire clauses where they do exist. Also important are clauses in employment and consulting contracts that, in the event of a dispute, the parties must engage in mediation to negotiate a licensing arrangement before being able to go to court.

Thinking legalistically about fractional ownership can quickly get philosophically complex and abstract, and rights will almost never be assigned perfectly. For instance, if a famous artist was only able to make valuable work because he ate pizza late at night to fuel himself, does that pizza shop own any rights to his work? Why was Robin Thicke sued successfully by the heirs to Marvin Gaye for the musical origins of his song "Blurred Lines," but the Rolling Stones borrowed generally from blues musicians and that was okay? At some level, many actors have a claim of added value—the music of Elvis wouldn't exist without blues musicians—and not everyone will get paid all the time. But it is still important to try to share the value that is created. And as technology makes it cheaper and easier to manage the oversight of fractional shares and to transfer small payments, the economic side of ownership opens up.

A recent copyright case in the arts, *Cariou vs. Prince*, highlights another dimension of the limitations of copyright and the ways in which fractional ownership is foundationally important for creative work.

In 2000, an artist named Patrick Cariou published a book of photographs called *Yes Rasta*. Cariou had spent six years of his life living in the midst of a Rastafarian community in Jamaica and photographing the people who lived there. Over time, Cariou received about $8,000 from this work.

In 2007 and 2008, the artist Richard Prince started to exhibit a series of large canvases, called *Canal Zone*, which borrowed significantly from Cariou's work, and Cariou sued him.

By professional label, both Cariou and Prince are "artists" but Cariou is referred to as an ethnographic photographer and Prince, who is represented by the preeminent dealer Larry Gagosian, is well known in the art world as an "appropriation" artist. (The art world is full of terms like "appropriation" that describe behavior that advances the boundaries of the definition of art and that sometimes create works of beauty but which would not be allowed of a fifth grader completing a homework assignment.)

Appropriation in this case means copying directly. In the 1970s, Prince rephotographed the iconic Marlboro Man advertisements and presented those images as his own work. In the 1990s, he made a series called *Nurses* by transferring the cover art from pulp fiction featuring nurses onto canvas and then painting over those images. Here, Prince collaged over-sized reproductions of Cariou's figures onto somewhat expressive, abstractly marked canvases. The case was decided in both directions—in nuanced ways and with significant procedural detail—and then settled.

From a legal point of view, copyright law offers clear frameworks. It sometimes weirdly puts judges in the position of being art historians, ascertaining whether Prince has modified Cariou's photos of naked men and women enough. But from an economic point of view, both Cariou and Prince clearly have some claim of "added value." Without both of them, the work in question would not exist.

Economically, they should each own a piece somehow. Exactly how might such an arrangement be structured? We have to look at how all the different forms of value circulate, and what is gained and lost in the appropriation. While it is tempting to start with artistic merit, aesthetic achievement is hard to define and actually not the most important place to focus. You can admire the artistry of Cariou's original work, or even the artistry of Prince's appropriation, but the questions to ask first are economic:

- Cariou made $8,000. Prince sold several of the paintings for more than $10 million each. (How much of that he kept is not known, but a typical artist-dealer split is 50-50.) How much would it cost Prince to re-create the photos himself instead of relying on Cariou's work? How much did it cost Cariou to make the photographs, even if he ran at a loss relative to the $8,000 he was paid? Considering

the opportunity cost of his time, did he give up other lucrative work to be there?

- What value of magnification did Prince's exhibition have?
  You could mentally model Prince as Cariou's agent for a
  moment. Prince brought Cariou's work into a high-art
  context, under the umbrella of Prince's existing reputation. Both of those factors have real economic impact, the
  same way that a Hollywood agent, upon discovering an
  actress, can radically level-jump her income.

- Does Prince's work inhibit Cariou's ability to carry on
  with his own creative franchise? Does the appropriation
  interfere with the continued life of the original?

These questions, taken together, center on production
economics—Cariou's actual expenses and his opportunity
costs, and Prince's foregone ones—and on reputational bump
and possible impingements. In essence, how much did it cost,
how much was saved, how much value was added, and at what
if any future costs to Cariou? These are questions you can
apply to any similar situation.

If someone asked me to be a philosopher king who decided
this case, I would give Cariou somewhere between $100,000 and
$250,000. That is a relatively small sum compared to Prince's
income from the sales, and a relatively large sum relative to
Cariou's prior income. Where in the $100,000–250,000 range
the payment fell would depend on the rest of Cariou's personal economics. Also crucial is designing the framework for
the negotiation itself. For as long as traditional copyright laws
exist, this kind of economic conversation will fall under pretrial

negotiation. I would like to think that from Prince's standpoint, or even that of his dealer, the $250,000 compares favorably to the legal fees themselves, and that for Cariou the $100,000 compares well to the $8,000 for work he did over three years of his life.

As a philosopher king, I would also have already devised a scheme for artists to own resale royalties, or other forms of equity, in their work. I would give Cariou a portion of Prince's resale royalty, perhaps one percentage point of Prince's 15 percent share. The aim is not to pull precise numbers out of thin air; they don't exist. At the outset of the lawsuit, each of these parties—Cariou and Prince—is a starring character in his own movie. The aim is to attempt to be fair to both plotlines and economically to give credit where it is due. The reality is that by virtue of Prince's appropriation, he has pulled in Cariou as a collaborator. They need to share in the upside they have made. And Cariou needs to be able to be generous—to spend three years making a not-lucrative project, without risking that someone else will come along and commercialize it when he has not.

Outside of copyright, fractional ownership platform schemes exist in a number of fields and can be generalized to manage shares in any kind of creative work.

In the pharmaceutical industry, the company Royalty Pharma has created a marketplace for shares in pharmaceutical royalties. In the late 1990s, Memorial Sloan Kettering, the storied cancer research hospital in Manhattan, found itself in the position of having concentrated ownership in one specific asset. The hospital owned a royalty on two related cancer drugs, Neupogen and Neulasta.

Those drugs were produced by the company Amgen in most

countries. In 2009, global sales of those drugs were $4.6 billion. Memorial Sloan Kettering's share of those sales was valued at $500 million, an especially significant sum relative to the hospital's $1.6 billion total endowment. What Royalty Pharma did was to buy 80 percent of the hospital's royalty for $400 million. That meant that Memorial Sloan Kettering still owned exposure to both the risk and potential upside of the royalty—the remaining 20 percent of it—but they also got to realize cash that they could then invest in many other things, diversifying their portfolio.

THE PARTICULARITIES OF
OWNERSHIP FOR DIGITAL WORK

Newer model ownership schemes also exist in the issuance and distribution of music. Matt Mason, who until 2015 was the chief content officer of the platform BitTorrent, worked with musical artists to create BitTorrent bundles—collections of music that are published on the platform. The musicians own the vast majority of the value in that work, giving BitTorrent a share in exchange for distribution. BitTorrent takes a far lower share than other publishers like iTunes would take. In 2015 *Fast Company* named Mason one of the one hundred most creative people in business that year.

More general ownership platforms depend on the nature of digital work of any kind, meaning that digital files are infinitely copyable. I have observed this closely in a company I advise, a platform called Bitmark. Sean Moss-Pultz, the founder, got the idea to start the company when he had his first son. A California transplant to Taiwan and a sleep-addled new parent, Sean thought idly about how he'd like to pass along his vast music collection to his son one day. As with most of us, the majority of his music is stored digitally. It suddenly occurred to Sean that he didn't actually own any of it. He owned licenses to use digital copies of songs, and those licenses went with him to the grave. He felt sad that he could never pass his music collection on to his son.

Instead of leaving it there, Sean started a company. He reasoned that the same forms of technology he used in his work—complicated encryption mechanisms—could make it easy to know whether a digital file was real or a copy. A math whiz who dropped out of physics graduate school and also a serial entrepreneur, Sean built a blockchain structure that, like Bitcoin, would be ferociously complicated to understand but conveniently also ferociously difficult to code-break, and too distributed a network to govern narrowly. That platform would become a registry to make digital objects unique. Because of this authentication, you could own an album again, now digitally, because your computer could tell that the album was unique and unpirated.

A platform like Bitmark makes it increasingly possible to manage the ownership of fractions of things. If you can issue a digital object like an album securely, the computer can manage fractions of those objects almost as easily as whole ones. A musician, down to the thirtieth backup singer, can seamlessly get paid a royalty however small. Or, if you invest in your friend's company, you can essentially receive a tiny fraction of ownership instead of a Kickstarter prize. Computing technology is good at managing these tiny pieces in a way that fax machines and paper checks never were.

The regulatory environment is catching up with making this kind of democratized ownership more flexible. In 2012, the U.S. Congress passed the JOBS Act—the Jumpstart Our Business Startups Act. That law aimed to relax private placement law, making it easier for a larger, not already wealthy class of investors to buy shares in private companies.* Instead of giving money to your friend's crowdfunding campaign, you might own shares in his or her business. If it goes well, you own a small piece of it. If the business goes bust, your contribution reverts to being a gift. As the legislative environment continues to evolve, the technology exists to make such a platform possible.

The larger need is to get comfortable with this kind of fractional thinking, in our own projects and in larger compensation schemes. Fractional ownership is, in some ways, close to the financialization of the person, but it is also closer than any other instrument to the alignment of value created and price received. If we could get comfortable, then more people's working lives could start to shift from production economics in which you get paid as a labor input of the productive firm to a hybrid of worker and investor—in which you are a co-owner in the projects you are laboring to create.

---

* Under existing law, you are only eligible to invest in private equity if you are an "accredited investor" or a "qualified purchaser," a requirement to have $1 million or $5 million in assets, respectively. The accredited investor standard comes from "Regulation D," a carve-out in the Securities Act of 1933 that compels companies to report to the government, unless they only take money from accredited investors. The rationale was that, in the wake of the Depression, the government should protect citizens from losing the shirt off their back in a fraudulent investment by monitoring companies, but if it's your fifteenth shirt, they will leave you alone. Wealth is a proxy for sophistication, or a sign you could hire someone to advise you. The "AI" standard is also met if you are single earning $200,000 a year or jointly earning $300,000 and expect that to continue. The "QP" standard comes from the Investment Company Act of 1940. Whether both standards apply depends on the legal and regulatory status of the firm you are investing in.

Over time, as technological management of shares in intellectual property grows, it will be possible for more people to make the decision that entrepreneurs do—to shade down your take-home salary in exchange for ownership stakes in the value you create. As more workers become freelancers and more firms, like Uber, take advantage of that free-agent status, we may all become, financially speaking, constellations of pixelated ownership. Eventually as a creative person, your day job could form the couch and your portfolio of royalties could come together like tiny pixels to create a coherent larger picture of investments in many different ventures.

The core shifts here are from maximization of utility to creation of value and from consumption to investment. Once you assign property rights correctly, the market can get a lot closer to the ultimate ideal of business as a medium: to make price equal value. The combination of building portfolios and rethinking ownership stakes keeps the boat in balance and fuels the creation of unknown value, ultimately rewarding anyone's inner artist.

The development of creative work is complex and uncertain. It needs the structural supports of income and investment portfolios. Assigning ownership stakes allows you to think from the perspective of collaboration, of the creation of value, and of managing the real risks of exploring the new.

The next step is to build organizational environments and culture in which that collaboration and open-ended process are possible—for individual workers and at the scale of larger groups and whole companies. The next kind of property right that gets assigned is not ownership stakes in your work but roles and responsibilities in your workplace.

CHAPTER 5

To Be in the Fray

Management is a craft, not a science. Beware of those
who try to mathematize and quantify human behavior. . . .
You simply cannot put numbers on everything.
It is, to my way of thinking, a failure of imagination.

—Donald Keough, president emeritus of the Coco-Cola Company

Ed Epping never planned to become an artist—let alone an art
professor charged with managing the creative development
of scores of students—when he enrolled in college in 1966 at
Western Illinois University. The day he and his parents drove
to orientation, a heat wave rolled across the state. His parents
were getting divorced and were either fighting constantly or
sitting in hostile silence. His mother insisted Ed wear a sports
jacket and that he keep it on for the entire two-and-a-half-hour
car ride. Their 1954 Buick had no air-conditioning. The radio

blared news of a man who would later be identified as Richard Speck who had just killed nine nurses in Chicago. Ed said, "It was not a good day."

As they arrived on campus in Macomb, Illinois, about a hundred first-year students and their parents streamed into a basement that smelled like a gym locker room, and an assistant registrar began to hold forth. If there are some jobs, like delivering babies and welcoming people to college, that require a person, as part of the job, to honor the singularity of the event for the other party, the registrar didn't get the memo. After droning on for forty minutes, she handed out booklets that exactly replicated the contents of her talk. Ed, still in his sports coat, wanted to get out of there as quickly as possible.

He looked at the first few pages of the book, which instructed him on how to fill out his course registration card. The sample schedule belonged to an art major. Registering for classes at a big state university then was tantamount to declaring a major. Ed wanted to leave so badly he copied the sample schedule. The registrar didn't notice that his schedule was exactly the same as the one in the book and commended him on handing it in early.

That semester Ed had two different art professors. One was a stickler for technical skills and believed in old-fashioned methods like drawing from the figure. The other was from California, full of big ideas and the enthusiasm of being a first-year teacher. Ed was hooked.

Ed is the reason I ever took an art class in college. I was a political science major when I saw Ed's watercolor class one spring afternoon painting by the side of a stream. To enroll, I had to take a drawing course first, my first art class in college. Ed never actually taught watercolor again while I was a student, but he did teach me, and a few decades' worth of other people, how to paint in oils—and how by extension to work creatively by ourselves and in conversation with other people.

At the beginning of the first day of painting class, Ed would give a talk about judgment. He would say that especially if we were just starting out, it would be easy to say things were "good" or "bad." If we said we weren't very good at something or were bad at it, what we were really doing was giving up responsibility for our work. Instead, he wanted us to be "critically self-aware." He wanted us to be able to observe what was working, to see what strengths to build on and what areas needed help. What Ed did in that classroom was to create a space and a conversation in which we could bring ourselves to our work. He knew the vulnerability of making things and scaled up his ability to shepherd a lot of us through that, individually and as a group.

Thinking back to some of the earlier tools of this book, one of the things Ed was doing was making it safe for anyone to risk finding their lighthouse—committing to a large question with an as yet unknown answer. As in the figure-ground compositional tool from chapter 1, Ed was setting the ground from which the figure of our work could emerge. Although it was a classroom setting and not a workplace, some of Ed's challenges and decisions managing the group shed light on the larger questions of managing creative process within a workplace.

The need for coordination and performance review lends the management of creative process particular challenges within organizations. You are not just grappling with each person's vulnerability as a maker, but dealing with complex systems, larger goals, and hard requirements for organizational performance. An art studio may feel alien and separate from a corporate culture of any kind. But as in an art classroom, you have the same need to evaluate performance while encouraging people to bring their whole selves to their work and to feel safe to risk failure along the way.

In that context, the manager of work in progress—what I will call W.i.P or "whip"—is a lot like Ed. His or her job is not to fix the problem directly but to hold the space for something new to grow. That can be an intensive and invisible kind of work. Your main tools are those of conversation and those of process. Your aim is to foster the individual mindsets of being in the weeds and pursuing lighthouse questions in the setting of complex organizations that, whether for-profit or not-for-profit, must function in the marketplace.*

THE GOOD ENOUGH MANAGER

This framework of management is rooted in the ideas of Donald Woods Winnicott, the storied early-twentieth-century British psychiatrist and pediatrician credited by his biographer Adam Phillips as writing like Lewis Carroll and bringing "a comic tradition" to psychoanalysis.

Winnicott had many ideas on how to parent healthy children, perhaps none as influential as his concept of "the Good Enough Mother."** Winnicott believed that no parent was perfect but that during an important period early in a child's life, from the child's point of view, he or she is inseparable from the mother. The mother perfectly mirrors and responds to the child's needs. That the baby is at one with the parent is an illusion. Over time, the parent's job is to gradually disillusion the child. Thus for Winnicott, the act of raising a child is a guided withdrawal from illusion to disillusionment.

---

* A nonprofit structure is also a market structure. It is a specific response to a market failure, designed with a combination of regulation and strategy.

** Winnicott lived from 1896 until 1971. Given the time in which he wrote, it feels safe to assume his ideas extend to parents of any gender. Winnicott himself had two older sisters, as well as a mother, a nanny, and a governess. (Phillips, *Winnicott,* 28.)

The manager of creative process is like the good enough mother—except a good enough manager instead. The creative project is the new baby that needs to be held. In order to develop, it needs to be mirrored back and supported. Over time, that idea must grow to self-sufficiency and be able to exist fully formed in the world. The illusion that needs to be overcome is that the "baby" of the creative idea can exist apart from the market. Eventually the idea needs to hold its integrity while supporting itself.

The good enough manager's main job is to create a "holding environment," a space in which people feel safe to explore and to work from an authentic self.* In cases where the holding environment was not present, Winnicott found that the children coped by adopting a "false self"—a protective cover for their true identities. The consequences of the false self were dire. As he wrote, "Only the true self can be creative."

That's not to say that all management practice needs to be a holding container or that all good ideas have to come about that way. Demonstrably, many great ideas have been executed and great ventures started by the brute-strength methods of robber barons, thuggish industrialists, and Machiavellian opportunists. Other seemingly thriving cultures, like Ray Dalio's investment firm Bridgewater Associates, take shaming as a management strategy to its logical extreme. (Dalio favors what he calls "radical transparency" in which employees' faults are

---

* The idea of the holding environment originated in Winnicott's study of children who were separated from their parents during World War II. He studied children between the ages of two and five who were sent out of London during the Blitz to be looked after by nurses. Notably, Winnicott called the process the "management" of children.

pointed out bluntly in front of their colleagues, or as Dalio says, "Pain + Reflection = Progress.") Here the strategy is to favor protecting new ideas and giving them longer to grow between and among people, in iterations and in conversation, inside the safe space of the holding environment.

In building that environment, the manager is not literally like a parent. A boundary-testing toddler and a car-borrowing teenager have little in common with a successful worker. Yet if the traditional manager's emphasis on reviewing and motivating performance comes at the cost of helping people feel safe to stretch and explore to their full range, then the organization doesn't access anywhere near the full capacity of its workers. The good enough manager is hardly perfect, just well-meaning, consistent, attentive, and reliable enough to hold an environment for other people.

In a work context, the sign of an intact holding environment is that people have the freedom to focus mainly on their work instead of spending all their energy keeping up appearances, managing difficult people, or navigating politics. Invariably any working environment will get ruptured from time to time, and all organizations have their complexity and interpersonal challenge. Ultimately, the key attribute of a successful holding environment is its capacity for repair.

To an ear trained on the aspirational language of management science, the focus on consistency over excellence may sound like a suspiciously low bar. "Good enough" or "adequate" is not usually a high compliment, but setting a holding environment is hard work. You have all the responsibility and not all of the authority. You have the exacting and constant task of protecting ideas while also being honest and sometimes challenging about their development. You are not executing on a vision but balancing how to be rigorous without being controlling, and how to be encouraging without interfering. Your work is essential and indirect.

Your main tools are conversational and they are easiest to describe as a set of roles. These three core conversational roles are the guide, the colleague-friend, and the producer. The guide, like a good teacher, offers you your own wisdom. The colleague-friend offers honesty and encouragement. The producer takes on the secondary creative task of fitting an idea to the constraints of the market. Whether you are being managed or managing yourself, you can seek out or assign these roles to build a conducive environment for work in progress.

THE GURU AND THE GUIDE

The first step in managing W.i.P. is to focus on being a guide more than a guru. In eulogizing Kirk Varnedoe, a legendary curator at the Museum of Modern Art who died in 1994, Adam Gopnik wrote, "A guru gives us himself and then his system; a teacher gives us his subject, and then ourselves." The guru tells you how you should do things. The guide helps you discover how to do them yourself.

I need to clarify the distinction between a guru and an expert. Everyone is an expert in something, and sharing expertise is an important part of making a contribution. Especially in technical fields of any kind, deploying expertise is a central facet of managing and leading other people. Here the expert is someone who can impart skill—who can teach what I would call the grammar of any given field. All fields, from ballet to computer programming, have their grammar—their basic structure of techniques and commonly understood forms. The expert shares this kind of knowledge so that other people have the requisite skills with which to build things themselves. Unlike the guru, the expert imparts skills without micromanaging their application, being guidelike in honoring other people's fundamental autonomy.

You can especially see the difference between the guide and the guru in the archetypal conversation in art school—the "crit," short for critique, in which you pin up your work and other students and professors engage in conversation around it. Although the art school crit may sound foreign to the culture of office life, the dynamic of the crit sheds light on any conversation around creative work in progress, because the crit is an even more personal version of the performance review. In 2006, a journalist named Jori Finkel set out to characterize this style of conversation in an article called "Tales from the Crit." Finkel visited the Yale School of Art, which was at the time housed in Paul Rudolph's brutalist Art & Architecture Building, a violently grooved, immensely solid concrete building, impervious to the outside world.

The Yale crits of the 1980s were called "pit crits" because they took place in a recessed atrium deep within the building's interior, a kind of idealized architectural environment for the shame-inducing possibility of getting dressed down while being randomly overheard. As the painter Lisa Yuskavage, now

represented by the megadealer David Zwirner, described the emotional tenor of her own 1984–86 pit crits, "Think about the general nightmare of standing nude in public. But add something else you fear, like standing nude on a scale."

The significance of the difference between the guide and the guru first occurred to me during a crit when I was in art school. We were watching another student's video of fuzzy, unexplained shots of electrical outlets and a teddy bear. By the end, the energy in the room felt fidgety and bored. One of the professors glibly but authoritatively shouted out, "You can't make videos about childhood! It's overdone." And I thought to myself, "Actually, you *can*. It's just that this one isn't working." It would be no different for someone to have presented a half-baked project in the workplace and for a manager to have questioned the underlying strategy instead of examining the execution.

That teacher was taking a guru stance—telling the student what the rules were. A guide could have helped the student uncover the project's strengths and weaknesses, and held the student accountable for what was probably also a lack of work. Because the superpower of the guide is in reflecting you back to yourself, the guide exudes rigor—the honesty of a mirror—but in the language of kindness and with the generosity of accepting your own premise as the starting point. As Flannery

O'Connor once wrote in a letter to an editor she later stopped working with, "I am amenable to criticism but only within the sphere of what I am trying to do." She was looking for a guide, not a guru.

Not all art school crits have this guru nature. The artist John Baldessari teaches an almost entirely crit-based seminar at the California Institute of the Arts, in Los Angeles. His idea of a successful conversation is not one in which he as the teacher delivers an insight but one in which he could leave the room and have the conversation keep going. He said, "I see my role as being a good moderator or navigator."

An example of this kind of critlike conversation within a company is what Pixar calls its Braintrust, a meeting of directors and others who come together to help each other with their films in progress. Ed Catmull, the head of Pixar, says something similar to Baldessari about Pixar's Braintrust meetings. His job is "not to actually examine the idea at the time. It [is] to sit back and examine the dynamics of the room."

The reason it is so important to hold that space of conversation is in order to protect the exploration of new ideas on the way to an as-yet-unknown point B. The safety of a creative space is as vital as the sterility of an operating room. As Catmull says about Pixar's award-winning, blockbuster films, in the beginning all of their movies "suck":

That's a blunt assessment, I know, but I make a point of repeating it often, and I choose that phrasing because saying it in a softer way fails to convey how bad the first versions of our films really are. I'm not trying to be modest or self-effacing by saying this. Pixar films are not good at first, and our job is to make them so—to go, as I say, "from suck to not-suck." This idea—that all the movies we now think of as brilliant were, at one time, terrible—is a hard concept for many to grasp. But think about how easy it would be for a movie about talking toys to feel derivative, sappy, or overtly merchandise-driven. Think about how off-putting a movie about rats preparing food could be, or how risky it must've seemed to start *WALL-E* with 39 dialogue-free minutes. We dare to attempt these stories, but we don't get them right on the first pass. And this is as it should be. Creativity has to start somewhere, and we are true believers in the power of bracing, candid feedback and the iterative process— reworking, reworking, and reworking again, until a flawed story finds its throughline or a hollow character finds its soul.

In shepherding conversations, the guide is walking an interesting line of reflecting you back without being too enmeshed. When I told Ed Epping, the painting professor, about the idea of Winnicott's good enough mother, he told me that he always explicitly sees himself as a mentor and not a mother. He sees his job as allowing students to risk being near the edge. He is trying to build an environment in which they feel safe enough to risk failure. When I asked him what he meant, he said:

If you see someone tinkering with the edge—they're at the top of the stairs and they are about to fly off and that requires an intervention—I don't tend to intervene. I tend to at that moment think, Let's see what happens if you fly off the steps in your work. And then be there if it fails.

This is the crux of creating the safe space. Ed is like a manager who is actively working all the time in order to hold the space in which people do not have to hold themselves back. Like Ed, your job as a manager of creative work is to try to let people channel their innate talents. They may veer toward the edge sometimes. The alternative would be that they make good work all the time. Great work has a higher volatility—higher highs but occasional lows. Of course, there are areas where a safe pair of hands and a good job are more important than a heroic effort. But if you are focusing on the risky, experimental part of your work, in the larger portfolio sense in chapter 4, then you want to let people go out swinging. The good enough manager is what makes it safe to try for truly great work.

Teachers and managers easily encounter the boundary Ed describes, of having to practice not overly identifying with people's creative struggles. It is one of the harder boundaries to manage because it requires you to support others more than to be the author yourself. The Buddhist teacher Matthieu Ricard calls this dilemma "empathy fatigue." In a study of doctors and nurses, Ricard and his collaborator Tania Singer, a neuroscientist and director of the Max Planck Institute in Leipzig, Germany, found that those who have empathy—who identify directly with their patients' difficulties—get burned out. Those who have compassion—who feel connected to their patients in a broader human sense—instead stay energized. Anyone in the role of the guide is doing a lot of the work of empathy—mirroring people back, seeing them, stepping into their shoes. But in the role of the manager, like Ed, you may need to consciously navigate when to take on other people's work as your own, through empathy, and when to adopt the no less warm but healthy boundary of compassion.

That said, the second role of managing work in progress is in fact more personal. It is the role of the colleague-friend—a fellow practitioner in some dimension of your field who is relating to you with warmth, humor, and friendship. Rather than holding the container of safe creative space, they are with you inside it. At some level, you let these people into the inner sanctum of your artistic self. They change you and you change them.

COLLEAGUE-FRIENDS

On May 29, 1970, the artist Eva Hesse died of a brain tumor at the age of thirty-four. Her close friend and fellow artist Sol LeWitt learned this news while in Paris preparing for an exhibition of his work that would open on June 2, three days later. In those few intervening days, LeWitt wanted to make an artwork to include in the show in Eva's honor. It was the first time in LeWitt's career that he used "not straight" lines. Before that, all of the lines in Sol's work—whether the Yaffa-block-like sculptures of towering cubes or the gridded surfaces of his wall drawings—were never anything but straight. Describing that piece, *Wall Drawing #46*, LeWitt wrote, "I wanted to do something at the time of her death that would be a bond between us, in our work. So I took something of hers and mine and they worked together well. You may say it was her influence on me."

That decision rippled through the rest of LeWitt's career. He carried the "not straight lines" into ninety more works, and eventually developed even less-straight lines for his later Loopy Doopy and Scribble series of drawings. Creatively, what does it mean to be open enough to another person to allow them to affect your work? Hesse and LeWitt had an unusually deep friendship. The more general dimensions of the colleague-friendship are that it is rooted in both deep affection and deep knowledge of each other's work. Seeking out colleague-friends and nurturing those relationships when they happen can have a profound influence on your own creative working life.

Sol had influenced Eva too. On April 14, 1965, he sent her a handwritten note responding to a letter she had sent him—from Germany, where she was living with her husband—confiding her insecurities as an artist. He wrote back:

> I have much confidence in you and even though you are tormenting yourself, the work you do is very good. Try to do some BAD work. The worst you can think of and see what happens, but mainly relax and let everything go to hell. You are not responsible for the world—you are only responsible for your work—so DO IT.

The word *DO* is drawn in giant block letters at the bottom of each page. That year began Hesse's most productive period, from 1965 until her death in 1970.

The colleague-friendship, especially at the level of Sol and Eva's connection, is a rare breed. But it is also part of a much more general category of affection and respect.

Colleague-friendship often falls into the broader type of friendship with neighbors, siblings, and college roommates where circumstances have conspired to put you into proximity with people who are not exactly like you. You are looking for people who may have different strengths and weaknesses or general skills, but who have similar values about work—fairness, honesty, punctuality, transparency, and so on.

Colleague-friendship tends to exist within the workplace equivalent of kindness. Success among colleague-friends is not zero-sum. There may be a time when you are both up for the same promotion or funding pool and only one can win. But most of the time, being a colleague-friend is a lot less like the World Cup finals—one winner, one loser—and much more like a rising tide that lifts all boats. One way to put out feelers to test and build kindness is to experiment with complimenting a colleague in front of your boss or a client. A colleague-friend will compliment you back, to the extent your culture makes that safe to do.

This idea is similar to an interview trick attributed to Lord Moran, probably best known as Winston Churchill's personal physician. Lord Moran was also the dean of St Mary's Hospital Medical School up until 1945, about a decade before Roger Bannister's time there. When Lord Moran was interviewing prospective students, he would at some point during the conversation reach down and pick up a rugby ball. He would toss the ball to the interviewee. If you caught the ball you were

accepted. If you threw it back you received a scholarship. The scholarship Bannister won was named for Moran.

See if you can cultivate similar habits of play with your colleagues. Do they catch the pass and throw it back? I have never understood why more people don't take a sincere, tag-team, charm offensive approach, especially in front of clients. Maybe that's my inner southerner talking, but if you can compliment other people and have them compliment you sincerely, that elevates everyone, and is also far easier to do than complimenting yourself.

Another tool to put out feelers toward colleague-friendship is to experiment with the sort of neighborly kindness that existed before cell phones. I think, for instance, of the time when my parents called and woke up our across-the-street neighbor to come stay with my brother and me in the wee hours of the morning when my mother went into labor with our sister. In the workplace, you can similarly take small risks to extend yourself toward other people, and vice versa, to see if there is a healthy, elastic, long-term reciprocity. You cover for someone who has a death in the family, or ask someone for help to see how it goes.

Like any friendship, a colleague-friendship has an unavoidable degree of emotional truth. Notice rigorously whether you feel better or worse after an interaction with someone. Watch them speak, in the same way you would watch a television screen in a country where you did not speak the language. Do they seem like they are telling the truth or acting? Do you feel safe or inspired?

Certain attributes that are negotiable in regular friendships can become more important in colleague-friendships—reliability and punctuality chief among them. You need to be able to count on people to do what they say and to be where they say they will be. Everyone has their limitations and some people are more naturally regimented in these areas than others. If punctuality or reliability isn't your strong suit, then you can cultivate colleague-friendships by leading with honesty and self-awareness instead, and trying to understand how important those qualities are to another person and to a larger working culture. If you are always running late or are over-busy, you will need to be candid about your limitations and to not overpromise by saying something like, "I would really like to do that and I plan to but I am not one hundred percent and don't want to let you down."

Especially because the colleague-friendship has dimensions of performance requirement that regular friendships don't, you may disagree. Being able to have a difficult conversation without emotional undertow is a hallmark of a colleague-friend. That requires a high degree of trust, which means, facile as it sounds, that the truest route to colleague-friendship is to be rigorous about hiring and accepting a job, and to find your people, whether inside your organization or not. Many people I know carry colleague-friendships on through their fields long after they worked together directly.

The opposite of the colleague-friend is the Katharine Parker character, played by Sigourney Weaver, in Mike Nichols's 1988 film, *Working Girl*. She says to Melanie Griffith's character, Tess McGill, "It's a two-way street and you make it happen," and then steals her idea and pawns it off as her own. (That was a spoiler, but then I think it's a movie everyone should watch anyway, over and over.)

In general, colleague-friends are people who disprove the famous Gore Vidal aphorism, "Every time a friend succeeds I die a little." There is great pleasure in watching your friends succeed. If you have common values, their success celebrates your values. If you like them personally, you get to watch good things happen to nice people, which is one of life's undersung joys.

On the chance you watch someone succeed and get a pang, you may need to ask yourself why. You might not like the person as much as you think. Or you may be experiencing your own insecurity. You can ask yourself whether the feeling of not-enoughness is a bottomless well you need to stopper, or a wake-up call that you are out of traction with your own work, or something else.

The category of the colleague-friend, with its ties of respect and affection, may be the secret sauce in the Pixar Braintrust. Brad Bird, the director of *The Incredibles* and *Ratatouille*, once said to Pete Docter, while he was working on the film *Inside Out*—after huge successes on *Up* and *Monsters, Inc.* but in a period when Docter was stuck—"I've said this to you on previous films, 'You're trying to do a triple back flip into a gale force wind, and you're mad at yourself for not sticking the landing. Like, it's amazing you're *alive*.' . . ." Bird was speaking as a colleague-friend, which had to have been an important support on a film that was in the weeds for a period of time.

Docter's film *Inside Out* was released on June 19, 2015. The film was critically acclaimed and grossed almost $300 million worldwide in its first ten days, but it took more than five years to make. The premise of the film was unusual and risky. The story takes place largely inside the mind of an eleven-year-old girl, using her emotions as the main characters. As Bird said, what Docter was trying to do amounted to a triple back flip into the wind. Somewhere around the three-year mark, Docter was walking around Berkeley in despair over whether the film he was directing would ever work. He knew they had an interesting idea, but he realized that, three years in, he didn't know the film's center.

Imagining he could even get fired, Docter asked himself what would happen if he lost his job and moved to the North Pole. He thought he could do without his house and his paycheck but not without his friends. And the friends he felt closest to were the ones with whom he had experienced not just happiness but sorrow. With that insight, he made the film as much about the character of Sadness as Joy—and found the film's center.

The fact that Pixar has an unusually close-knit culture does not imply that everyone you work with needs to be your closest friend. Where trust and affection occur, nurturing them can support creative work. And in environments where you can't do that, the compassionate reserve of the guide and the clear delineation of responsibilities and milestones later in this chapter can help.

THE PRODUCER

So far we have been talking to an extent about fine art, which by its definition does not have to succeed in the practical world. In adapting the process of art outside its more rarified habitats, you eventually hit upon the constant and awkward truth that most things that are developed in organizational settings, no matter how good the idea, will eventually need to find a way to pay for themselves. Their existence depends on it.

That means that to manage creative processes within organizations, you have to look at both the rising and the falling action—the exploration of the idea itself and the secondary creative process of making the work commercially viable. In the film industry, the midwife between the idea and its execution is specifically called a producer. Everybody in every field needs a producer, and film producers are great models as the go-betweens who make an artistic vision possible by fitting it into a practical reality.

The 2013 film *Dallas Buyers Club*, coproduced by Robbie Brenner and Rachel Winter, illustrates the dynamic of the producer particularly well. The project began long before 2013 and took root in colleague-friendship. Craig Borten, one of the first friends Brenner made in Los Angeles, and his screenwriting partner Melisa Wallack completed a script in the 1990s, and Brenner introduced him to her other friend Marc Forster, who bought the film for Universal and attached Brad Pitt to star. Through no particular fault, Universal didn't make the picture, and the script reverted to the writers in 2009.

This time Robbie gave the film to Matthew McConaughey's agent. The script arrived at an interesting time in McConaughey's life. A year and a half before then, he had made what could be called a risky choice, and turned down a guaranteed salary of $15 million, with the possibility of more, to star in an updated *Magnum P.I.* film from Universal and Imagine. After declining the role, he took a year and a half off.

When McConaughey received the *Dallas Buyers Club* script, he agreed to star as Ron Woodroof, the AIDS-afflicted rodeo-meets-international-pharmaceuticals-magnate at the center of the film. McConaughey was reported to have been paid less than $200,000 for the part though with some exposure to the gross. They still needed a director. Robbie knew Jean-Marc Vallée from a project they had collaborated on that had not gotten made (note the continued theme of colleague-friends), and he agreed to direct. Since Robbie was working as president of production at Relativity Media, she asked her longtime friend Rachel Winter to coproduce.

In order to play Woodroof as ravaged by the HIV virus, McConaughey went on a near-starvation diet. When he had already lost roughly 38 of 40 pounds in preparation for their shooting schedule, the funding for the film fell through. The producers called McConaughey to tell him they might have to delay production by a few months to regroup financially. McConaughey wasn't in a position to wait. He told them they would have to figure it out.

The critical decision that the producers took in order to keep the film on track was to cut the lighting budget entirely.

There is essentially no artificial lighting anywhere in the film. By making that decision, the producers saved about a million dollars, allowing them to make the film for roughly $4 million. The lack of lighting might have seemed like a hardship, but it also gives the film a certain gritty authenticity that brings forward the less digitally perfect 1980s in which the story takes place. The film went on to receive six Academy Award nominations and to gross more than $50 million worldwide.

This is the dilemma of the producer: You have a great idea. You want to get it made. That costs money. You have to figure out how to shape the project itself—toggling back and forth between the money side and the creative side. You have to get the work made in a way that reflects what you want it to be artistically while also making ends meet financially. In a world structured as a market economy, the producer often makes the creative work possible at all.

In industries like film, it can become increasingly difficult to finesse the overlap of artistic integrity and commercial viability. As Lynda Obst, the producer of *Sleepless in Seattle* and *Adventures in Babysitting* and the author of the book *Sleepless in Hollywood*, wrote, film producers now contend with an even narrower path to profitability no longer supported by DVD sales. Not having that revenue to fall back on makes new projects feel even riskier, and following templates from past success even more tempting. As Obst observes, getting a film made that is not a "tentpole"—a gigantic international franchise—or a "tadpole"—a small independent film—becomes an increasingly unicorn-like occurrence.

In any industry, one way to picture this toggle between the creative and the business side is in terms of the diagonal lines you can draw on an iconic diagram.

Each quadrant describes an activity, beginning with research, then analysis, followed by synthesis and realization. The numbers on the diagram describe steps in a design-thinking process: (1) sensing intent, (2) knowing context, (3) knowing people, (4) framing insights, (5) exploring concepts, (6) framing solutions, and (7) realizing offerings.

It is the diagonals of the matrix that map the producer role. Whether you are going from research to synthesis or from analysis to realization, you are in the process of taking something from idea to execution.

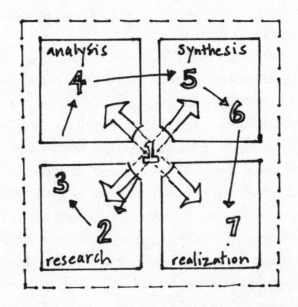

I was first given this diagram by Hugh Musick, a delightful and delightfully named artist and associate dean at the IIT Institute of Design in Chicago. The diagram appears in his colleague Vijay Kumar's book *101 Design Methods*.

The Institute of Design, where Hugh and Vijay teach, was founded out of the influences of the Bauhaus, the German school and social experiment started in 1919 and disbanded in 1933. The Bauhaus took as its founding mission the connection of the creative and commercial arts.

So it is especially fitting that Hugh uses this diagram in a class he teaches on the category of the producer. It doesn't matter just that you have a brilliant idea or a gorgeous design object. You also have a responsibility to try to make those creative works exist in the economic world. Anytime you find yourself walking one of those diagonals, you are taking on the work of a producer.

In addition to film production, another place to examine the producer role is in social entrepreneurship in developing countries. The financial constraint is that much more extreme and the downside that much more steep.

Take the example of Peter Scott and his colleagues at BURN Manufacturing, who set out to make an energy-conserving cookstove in Kenya. As of 2015, approximately half of Kenyan households relied on traditional cookstoves that are powered by wood and charcoal—and that, by extension, are associated with deforestation, pollution, and deaths from carbon monoxide poisoning. If pollution sounds abstract, in fact, it is estimated that more people die each year from indoor pollution—approximately 4.3 million people globally—than from malaria, tuberculosis, and HIV combined. With roughly 90 percent of the Kenyan population living off an electrical grid and without access to solar panels, there is not much of an alternative to cookstoves.

The need for a clean-energy cookstove is clear, but the reality is that an alternative product could never be absorbed into impoverished communities unless it could be manufactured cheaply. A lot depends on the producer role.

Peter Scott, the Canadian CEO, first resolved to work on cookstoves twenty-five years before BURN started manufacturing. Working on aid projects for the U.S. and German governments, he was shocked to witness the deforestation and loss of life associated with charcoal-burning stoves. His path from knowing he wanted to save the forests to wanting to build "consumer products that can save the world" was a winding and weedy one.

Scott first assembled a ten-person team to found BURN in 2009. Developing the stove took three years, ten thousand engineering hours—many of which were donated or discounted—and roughly fifty full design iterations. They started manufacturing in small runs in the fall of 2013, and opened a full-scale production facility north of Nairobi in 2014. In 2015 the social venture fund Acumen invested in the company.

There are two different pieces to the producer puzzle here, one economic and one financial. For BURN, the first was getting the manufacturing cost cheap enough that the stove would be affordable. The second was creating loan terms so that families could finance the cookstove purchase.

On average, these families were spending $500 a year on charcoal. The BURN cookstove takes around half the regular amount of charcoal to run, saving families $250 over the course of a year. Many of those families didn't have anywhere near that amount of cash all at once. They weren't able to afford the $40 stove out of pocket, even though using it would save them hundreds of dollars over time. It is the kind of challenge that banks and stock exchanges were invented to solve.

So in addition to the producer role of designing a cookstove to be both good and cheap, BURN also incorporated access to financing into its business model. The company loans people money to purchase the cookstoves so that they can spread out that $40 over an affordably long enough period of time.

Scott plans for BURN to make and sell 3.7 million cookstoves over ten years. By his estimates, those collective stoves will save $1.4 billion that families would otherwise spend on charcoal. The stoves will also decrease carbon dioxide emissions by more than 20 million tons, radically lowering indoor pollution and saving about 125 million trees that would otherwise be cut down for kindling. That impact on people, their household budgets, their health, and their environment all depends on the work of the producer.

What constitutes a producer role will vary from workplace to workplace. The spectrum of producing can tilt more toward the artistic side, as in the case of the gallerist who lets the artist have free rein but tries to sell the work. Or it may tilt more toward the commercial side, as in the mass-marketed product that is focus-group tested but still intends to be unique from a design standpoint.

In any workplace, being a producer does not always have to be a full-time job. It does, however, need to be an intentionally designated role. Designating a producer frees up everyone else to focus on the work itself. The task of commercialization becomes a creative assignment unto itself. If the producer role rotates it is less likely to feel like a person saying no and more likely to build common understanding and flexibility between people wearing creative and business hats. And since keeping a foot in the practical world is part of anyone's job, it's good practice.

Being the producer is a bit like being the designated driver in a brainstorming meeting. One team member or a portion of the team holds that role, freeing others to explore the big-risk, big-reward space knowing that they can rely on their teammates to troubleshoot their ideas for viability. In a strategic review planning session or retreat, team members can take turns acting as the producer or go-between in blue-sky and budget-planning modes. Outside of work, a friend or coach can also take on this role.

The decision-making pathways of the producer actually place a healthy framework of governance around any creative process. Those pathways help you negotiate the territory between projects so idealistic they are doomed to failure and those that are so tightly controlled that they are hobbled in hitting a stride. The producer is the difference between a good idea and an actual success, but the true art of the producer is to commercialize the idea while also not stunting its growth by compromising too early.

A tool that works well with the producer role is to relax the authorship constraint. Given the motivation to perform well, it is worth asking what you would do if you knew you were not going to get credit for it. If no one could claim authorship, what project would you choose? In a funny way, rotating the role of producer has the side benefit of letting everyone take a break from trying to lead with their ideas. The designated producer gets a moment of pause to see a larger picture. Designating producers also works in tandem with defining a grace period as in chapter 2. The grace period allows the brainstorming phase to carry on unabated, by pushing the producer deadline out into the future.

Knowing that the practical role has been designated creates a safe space for a whole-person culture. As you produce, you may also rely on the listening tools of the guide and the sturdy and sincere affections of the colleague-friend—exploring the point-B possibilities expansively, knowing that the producer process will also help define them.

So far we have been talking about roles that are in some cases assigned and in others innate. A label of colleague-friend describes a state of nature but can also be cultivated over time. The label of producer may describe a particular person's strengths, or may be assigned temporarily as part of a process. In fact, a number of project management roles can be assigned, as part of facilitating the logistical flow of creative work and the added complexity of holding space for open-ended exploration within an organizational structure.

DESIGNATING ROLES
FOR PROJECT MANAGEMENT

If the guide, the colleague-friend, and the producer are key roles to seek out in others and to cultivate in yourself, there are a number of other roles that can be assigned in order to field the size of team necessary to work on demanding, large-scale, complex projects. These roles draw from sports and from Scrum, a common project management framework from a particular class of creative workers whose output demands coordination: computer programmers.

Frederick P. Brooks Jr. is a retired professor of computer programming at the University of North Carolina at Chapel Hill and the author of *The Mythical Man-Month*, an essay collection that is a cult, almost spiritual favorite among some computer programmers. For Brooks, programming is beguilingly close to art:

> Why is programming fun? . . . First is the sheer joy of making things. . . . Second is the pleasure of making things that are useful to other people. . . . The programmer, like the poet, works only slightly removed from pure thought-stuff. He builds his castles in the air, from air, creating by exertion of the imagination.

Programming also demands theoretical perfection. A single typo and the code won't work. As Brooks writes, "Human beings are not accustomed to being perfect, and few areas of human activity demand it." Yet as programming projects grow larger, they by necessity require teams—not just perfection but coordinated perfection. One person couldn't build most modern software any more than one person could win an entire war, single-handedly operate a ship, or write a comprehensive encyclopedia in a lifetime. Therefore the process management tools of software development generalize well to the organizational management of any creative process. Those tools depend on designating roles.

In 2001 a group of computer programmers published a manifesto announcing a way of working called Agile. Within the Agile framework, one of the most popular systems for day-to-day management of process is called Scrum. The term comes from its common meaning in the sport of rugby, in which the scrum is the formation of players fighting for the ball when it has gone out of bounds. (The scrum is a heaving mass of people who are one roll of medical tape away from cauliflowered ears.) Similar methods of product design have surfaced since the 1970s, and in 1995, programmers Jeff Sutherland and Ken Schwaber came together to formalize the framework and start a Scrum movement (scrum.org).

What I want to do here is to take the ethos of Scrum, with its short-term time frames, its designation of project roles, and its focus on milestones, and to adapt it to ways of working more open-endedly. Scrum is a framework for iterating solutions to customer problems. It puts us squarely in the Henry Ford territory in which a customer won't ask for a car but for a faster horse and buggy, or the Steve Jobs realm of "people don't know what they want until you show it to them."

Scrum is designed to get to a known outcome of a specific, preplanned product. A working process to invent point B will look more like Ed Epping's art class than a software development project where the component parts are known ahead of time. What the underlying structural levers of Scrum have to offer are ways of coordinating and collaborating over relatively short periods of time. With minor modification, adapted Scrum suits open-ended creative work too.

First, the starting point of any Scrum process is a project brief. For traditional Scrum, that is a picture of what the solution needs to be. Here, we adjust that and make the project brief a question—an open-ended lighthouse question from chapter 3. Depending on where you are in a project, that question can be as broad as "Wouldn't it be cool if" or as producer-like as "How can we make this commercially feasible."

Second, you designate roles. There is a Project Owner who is the keeper of the brief. Then there are the members of the project team. They are the players on the field. Then there is the Scrum Master, whose job it is to remove roadblocks. You can think of the Project Owner and the project team together as the collective equivalent of the artist. They hold the project brief and explore it via a combination of studio time and milestones. The Scrum Master, what I think of as a coach, is a guidelike manager taking into account obstacles and working to remove them.

Scrum projects are organized over strict time frames, often a thirty-day sprint. Similarly, you can scope this phase of work on your lighthouse question. Within the sprint, the project exists in time and space by virtue of habits and milestones. In Scrum, the day typically starts with a "stand-up meeting"—often taken literally standing up. The team members do a round-robin to say what they did the day before, what they plan to do that day, and what if anything is in their way. In those meetings, the Scrum Master—the guidelike coach—is part mentor and part water carrier, taking account of those obstacles and going about trying to remove them. The Project Owner is there to speak at the end if need be, to

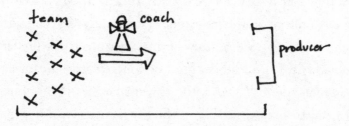

keep the question or central brief alive and connected to the work of the group. The daily check-in usually lasts only about fifteen minutes.

In classic Scrum, at the outset, the team clarifies goals and sets the time frame of milestones. At the closing meeting, the whole team reflects on the completed work and accounts for uncompleted portions. They look at what worked well and document what didn't go well. In that way, these meetings work like an art school crit—avoiding judgment in favor of engaged conversation about what is working and what needs to be addressed. The adaptation here is to clarify at the outset what kind of sprint it is and what types of milestones—research completion, for instance—are really needed. In fact, the classic Scrum sprint to build a product might happen after the kind of open-ended sprint described here.

SETTING MILESTONES

In the original Scrum framework, the team has clear outcome goals. The process was designed to result in a software product. In the case of inventing point B, milestones take the form of waypoints instead of goalposts. In a task where the outcome is unknown, the milestone can be a prototyping goal, a research goal, or a deadline for an experiment. As Frederick Brooks writes, "Milestones must be concrete, specific, measurable events, defined with knife-edged sharpness." But they do not need to be measurable in the outcome sense. "It is more important that milestones be sharp-edged and unambiguous than that they be easily verifiable by the boss." The milestone simply gives the team the ability to work wholeheartedly for a short period of time and then to stop the clock and see how the work has gone—to back up from the canvas together and look at what they have or haven't made.

Without having to drive directly toward a narrow solution, you can set milestones that involve information gathering, testing, and iteration as forms of experimentation. Or you can set a radically ambitious outcome goal to force the team into the creative resourcefulness of being up against a constraint and being forced by a deadline to try to maneuver around it, whether they actually succeed or not. In a culture where failure can happen without shame and where the team is highly re-sourceful, that kind of goal might yield an inspired success. In a certain way, kicking the need for outcome down the road—delaying the need to definitively solve something, the way the Wright brothers gave themselves a pass on building a flying machine for many years but did it two years later—can free you up to gather research more broadly and sometimes to get to a solution more quickly.

The core structures we are working with are:

- the clear designation of roles
- the placement of milestones
- the "sprint" of scheduling work over a relatively short period of time

Together they create an expansive and sturdy holding environment in the Winnicott sense. First, you have the structural supports of a coach whose sole job is to remove obstacles. This person is a guide. They are not doing the work for you. They are helping you discover how to do the work yourself, helping you become less encumbered.

Second, the time frame helps to contain what could otherwise be a sprawling creative process. Knowing there are boundaries—you won't have to do this forever—makes it easier to take a sprint and see what happens.

Third, the daily stand-ups subtly defer judgment by putting you in a mindset of description, transparency, and frequent interaction. Chris Argyris, the late Harvard Business School professor and pioneer in the field of organizational learning, developed the idea of a "ladder of inferences." The ladder maps how easily you can go from simple observation through steps of interpretation, to early conclusions held on to with defensive might. The beauty of the daily stand-up is that it mollifies the desire to conclude. It keeps you open. What might develop into judgments about someone else dropping the ball get labeled as obstacles to be removed with the help of the coach. Having to be accountable as a daily practice makes it harder for most people to default anyway. If you do, you are not there alone for too long.

Like the ownership tools around creative work from chapter 4, the process of designating roles and setting milestones is actually an organizational form of assigning property rights: People know which part of the work they are responsible for and when. Having the clarity of those boundaries makes collaboration easier. Structuring the time frame concentrates everyone's energy and increases the odds of success.

PITFALLS OF MANAGING THE W.I.P.

What I have described is idealistic. It is founded on a belief that, if allowed to bring our best selves to work, people have the capacity to be intrinsically motivated and innately creative, without stepping on their own toes. Yet, for all of us, the guide and the guided, there are some common pitfalls to look out for. Where we see them we can engage honestly in conversation about them, both with ourselves and with others. What follows is a list of three common pitfalls of the individual. They are things to keep an eye out for in yourself, or to be mindful of as possibilities in the people around you.

These pitfalls fall into three broad categories: the risks of excessive monitoring and reporting, the risk of laziness and distraction, and the risk of telling ourselves paralyzing stories about our own past success.

THE SOUFFLÉ PROBLEM

The risk of excessive monitoring is akin to baking something but opening the oven door so often that you interfere with the cooking. If you open the oven door on a soufflé to check how it is going, the fact of opening the door makes the soufflé fall. It could have been going beautifully, but excessive monitoring makes it fail.

Of course, when our work and livelihood are at stake, it is understandable to want to see if something is going all right. But for periods of time during the creative process you need to work against that impulse. To engage fully in the work itself, you need to be able to sit with uncertainty and to accept temporarily that you are too busy making the work to measure exactly how it is going. Setting clear milestones and setting nonevaluative check-in meetings can help. Instead of motivating people with praise and criticism, aim simply to make them feel truly seen and heard. Give them time to work uninterruptedly and then check in periodically to see how things are going.

One way to check in is to experiment with a radical no-praise conversation—making a rule that nothing you say will boil down to good, bad, or should. Instead, aim for radically accurate description and kindly attention. This exercise requires you to study the ways in which you give validation.

In general, you can validate other people: by giving them attention, just by noticing and seeing them; by thanking and appreciating them; by praising their effort; or by praising them and their work. In Carol Dweck's research on how children respond to praise, she suggests praising the effort instead of the intelligence—to keep people in the learning mindset discussed in chapter 2. This observation has taken hold in current theories about raising children.

In the no-praise conversation, see if, as an experiment, you can avoid praise at all—even praise of the effort—and focus on validation by attention. On an ongoing basis, you probably want to show your sincere appreciation of people all the time; but particularly in the moment where someone is struggling with a vast, point-B project, focusing on attention and not praise helps to keep the person in the mindset of their own experience—learning to trust their own sense of what is working or not, instead of trying to please you or gain your validation. Around creative work, praise can be a form of grade-inflated criticism.

Based on my own experience—again, as a southerner who thanks people for thank-you notes—you may find that what people really seek is not to feel praised but to feel seen as they are. In art school, I made a project once called *Amy Whitaker Invites Six Investment Bankers*, in which I invited lawyers, investment advisors, and economists in to make artworks that I then hung in one of our group exhibitions. Coming into the studio was somewhat hilarious but also anxiety provoking for some people. What I found was that what most people really needed was to feel safe and to be left alone.

Similarly, to cultivate creativity in any area, you want to keep people centered in their own authentic sense of their work. Anything else conditions us to be lab rats looking for pellets of praise rather than brave and open versions of ourselves. Again, the experimental question is: How can you make your colleagues and team members feel encouraged without being praised?

Another tool related to the no-praise conversation is to, as a team, use the same tools of sheer description to write what David Grant, the founder of the Mountain School and author of *The Social Profit Handbook*, calls a rubric. A rubric is a framework for nonquantitative evaluation of outcome based on *describing* what substandard, baseline, and exemplary performance might look like. Again, the goal is not to say you want to do a good job, but to focus on aligning with the description of a good outcome.

The no-praise conversation and the rubric give you ways of navigating with powers of observation more than conclusion. Dropping the praise lets you engage more and talk more deeply about what is really going on. With regard to the soufflé, you leave the oven light on instead of opening the door.

THE PRETENDING-TO-BE-A-WRITER PROBLEM

The second risk is the inverse of the first. Instead of failing by monitoring too much, you fail by pretending that you are doing the work when you are not. My friend Peter used to joke that his ideal job would be pretending to be a writer. He would go to a room every day and write just enough that he could talk about it to people at dinner parties. Writing would be The Thing He Does, but he would never have to actually finish or publish work.

Here the designation of roles for project management is helpful. Peter the writer needs process deadlines, like dates at which point he has to share his work with a colleague no matter what. Process deadlines are different from outcome goals. They give you a check-in point to cram toward even if you can't fully know the final version yet.

Peter may also be avoiding completing work because he fears criticism. Perhaps he is awash in anticipatory shame. This pitfall can be guarded against by guidelike conversation, what Ed the art professor calls being critically self-aware and not judgmental, so that Peter can take responsibility for the work itself.

THE NEVER-FALLEN-OFF-A-BIKE PROBLEM

The last risk is that of too much praise and past success. Let's say you are one of those people who just figured it out really early. You published an essay in the *New Yorker* in high school.

You were a Rhodes scholar. As an artist, you were offered representation by a major gallery before you had left school. You predicted the 2008 financial crisis, the dot-com bust, or the latest airline merger. You were named to a list of 40 under 40, 30 under 30, or 20 under 20. You are a rock star within your organization and among your friends, but rather than feeling encouraged by your reputation, you feel weighed down by it.

Professionally, you've basically never fallen off a bicycle, which means you haven't proven to yourself that you can get back on. For all your successes, you lack the muscle memory of resilience, and you have the pressure of being good at something. Receiving past praise has warped your ability to consult your own compass.

In this case, it can help to do a number of things. One is to return to guides and colleague-friends. You may need a sort of support that you look too self-sufficient to have been offered. Another is to pick up an activity in some area of your life that is new: learn a language, take a dance class, make a YouTube video, teach yourself to skateboard. The process of learning from scratch will build your muscle memory of resilience.

Third, you may also need to ask yourself if you are working in an authentic space. Lisa Yuskavage, the painter I mentioned earlier who likened the pit crits at Yale in the 1980s to the vulnerability of standing on a scale naked in public, actually was one of these people. About a year after finishing her MFA in painting, she received an exhibition from a major New York gallery. The show received rave reviews, and she sold a lot of art. But as she was on her way to her own opening party for the exhibition, she realized that the work in the show wasn't the work she wanted to make. She felt like a fraud, doing what she thought she was supposed to do. She described the party as one of the most excruciating experiences of her life, even though from the outside it was going well. Afterward, she took a year off from painting. She absorbed films and walked around New York. It prepared her to be able to come back to the work and to lose herself safely and authentically in it. The same tools of avoiding praise as well as criticism can help anyone trust their own sensibility.

MEASURING PERFORMANCE AND HIRING WELL

The challenge still left is that performance evaluation does exist. It is necessary to competition and comparison of any kind, and placing people and events into categories is part of how we make sense of the world. How do you square the tools of managing W.i.P. with the realities of performance review?

In 2006, former McKinseyite Laszlo Bock went to Google to become the head of human resources, what Google calls "people ops." Bock hired Prasad Setty, a data analyst from Capital One, and they ran an experiment to seriously analyze the universe of Google's performance reviews. Using reservoirs of data from 360-degree review processes, Setty and his team of Ph.D.s set about the task in the most rigorous way they could divine. In a study that became known as Project Oxygen, they tried proving that management didn't matter. As the Project Oxygen co-lead Neal Patel said, "Luckily we failed."

Google is a relatively flat organization for its size: approximately 35,000 workers, 5,000 managers, 1,000 directors, and 100 vice presidents. In its early days, the company attempted to enact the belief that managers didn't matter at all, and then realized that they did. (They are not alone in that experiment. The Museum of Modern Art in 1947 fired its legendary founding director, Alfred Barr, who had been there since 1929, explaining that they would replace him with a roving executive committee of six. That didn't work out as planned. Barr stayed on in a lesser role at half his salary out of a sense of service to the museum. The museum found that in fact they did need a director. Barr returned to the role, and the executive committee blip got largely edited out of Barr's mythology.)

Project Oxygen revealed that most managers at Google were doing okay, and that many factors affected worker happiness and productivity. But it also found that the jump from good to great in managers led to similarly steep gains in productivity and worker happiness. They distilled good manager success into eight attributes:

1. Is a good coach
2. Empowers the team and does not micromanage
3. Expresses interest in and concern for team members' success and personal well-being
4. Is productive and results-oriented
5. Is a good communicator—listens and shares information
6. Helps with career development

7. Has a clear vision and strategy for the team

8. Has key technical skills that help him or her advise the team

Number 8 aside, those attributes fall into three buckets:

- setting vision and goals (#4, #7)
- seeing the individual (#3, #6)
- holding the container of the team's work (#1, #2, #5)

The larger bias of the study is a positive one: Google spends significant time and resources rigorously hiring the best people they can. The company receives 20 million résumés each year. It bears repeating: When you are hiring people you are like a venture capitalist investing in an early-stage start-up. The team is everything. That moment of bringing people in sets the ceiling of possibility. The new hire is as serious to the health of the team as an organ transplant is to the health of the body. You want the best people you can find, and the ones who will contribute most positively to the team. It's not because you want everyone to be a star. It's because you want everyone to feel safe and confident enough to risk looking like a complete idiot—in service of aiming for a larger success.

The eighth point—has clear technical skills—calls back to the role of expertise, which would be especially important in a technology-driven firm like Google, and which can be shared in a guide- more than guru-like manner.

FINISHING WORK

Amid all these tools for process, all of us confront that moment when, alone or together, we just have to get the work done. The time comes when, in the words of Sir Nicholas Serota, the director of the Tate, you have to "lock yourself in a dark room with a cold towel around your head and just get the work done." The goal of the good enough manager is to make it safe to risk losing a perfect idea to an imperfect execution.

Almost everyone has had to complete a project that's a little bigger than they are—a report, an event, an important presentation—and had to confront the reality of finishing. Amy Poehler described the process of writing the book *Yes Please* as defrosting a freezer by hand with a screwdriver. Getting work over the finish line is a particular feat. The halfway point of any creative project is very far into it, the same way that mile 23 is the rough halfway point in the 26.2-mile marathon. Finishing any creative project is like simultaneously defying Zeno's Paradox and the myth of Sisyphus—the idea that you cross a distance halfway and then halfway again, and again, and you never actually reach the other side, except that at some point you just round up, and the project gets pushed over the finish line. Sisyphus pushes the boulder up a hill futilely every day and then one day it tips over.

In October 2014, the writer Anthony Doerr—the author of *All the Light We Cannot See*—wrote an essay in *Real Simple*, a magazine that covers books and life philosophy but is better known for home organization tips and reviews of shampoo. *Real Simple* had invited him to write about finishing creative work, which he did by telling the story of a particular Halloween costume. Six years earlier, Doerr had been introducing his friend Aimee Bender for her talk in Boise, Idaho, where he lives. He was reflecting on the fact that the word people used most often to describe Bender's writing was "original." It made him think of winning the "most original" award for his ill-fated costume. He told the story at that talk and it went on to become the *Real Simple* essay. The essay encapsulates what it is to finish creative work.

Doerr grew up in a household of Calvinist DIY creative rigor, where "to attach the adjective *store-bought* to the noun *costume* was to indicate a certain air of indolence and underachievement, and perhaps even a faint suggestion of bad parenting."

When Doerr was seven, he decided to make a costume called "knight in armor," using a book at the library. The library was a common destination on his mother's DIY circuit, next to the unpredictably stocked but undeniably cheap Drug Mart, where he procured supplies. For his knight costume, he needed black poster board, which was almost out of stock, so he bought what they had plus a dozen sheets of white poster board, which took him two whole evenings to color in with black markers. That Halloween, it rained. By the time Doerr reached the post-trick-or-treat party, his costume was a soaked pile of poster board pulp, tinged purple by runny marker. When Doerr got home, he said to his mother that his costume was awful, the worst by far. She said, "It was beautiful."

Likening the rain-soaked knight-in-armor to the completed book, Doerr wrote:

Every day I fail. . . . I can't ever fully execute the glorious and inarticulable dreams in my head. Even on my
best days, I just manage to cobble together the failures of
many other days and assemble an imitation of the original vision. . . . A strange and unpredictable breach will
always exist between what we want to make and what we
are able to make. The important thing is to embrace that
breach. . . . To build our castles in the clouds—to sew a
quilt, to start a painting, even to write a single satisfying
paragraph—we will need to live with the fear that we will
stink, that no one will pay any attention, that we will fall
like trees in an empty forest: the fear that we are going to
take our glorious, flawless, nebulous ideas and butcher
them on the altar of reality.

Whether your work entails, as Harper Lee put it, "sit[ting]
down before a typewriter with [your] feet fixed firmly to the
floor" or keeping your head screwed on in the midst of meetings and reports and schedule overload, you have to finish one
thing to start the next. Those beginnings are the flipside of
endings. And they carry the risks of what is in between.

In finishing work, perfection isn't really the aim. It is not
that you are creating a better version of what you started with.
It is that what you started with has grown into its own point-B
reality. What you create has a beauty and integrity by virtue
of the particularities of being whole—like the naturally lit
Dallas Buyers Club or the life of Ed Epping thanks to a sports
coat and class schedule. Managing W.i.P. has to allow each of

us—finding ourselves in the fray of our own work and the work of all the people around us—to be able, in the words of David Leverett, an art school teacher of mine, to have wrapped yourself in barbed wire for weeks on end and then suddenly to emerge into a field of lilies.

While you're on your way from the barbed wire into the lilies, one of the kindest compliments you can pay to someone who is engaged in the deep middle of a creative project is, "You're not crazy. Carry on." And then you can try assigning roles and process goals and building an architecture to help them.

CHAPTER 6

To Build a House

Being good in business is the most fascinating kind of art.

—Andy Warhol, artist

The oldest companies bear the moniker "The House of"—the houses of Rothschild and Fraser, Frick and Busch. The businesses exist under the umbrella of family name. Those empires are built out of the same fabric—the same blocks of cost structure—as the early-twenty-first-century technology platforms. The art forms of capitalism have changed and brought new species of business model itself, but the core tools of the medium have stayed the same.

In the last chapter the producer was the person tasked with making a creative project fit within a market structure. Here you have to take the producer role a step further and produce the market structure itself. Market structures are containers for the things you care about. They are the anonymous vessels in which beloved products arrive. Yet those structures have an artistry all their own.

There are two kinds of creativity: writing the letter and designing the envelope. Writing a letter is like making an object—a painting, a book, a computer, or, in a case we are about to see, a pair of glasses. Designing the envelope is creating the system in which the object can exist—the company's business model, the artist's day job.

The design of business models is the art form of the envelope maker. Those containers are not so anonymous after all but the sheltering house in which everything else unfolds. It turns out that designing those vessels requires material resourcefulness with the tools of the market—engaging with the possibilities and limitations of capitalism as a design medium itself.

PRODUCT PLACEMENT IN HIGHER EDUCATION

In 2010, I had just started teaching economics in the Design Strategy MBA program within California College of the Arts in San Francisco. It was an intensive but enjoyable way to cut your teeth teaching—one eight-hour class one Saturday a month, an entire semester of economics in five weekends, bookended by plane rides from New York. When it came time to write the midterm exam, I took a break first. Everything from that break became a question on the exam, including having coffee with an old friend whose sister had just gone to work for what was then a brand-new eyeglasses company called Warby Parker.

Warby Parker began in a computer lab at the Wharton School of the University of Pennsylvania, when one of the founders-to-be, Dave Gilboa, confessed to his friends and MBA classmates Neil Blumenthal, Jeff Raider, and Andy Hunt that he had left a $700 pair of glasses in the seatback pocket of an airplane. Neil, who along with Jeff and Andy would go on to be Dave's cofounders, commiserated. Then Neil told him: There was no reason glasses should cost $700 in the first place. That observation led to a company that operates an unusual combination of artful product and artful business model.

Before Neil went to business school, he had spent five years running a nonprofit called VisionSpring, which gives glasses to people in the developing world. Neil had stood in the factories. "I had seen glasses that we were making to distribute in Bangladesh coming off one production line and then frames for some of the largest fashion houses in the world being produced on the production line right next door."

Why were Dave's glasses so expensive if it cost the factory the same amount to make them? When Warby Parker entered the eyeglasses industry, the company Luxottica alone controlled an estimated 80 percent of the market. That company, founded in Milan in 1961, is almost completely vertically integrated, owning all parts of its supply chain. It owns LensCrafters, Pearle Vision, Sears Optical, Target Optical, and Sunglass Hut, among others, and it produces Ray-Ban, Oakley, and Prada sunglasses, among many others. Its strategy is to license the glasses design from companies like Prada in exchange for negotiated percentages of the sales price. That licensing arrangement is similar to the ownership-stakes strategy advocated in chapter 4 but in this case part of a larger, oligopolistic industry that was unwittingly wide open for a disruptive competitor. As Neil described the eyeglasses landscape they wanted to change, "It is a beautiful industry from a businessman's perspective, but from a consumer's perspective, it's a little less exciting."

Embracing the envelope maker's craft, Warby Parker took apart and reassembled the business models of their industry and rebuilt a fulfillment process that had become inelegantly circuitous over time. First, they decided to design glasses in-house under their own brand, saving them the percentage licensing fee. Second, they started selling directly to customers online. Instead of working with retailers who would mark up their product three to five times, Warby Parker circumvented wholesaling altogether.

Selling glasses online also changed the order of operations by which a prescription is filled. If you buy prescription eyeglasses in the United States, you typically go to a store and choose frames. The store then mails those frames off to have lenses fitted. They then mail those glasses back to the store. Warby Parker figured that if they could have you try on frames that were identical to the ones in their warehouses, there was no need to mail off that particular pair. In fact, initially Warby Parker would simply mail customers sets of frames to try on, avoiding the need to open stores during the company's start-up phase. In addition, regulation of prescription lenses happens at the state level in the United States and so it also helped Warby Parker to operate through centralized fulfillment locations only in some states—mainly at first in Minnesota.

Neil and Dave, who became the co-CEOs, wanted to be a force for good using the tools of business, so they worked into their cost structure giving away one pair of glasses for each one they sold. Even there, they consciously designed the envelope. If you simply give glasses to people in the developing world, you disrupt a local economy in which someone is already selling glasses. Instead of giving the glasses to people directly, Warby Parker would donate them to nonprofits that in turn trained local women to sell them at agreed-upon market rates. In one fell swoop, Warby Parker was creating jobs for women in the developing world and providing glasses for anyone—all within a price of $95 a pair. Over time, Warby Parker has expanded to have retail locations. In 2015 they topped *Fast Company*'s list of the most creative companies in the world.

For Warby Parker both the letter and the envelope are objects of design. When Neil was working in his job before business school running VisionSpring, he found himself in a village where a man who was nearly blind was being offered a pair of glasses. He was refusing them because he thought they were ugly. Neil realized in that moment that design matters to everyone.

What Warby Parker was doing was analytically imaginative yet also imperfect—human and hopeful in the manner of an art project. As they started to scale up, in a funny way the tools of business helped them to realize their charitable aims more clearly. Neil said that when they first started, they wanted to have excellent human rights and worker conditions in their factories, but they were unable to afford people to advise them. He said in 2013, "Now we hire the most rigorous labor auditing firm in the world to go into our factories to audit them for safety and for how they treat their employees. We weren't able to do that at the beginning. I was sort of looking around and saying, 'This sounds good. They have nice exit signs. I see a fire extinguisher.'" The company now brings all of their suppliers together—the hinge, case, and frame manufacturers, and the acetate producers—each year to walk through the history of labor safety in the United States.

Neil's and his colleagues' vision is still very much a work in progress, a canvas at the easel of his working life. Or as Neil put it, "The problems humanity faces are larger and far more complex than ever before in human history. Volunteer hours on the weekends are not going to solve these problems. We need to spend our twelve-to-fourteen-hour working days."

MATERIAL RESOURCEFULNESS

Warby Parker's business trajectory follows from one of my favorite qualities of artists: material resourcefulness—the ability to adapt a material to an unexpected purpose by focusing on its first principles.

Art school overflowed with material resourcefulness. Need to make art and have no money to buy supplies? Pick up discarded McDonald's cup lids on the way to school and see their beautiful shadows dance kaleidoscopically on an overhead projector. On a not atypical Friday afternoon, a classmate would charge animatedly into the studio to announce a bounty of discarded chairs in a trash heap behind the student center. Those chairs would then turn up as studio furniture and, sometimes, as parts of people's art. Bruce, the head of the painting program, said only somewhat facetiously that he didn't know any artists who were not good cooks, adding even culinary resourcefulness to the list.

In a pivotal scene in Robert Pirsig's classic book, *Zen and the Art of Motorcycle Maintenance*, a character realizes he can fix his broken bike with part of a beer can if he ignores what the beer can means in favor of what it is—a flexible, coated piece of metal. This artist-as-MacGyver mindset requires you to understand component parts, to see something in raw ingredient form and to note its potential.

In business terms, material resourcefulness is the basis of letter and envelope design. The resourcefulness is in noticing, as in the case of Warby Parker, where an industry contains pockets of an almost stagnant surplus. And then it is the process of designing the new business model itself. You are looking for ways to disassemble bulky business models to squeeze more efficiency out of them, to build them more nimbly and flexibly, and, more and more, to build a sense of community and purpose that is sustainable and expansive.

The platonic ideal of material resourcefulness in business is taking something that is trash and turning it into treasure. The firm Nutrinsic, formerly known as Oberon FMR, is an interesting case in point. The company manufactures animal feeds. The firm grew out of an unlikely observation: To produce many different forms of human food, factories generate a lot of waste, which takes the form of water full of discarded foodstuff. Many of those firms pay to dispose of that water. The company's founders realized that although the wastewater had no use for human food, its content bore an uncanny resemblance to the food needs of fish. They started taking something people were paying to dispose of and turning it into feed for fish—and then for a variety of other animal species. An area of cost has become a source of profit, trash to treasure.

The same kind of material resourcefulness underlies many other inventive business structures. That inventiveness, over time, leads to new species of business models—like the variations on the large technology platforms of companies such as Google and LinkedIn.

What is tricky about designing with business is that you are almost immediately talking not about business or art but about politics and mission. Putting art and business together is a political act. It is an act of defining how far the market comes into your creative life. Any combination of art and the market is characterized by what I would call the bluish-green crayon problem. You can have a crayon that is bluish green or a crayon that is greenish blue but the crayon will always tilt one way or another, slightly more green or slightly more blue.

Similarly, a business will tilt more toward a profit motive or more toward pure artistry. The political part is in clarifying those boundaries between mission and the market. At a personal level, the same individual might decide to become a public school math teacher or a stockbroker. At an organizational level, you might choose something that has a more than fiduciary purpose, or conversely make mercenary decisions. These are all political questions. There is not a definitive right answer but a spectrum of possibilities.

COST STRUCTURE AS BUILDING BLOCKS

At any scale—the person, the organization, the whole society— cost structure is the core unit of building with business. It governs the life of the individual maker, the growing firm, and the market overall. The man credited with first distinguishing between fixed and variable cost is not an accountant but the British potter Josiah Wedgwood. By the 1760s, Wedgwood had built a thriving luxury business. His pottery had become a signal of social status. His London showroom was mobbed in a "violent Vase Madness."

By 1769, Wedgwood discovered he was having cash flow problems, a common symptom of business expansion. His capital investments were leaving him cash-poor. Wedgwood examined his own books to see where he was going wrong. What he found was that his greatest costs—building molds, paying rent, covering wages—were expenses that, in Wedgwood's own words, "move like clockwork, & are much the same whether the quantity of goods made be large or small."

That simple observation led to the distinction between fixed costs—those that you incur no matter how much you produce—and variable costs—those like materials that you only incur when you produce something. The distinction led Wedgwood to realize the advantages of specializing in product lines where he could produce larger quantities of the same goods.

The tool that connects fixed and variable costs—and that eventually leads you to identify species of business models—is the common business practice of breakeven analysis. Breakeven is the inflection point at which you sell exactly enough goods to cover your fixed cost, causing you to stop running at a loss and to start turning a profit. The breakeven point connects fixed cost, variable cost, price, and quantity to show you the baseline level of production at which the business runs sustainably.

To calculate the breakeven point, you need a number called the "unit contribution" and a temporary tolerance for a fifth-grade-textbook kind of math. The unit contribution is the difference between the price and the variable cost. It is the amount you pocket each time you sell something, and the amount you can therefore use to defray your fixed cost.

Let me offer a more pictorial way of showing breakeven—a perhaps cheerier simplification of the "cost-volume-profit" analysis commonly found in marketing textbooks. Imagine that your fixed cost is a wall. Its height is the total of your fixed costs—rent, overhead, and other expenses that you pay no matter how many units you produce. Now imagine that the unit contribution is a brick, of the height of the unit contribution. Let's say you sell snow globes for $10 each. And let's say that the direct variable costs—materials and packaging—total $5 per snow globe. Therefore, your unit contribution is $10 minus $5, or $5.

If your fixed cost is $100 (as an Etsy seller making snow globes at your kitchen table), then you need enough $5 bricks to reach the top of a $100 wall. Anything over that is profit. In this case, you need 20 bricks of $5 each to cover $100.* The business breaks even at a quantity of 20 snow globes. Below that, it fails; above that it makes a profit.

So far so good: That mechanical relationship of cost and volume shows you the Newtonian truth of a business model. The fixed cost is a wall that is always there. The larger the volume of units, the more bricks you will have. The higher the price, the taller the bricks will be. With either taller bricks or more bricks to stack, the more power you have to break even. In Wedgwood's case, that analysis allowed his business to weather the storm of the enormous credit crisis of 1772.

Fixed and variable cost will tell you a great deal about the skeletal structure of a business. For instance, a business like

---

* The breakeven point equals the total fixed cost divided by the unit contribution. Or, BE = TFC/(Price-VC).

Google or LinkedIn is almost entirely fixed cost. There is no variable cost to subtract; the price is the unit contribution. A company like Amazon has the significant fixed cost of a distribution system, and then an enormous quantity of very flat bricks—selling a high volume of goods on very low margins.

Fixed and variable cost will also help you analyze a nonprofit organization with some earned income. The donations and grants serve as a gigantic block that the bricks of their unit contributions sit on top of. Breakeven is a tool for knowing the health of a business model that is as rudimentary and true as taking a person's temperature.

THE COSTS OF IMAGINATION AND IMPERFECTION

To more fully build the house of a business model, you need the connective tissue of two other categories of cost: transaction costs and opportunity costs. Transaction costs are costs of dealing with the friction of actual people and events. They include search, contracting, monitoring, coordination, commissions, slippage, and switching. They are costs of imperfection—of looking for things, of watching them, of moving them around, of learning new ones.

If transaction costs are costs of imperfection, then opportunity costs are those of imagination. Opportunity costs are those invisible costs that show up in lost alternate realities. The opportunity cost of Bill Gates's finishing college could have been not founding Microsoft. If you use your computer for work, the opportunity cost of having your computer be broken for a day is the day's wages. If you sell snow globes on Etsy, the opportunity cost includes what else you might have gotten paid for in that time, or how else you might have used your kitchen.

Together, those categories of cost form the building blocks of the universe of business. One of the most popular business models of our time is the technology platform. Not only is it a fixed-cost-intensive business with almost no variable cost like LinkedIn or eBay, but also its success hinges on mitigating search cost.

In the case of eBay, consider the cost in time and effort of spending three weeks trawling flea markets to find vintage coasters instead of the three minutes to find them online. In the case of LinkedIn, consider the cost of fielding résumés for a new hire instead of studying a searchable database. These businesses also tend to have a network externality, meaning a benefit to each person of having more people participate, like a friends-and-family plan on a mobile phone.

For LinkedIn, along with OkCupid and Spotify, the cost structure and network externality come together to create a species of platform businesses called the freemium model. Once LinkedIn is built, the cost of adding one user is negligible while the benefit of having many people on the platform is significant. So most people join for free and then a small segment of premium users such as recruiters pay enough to gain access to advanced searches that they support the platform overall.

eBay, along with Amazon, belongs to a species of what the writer Chris Anderson calls a "long tail" business model.

Whereas theoretical economics would tell you to produce one object in bulk, the long-tail business profits by offering an impossibly wide range of products, each with the long tail of a niche audience. In 2004, the average Barnes & Noble bookstore carried 130,000 separate titles. At the same time, more than half of Amazon's sales were coming from books beyond their top 130,000 titles. Because Amazon does not have to house the books in high-rent retail space, and because their algorithms can make the books easy to find, they can run a long tail—a high variety of products each sold in low volume—against the more traditional business idea of specializing in one thing to gain scale economics. Heightening the draw of the long tail, computing technology makes it easier to hopscotch from the long tail of one related niche product to another.

A third species of technology platform—again, based on a combination of types of cost—is the excess capacity platform. Airbnb was founded by Brian Chesky and Joe Gebbia, friends at the Rhode Island School of Design, who started rooming together in San Francisco when Gebbia got a job at Chronicle Books. Not long after, there was a design conference in town and all the hotel rooms seemed to be sold out. So Chesky and Gebbia rented out their own space to conference attendees and made a thousand dollars.

Reflecting on how much they actually enjoyed hosting people and showing them the ropes of the city, they enlisted a friend, Nathan Blecharczyk, to build a website and tried out asking people to list their own spare rooms, first for the 2008 South by Southwest festival in Austin and then for the 2008 Democratic National Convention in Denver.

They had discovered excess capacity—people who needed places to stay and people who had spare rooms—and were able to solve the vetting and coordination problems to match them up. The system grew initially from a friends-and-family network, lending it an umbrella of goodwill.

In the case of Airbnb and Zipcar, technology allows you to reverse the order of steps to buy something and to more easily take it apart and sell it in pieces. For instance, you used to only be able to rent a car for a minimum of a twenty-four-hour day. You would go to a desk, show your driver's license, sign contracts, and be given keys. Now you can start by showing your driver's license and signing contracts when you join Zipcar, and then computers can allow you to access a car using an electronic card tied to their reservations system. Because you don't have that transaction cost of appearing at the rental car counter—or the firm's cost of the worker who receives you—you can more easily break up the twenty-four-hour block into pieces.

Let's say I rented a car for 24 hours to do a 4-hour errand and I paid $100. I would be happy to pay $15 an hour and just rent a Zipcar for four hours, paying $60 and saving myself $40. From the standpoint of Zipcar, they could theoretically rent the car for 20 more hours that day at the $15-per-hour rate, making up to an additional $300. Or, if they only rented the car for 7 hours total, they would have exceeded the $100 benchmark for 24 hours.

To think in terms of building new patterns of business model, the first place to start is in radically observing all the business models you encounter and mixing and matching them mentally. In any room, there are at least tens of business models

coming together—manufacturers of outlets and paint and furniture, providers of electricity and plumbing and shipping. You
can play a game called "object in the room." Each person has
to choose an object in the room—the more boring the better—
and report back to the group on how that object is made. You
can choose chairs or the clothes people are wearing, but you
can also choose outlet covers, door hinges, flame-retardant
paint, and so on. In playing this game with product designers,
I've learned a surprising amount about the zinc coating on the
wheels of movable tables and the subtle variation in the shapes
of plastic coffee-cup lids.

Another exercise to flex your business-model-design
muscle is to mix and match business models to see what would
happen. What would it look like to take a business model
from one area and to apply it in another industry? What if
Halliburton ran preschools? That sounds ridiculous but that
is the point of the game. What would Halliburton actually
be good at as a preschool administrator? First, based on how
hard it is to find information on Halliburton, I infer that they
would be good at following federal standards for student con-
fidentiality. Second, Halliburton reportedly secured a $7 bil-
lion piece of work, inclusive of $490 million in profits, from
the U.S. government in a project for which Halliburton was
the sole bidder. They might be good as securing governmental funding for prekindergarten education. Third, they had an
accounting scandal. Under the belief that parents who were
wild in their youth are the strictest and most informed disci-
plinarians, they would be good at keeping order. Needless to
say, the Montessori curriculum—and the basic impossibility

of scaling the care of very small people—would fall outside their expertise, but their expertise in staffing and logistics is considerable.

You get the idea. You can try to find the commonalities in outlandishly different enterprises—a defense contractor and a preschool—or compare the subtleties of related businesses—a fast-food and a farm-to-table restaurant. The farther away the businesses are, the more you can look for what unites them. The closer they are, the more you can look for the nuance of what separates them.

As you walk around, see if you can identify businesses that are the same but one is big and the other small (Whole Foods and a street fruit vendor), and others where the businesses serve the same function through different means (United Airlines and Peter Pan Bus Lines) or serve radically different functions using the same business model (selling weapons and selling diapers). These games are mental gymnastics to cultivate material resourcefulness and to build a mental encyclopedia of usable business forms.

THE FOOTBALL FIELD

The mechanics of cost structure and the breakeven calculation tell you that a business works. But how do you know if it will run fast enough over time? How do you know if it will scale up to the profitability you want, or give you the investment return you desire?

The design of many business models is toward growth.

But growth happens in two different ways. Businesses grow through scale—through efficiency. They also grow through invention—through the process of art, of experimentation with new forms.

In his book *Zero to One*, the venture capitalist Peter Thiel argues that business is obsessed with globalization when he wishes it were more concerned with technology. He defines globalization as the process of going from 1 to N, what I would call scale. Business excels at taking you from one to many. Once you have designed the eyeglasses, you can produce them in bulk much more cheaply. To get to the point where you can do that, you have to go from zero to one first, meaning you have to design the mold.

Thiel offers a picture of these two forms of growth happening on two different axes:

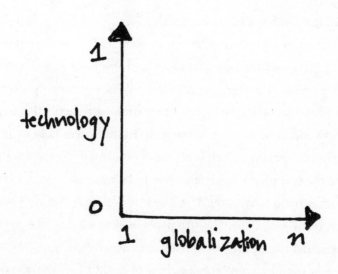

The hitch is that going from one to many can only happen *after* going from zero to one. That picture looks more like this:

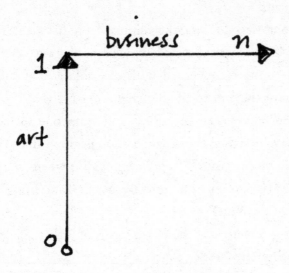

Invention happens before scale.

The game of soccer—European football—provides an interesting metaphor for how efficiency and invention come together with mission. Playing soccer, your job is, to varying degrees, defensive and offensive at the same time—to keep others from scoring and to score on goal yourself. In the soccer field of an enterprise, the defensive half is all about efficiency. You just want to move the ball up the field and away from your own goal. Having the other team score would be like losing money. Scoring on the other team would be, for the profit-making firm, like making money, and for the mission-driven firm, serving their mission—or for most entities, some combination of both. Moving the ball up the field takes efficiency into artistry. You can go directly toward the other team's goal but it is likely to be defended. At some point pure efficiency breaks down and ingenuity is needed to score.

As was said by the sports reporter Jeré Longman of Lionel Messi, the precociously legendary Barcelona midfielder, "Today, soccer increasingly relies on size and muscle and speed," but Messi has "immersed himself in the Barcelona style, which demands flair and creativity, not mere utility." In this metaphor, size and speed are markers of efficiency—of pure strength or utility. The agility to get the ball up the field, past other players and into the goal, requires creativity too.

Increasingly business requires this midfielder stance in which you must think about efficiency and invention at the same time. As a company, Warby Parker is a gifted midfielder that makes decisions holistically, considering things of quantifiable monetary value alongside things of unquantifiable but sometimes even more vital importance. As Neil said:

> I can tell you that all the stuff we do starts to take a point here off of our margins and a point there off our margins. I never really added [it] up all together because I also deeply believe that whatever those costs are it pays dividends in terms of the talent that we have and our productivity and willingness to sort of just bust our butts and get stuff done, so I don't think I've ever been faced with a Sophie's Choice like that.

Their success is based on knowing the tools and aims of the market and then choosing when something else is important.

They sometimes move to the side in order to move forward. Warby Parker's unit contribution is smaller because of the extra cost of the donated pair of glasses, but the model still works. In fact, it may work better than driving the ball directly up the field. For Messi on the soccer field or a company developing strategy, those lateral moves result in a much more beautiful game.

THE INSEPARABILITY OF THE LETTER
AND THE ENVELOPE

Warby Parker designs both the letter and the envelope, but in some cases the letter and envelope—product and business model—are even more conjoined. The story of the Atavist, a multimedia digital publishing platform, is a case in point—a collection of stories and a structure in which to tell them that are inseparable.

In 2009, the writer Evan Ratliff published a story in *Wired* called "Vanish." The premise of the article was that Evan would try to disappear as a physical person while maintaining a digital-bread-crumb presence under a new identity. Between August 15 and September 15 of that year, readers would try to find him, and the winner would get $5,000—a portion of which, $3,000, would come from Evan's own pay. To win, someone would have to find Evan, say the code word "fluke," and take his photograph. That August, Evan left San Francisco armed with a fake identity as James Donald Gatz, a name lifted from *The Great Gatsby* melded with Evan's real middle name.

Evan prepared for months, learning to buy things with pre-paid Internet cards, securing an office space in Las Vegas, and becoming schooled in Tor networks and other ways to mask his online presence. The chase caught on, and a subculture of people began tracking his whereabouts, organizing themselves into faction-like citizen groups, some trying to find him and some trying to protect his identity. At one point, he road-tripped from Los Angeles to Texas and St. Louis undetected with a band called the Hermit Thrushes as something between a "lazy roadie and a moneyed patron," trading gas money for a lift in the modified senior-citizen van they used as a tour bus. At another point, in order to watch the U.S. men's soccer team compete in Salt Lake City he shaved his head to replicate male-pattern baldness and wore giant American flag novelty glasses and a red clown nose.

The story took on a life of its own, and sounded unbelievable even when it was true. Without giving away the ending, when Evan went to publish his article, he and his *Wired* editor, Nick Thompson, found that they could tell the story well in some ways but not in others. Although "Vanish" was a hit, it was also, in the words of *New York Times* writer David Carr, "the kind of deeply reported journalism that was going the way of the fax machine."

Evan had amassed all sorts of video and other forms of documentation during the hunt, and his editor Thompson would occasionally feed these details as clues to the gamers searching for him. Evan complained to Nick about not being able to do more. For a few years, Evan had been thinking about new forms of journalism, even applying in 2005 for a related grant that hadn't materialized. Now Nick and his can-do self invited a third person, his friend Jefferson "Jeff" Rabb, to talk with them about it. The three met for beers up and down Atlantic Avenue in Brooklyn and decided they wanted to build a publishing platform. It was, in Carr's words, "the first tangible result of journalists gathered in a bar to complain about the state of reading [that went] beyond ordering another round."

At that point, the venture held a peripheral slot in the portfolio view of all of their lives. Nick worked full-time as an editor at *Wired*, then at the *New Yorker* online. Evan was freelancing and knee-deep in a story. Jeff, a computer programmer, had been building author websites, including Dan Brown's site for *The Da Vinci Code*.

The seminal first meeting where they decided to really do something took place in October 2009. Evan, a fellow southerner, explained the timing to me, invoking the almost liturgical seriousness and regularity of the college football season: "I can remember the exact weekend because it was the Alabama–Tennessee football game, which is the third weekend in October every year." In that particular game, the Alabama guard Terrence Cody blocked a field goal in the last four seconds of play, giving Alabama the victory, and an undefeated, number-one season. And Evan, Nick, and Jeff decided to explore how the endless space of the Internet could hold the longer form, multimedia stories they loved, all the while transmitted back to the tiny devices like the phones that they were reading on.

In the in-the-weeds phase of the business, they kept meeting once a week for beers, propelled forward by the lighthouse question of how storytelling itself could exist in both digital and business forms. They sought advice first from friends and publishers and then from investors. One potential investor told them they were running a "lifestyle business," the ultimate backhanded compliment, relegating their idea to "oh, how cute" status in a field where vast, scalable returns are the aim. Evan said it took him weeks to recover. Of another investor, Evan recalled, "He's like why are you wasting your time doing this, publishing? Make a lot of money and you can . . . publish all the stories you want." In the parlance of American football, he was advising a punt.

Instead they started the Atavist. To be able to tell the stories they wanted to tell, they also had to build the platform the stories would live on, letter and envelope. To some eyes that meant they had two businesses—one in storytelling and one in technology platforms. For the first, Evan, a wordsmith by trade, had to grudgingly accept the business label for it: *content*. At first, the stories could seem like an albatross relative to the scalability of the platform itself. But actually, the stories and the platform were letter and envelope together, their success intertwined. The Atavist would pay one writer each month to write a long-form Atavist story, and also license out the platform itself to companies like TED Conferences and Dow Jones. Later that year, they rolled out a version of the platform anyone could use to build a story.

Through the lens of business strategy, the entire storytelling program might seem like a marketing spend to support the platform, except that a marketing spend would be separable. Here the scalable technology platform and the homegrown, organic, and noncommercial venture were parts of the same thing. In the Atavist's model, the decoration of rooms is inseparable from the house. The content and structure work together.

Nick, Evan, and Jeff would become part of a larger movement of such businesses—ones whose business model closely tracks the product itself, ones that democratize the tools of creation. In the same way that the Atavist would offer a story-builder platform anyone could use, companies like Maker's Row and Byco would make it easier for fashion designers and makers in any field to find factories to build their prototypes. And companies like Bond Street and Upstart would make it easier for those companies to get access to capital.

Business models were becoming more limber in their design potential; technology was making it more possible for many people to enter the fray, at lower levels, and with greater range. But what they were entering was still a much larger system with well-worn infrastructure and entrenched mechanics. Those inventive forms of envelope design within firms and industries still come together into the vast mural of the market overall. The house that each organization builds, however unique and inventive in its structure or embedded philosophy, still exists on the larger ground of the market itself. Sometimes it is not enough to build the house. You need to consider the ground.

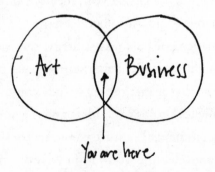

THE DESIGN CONSTRAINTS OF CAPITALISM

If cost structure and revenue models are forms of design, what are the inherent limitations and possibilities of the medium of business itself? The same thing is true of capitalism that Winston Churchill said of democracy, that "[d]emocracy is the worst form of government, except for all the others." As an artist of enterprise, it is necessary to understand these limitations, in order to design around them or to change them.

I would divide the main artistic limitations of business into the following categories:

1. Imagination Problems

No one can predict the future. Most hedge fund disclaimers feature a variation on the sentence "Past performance is not indicative of future results." Yet some people feel that even if they can't predict the future, they can manage the risks of it. The problem is what Nassim Taleb calls a "black swan." A black swan is a rare outlier event like a stock market crash. The likelihood of the event is way down in the very thin tail of the normal curve, maybe 0.0003 percent likely to happen. The problem is that when these events *do* happen, they open up a point-B world in which the entire risk model no longer applies. This is what happened in the 2008 market crisis. Private risk takers had imagination problems that, in the point-B world, were inextricably tied to all of us. In the point-B world, everyone had to clean up.

2. Concentration of Interest Problems

In many cases, including the 2008 financial crisis, there was a structural imbalance in which some people had diffuse costs on one side of an issue and the people on the other side had a concentrated benefit. When the Troubled Asset Relief Program (TARP) was originally allocated $700 billion, the United States had a population of roughly 300 million people—making that original allocation approximately $2,300 for each person. That is not an insignificant sum of money but, in the grand scheme, $2,300 is not an amount that would likely cause you or me to spend three years suing the federal government. However, for the company receiving the bailout, it was, organizationally speaking, a life-or-death matter. Their gain was concentrated, our cost diffuse.

In everyday life, if someone jumps through the elevator door or the subway car door just as it is closing, they cost everyone on the elevator or the train only a couple of seconds, but they save themselves five minutes waiting for the next one. They have a concentrated gain and everyone else has a very diffuse cost. However, if you add up the few seconds for all of the hundreds of people on the train each time one person saves himself five minutes, it sums to more than five minutes. Everyone is worse off collectively, but in a diffuse way.

Business is rife with these structural problems of unbalanced cost-benefit matchups. Many of these problems have the structural characteristics of a global commons: If you live in a small English village, it is tempting to have your sheep graze in the town green. But if everyone does what you are doing, the town green will be eaten up. Pollution works this way. It is tempting to drop trash yourself. What's one apple core? But if everyone did that, the hiking path would be littered with them.

Other problems of diffuse cost and concentrated gain are not global commons problems but simply endemic structures. An iconic 1970s bumper sticker invited the U.S. government to hold a bake sale to buy bombers, citing the way school projects fundraise. Some things—bombers, banker bonuses—are funded by taking a very tiny sliver of a very large number, out of, say, a defense budget or a deal fee. And others are funded by finding every single dollar—for a teacher salary or a bake sale project.

This is not the moral question of how much bankers and teachers should be paid but the structural question of why it is easier to pay bankers more. The whole of a banker's pay is a tiny piece of a much larger swath of money. The pay of the bake-sales-for-bombers teacher is assembled dollar by dollar. Technology platforms increasingly make it easier to coordinate the diffuse side of the equation and to crowdsource funds, but the structural imbalance is a design constraint.

An investment variation on the bake-sale-for-bombers advantage of starting with a very large number is that, depending on how you count, the U.S. government has so far made a profit on the investments it made as part of the TARP bailout. According to ProPublica, as of October 2015, the Treasury had spent $617 billion, and received back $673 billion as a combination of refunds, dividends, interest payments, the sale of stock warrants, and other proceeds. Even for the government, this power of making small returns on large sums still holds, or as Edgar Bronfman Sr. once said, "To turn $100 into $110 is work. To turn $100 million into $110 million is inevitable."

3. Externality Problems

Economic theory is, at its core, utopian. There is the belief that markets can coordinate behavior so that we use scarce resources in the best possible way. What is most expensive is most valuable, the theory goes. But markets do not include in the price the value of everything. Things of value outside the market, positive or negative, are called *externalities*. These are the leaks that the economic system fails to capture.

Your time is an externality to a business's cost structure. If Time Warner is running late to set up your cable, the cost of your time is not part of Time Warner's explicit cost structure. They have to pay for workers. Paying for slightly fewer workers—say, eight workers instead of ten—is cheaper for the company but leaves a greater chance that a worker will be running late. Time Warner saves money and costs you uncertainty and possibly time.

The cost to you is relatively diffuse and the benefit to the company relatively concentrated. Similarly, no one ever pays you for the time it takes to call the health insurance company the fourth time. Often the health insurance company also gets the benefit of the float—hanging on to your money in an interest-bearing account during the delay.

I have often dreamed of having a magic wand where, after I wish for world peace, I would wish for companies to have to pay everyone even minimum wage for their time when the company is running late or when you have to call to follow up on a company's mistake and end up on an interminable hold. It would price in the externality. And that, along with charging higher rates for junk mail to price in the externality of paper waste, environmental waste, and postal carriers' time, would radically change the modern, Western experience of what it is to be a person in the world.

Assigning property rights to *everything*—from pollution to the creative work of artists—can help price things in, but we don't do it enough, and the costs that are not priced in present a design problem. Regardless, as a starting point, anytime you see that price does not equal value, economics isn't working.

4. Political Problems

Try to prove this statement wrong: All social problems can be fixed with either education or campaign finance reform. The political problems of special interests and uninformed voters—understandably so with unreadable thousand-page pork barrel legislation wrangled from a bitter infighting process—are the biggest economic problems we have. People who legislate or regulate the financial services industry do not always understand it well enough. People who vote, all of us, could understand it better. There is also the problem of conflicts of interest in the decisions that get made, for instance: defense attorneys and medical malpractice laws, health insurance companies and health care reform. At the very least, a lack of campaign finance reform starves us for discussion. Funders and lobbyists become the general equivalent of blowhards who dominate dinner conversations.

We have a responsibility to educate ourselves, but people get busy. Again, there is a diffuse benefit to the individual of understanding the political system and relatively diffuse cost to the individual of taking the time to do so. There is a concentrated gain to the whole system if we all take the time or loss if we don't.

There is so much information in the world, it is hard to understand enough. I would personally like to understand the chemical mechanism of Tylenol and the encryption math of Bitcoin, to say nothing of the electoral process and how to change a flat tire, and that may all be more than I get to do in my lifetime. Like everyone else, I still have a responsibility to put my head up and at least try.

5. Character Problems

It is easy to reminisce about the olden days when people walked to school bootless in the snow, uphill both ways, or when public figures had mistresses but we didn't have to know the tawdry details. Still, it is easy to feel that old-fashioned values of dignity and courage—those of Roger Bannister or the "greatest generation"—have declined. The more that technology and corporate forms take over, the less that people feel responsible for their own decisions.

What is true of computers and paper is true of the massive econo-industrial complex and human character. Computers can replace the need for paper because you can read on-screen. Yet the more we have computers, the more we actually print. Similarly, corporate infrastructure and technology were intended to replace human error or slowness by automating systems and decisions. Yet the more we have those systems—from algorithmic trading to computer-run airplanes—the more we need human beings to navigate them.

6. Common Risk Problems

In *The Omnivore's Dilemma,* Michael Pollan suggests we shop the perimeter of the grocery store, where the meats and produce are. Otherwise, he explains, all the food is made of corn syrup and other corn by-products. And if we eat it, then *we* are all made of corn. The same thing happens in finance. A whole set of unrelated transactions can all of a sudden be tied to one common risk factor. The whole finance system is accidentally made of corn, with all the usual risks of putting everything in one place.

For example, a Wall Street trader looks at the exchange rates and relative interest rates between the U.S. dollar and the Japanese yen and sees a good opportunity to do what is called a "carry trade." This means that the trader borrows yen at a low interest rate, converts them to dollars, and buys higher yield U.S. dollars. The problem is that if everyone does that, parts of the U.S. bond market are secretly made out of yen.

It is hard to fix this problem because it centers on the peculiar economic character of information. Investment strategies are often zero-sum. As in a soccer or football match, only one team can win. (One team is +1 win, the other is -1 loss, hence it sums to zero.) Because many opportunities may not be win-win, traders want to keep their good ideas secret. They want to be the +1. But that also means they might all be doing the same thing and not know it.

Sharing this information, with regulators or otherwise, is also perceived as tricky because once known, information cannot be unknown. If I have a secret recipe, you won't know what it is worth until I tell it to you. But once I tell you, if you can remember it, why would you still pay me for it? The economic life of information makes oversight hard. But perhaps if we all understood carry trades better—asked the people who actually carry them out to teach us what they do—maybe we could come up with better ways to manage common risk problems without the risk of revealing their secrets. This limitation is different from simply having more or less money. It is a problem of privately taken risk that can suddenly become collectively held.

7. Pervasiveness of Capitalism Problems

The last problem is simply that capitalism is everywhere. Changing the system in any significant way is serious and unknown, a kind of fracking of modern society, where it might work or it might not and we don't know yet. It follows that having people not understand the market economy is the greatest political challenge of our time.

Market failure and business strategy are flip sides of the same coin. Any of these problems gives you a way to extract more value, if you can figure out how to get on the right side of the equation. Benefiting from market failures is a form of activating your own enlightened self-interest. To that, I would ask you two different political questions, which I think are the most powerful and determinative political questions you can possibly ask yourself.

The first question is: How narrowly or broadly do you define your own self-interest? Is it in your interest to have public education? Or is it more narrowly in your interest to produce goods for society and to amass wealth? Is it self-interested to live in a society where people have access to education, or is it in our common interest for people to become personally rich by contributing in an Ayn Randian way? There's not a right answer, but those personal politics will establish the parameters of how you believe business should operate as a system and how people should act within it.

The second question is: How much do you care about things in theory or in practice? For example, many people would agree that certain government services are very badly run, bloated, and overly bureaucratic. But once you notice faults in practice, would you rather accept that imperfection, or have theoretically perfect government that leaves people without a safety net? The answer to that question could determine how you vote in elections but it will also tell you a lot about how to approach organizational problem solving—trying to lead by principles that get imperfectly enacted or by rules that must be perfectly followed.

The reality of any art project—a company or organization or even society included—is that, at least in my own experience of the smaller painting-like variety, a project will usually appear to you at the outset in some kind of idealized form. Then you start to make the work, and when you get halfway through you realize it does not look like what you imagined at all. The important part is everything that happens after that point.

The world we live in—our whole societies, our families, our workplaces—is all already like the half-finished painting. We rarely have blank canvases. We are almost always building what we hope for in the midst of what we have. We build the point-B world not from scratch but in the point-A world we inhabit. Therefore, all of us have to grapple with what will

likely fall short of perfection. We may want to make a perpetual motion machine but then we are constrained by the
laws of physics. We have to accept that aiming for perfection,
at its best, just maps a trajectory toward the good and the
whole. Our work never exists in the vacuum where absolute
perfection is possible. It takes shape in conversation with the
constraints of the materials we are working in, and with each
other.

ASK NOT WHAT ECONOMICS CAN DO FOR YOU

The only right answer to these extremely large questions is to
be able to know what you think and to discuss it with others—to disintermediate the messaging of television and the
Internet and to engage in old-fashioned conversation of the
open-ended variety. That is to say, capitalism needs the tools of
democracy. It needs an informed electorate. Being an artist is a
form of being an independent thinker; thinking independently
is the greatest political value there is. It doesn't matter so much
what you think. It matters *that* you think, and that you continue to think.

The design constraints of capitalism are what they are, the
same way that oil paint takes a long time to dry and ice sculp-
tors must contend with the heat. These are limitations to be
reckoned with and designed around. They are simply part of
the nature of the materials you are working with.

For business to function less as a straitjacketing system of rules and more as a set of creative building blocks, it has to be, no matter its efficiencies and robot structures, a human and fallible system capable of give, and ripe for reinvention. To paraphrase John F. Kennedy, ask not what economics can do for you but what you can do for economics. Consider what would be possible if more people understood business well enough to build things with it, alone and together.

As a place to start, one of the strategies I recommend most when teaching business to artists is what I would call the periscope move. You look at your own projects and aims. You consider what isn't working, and then you take the time to put the periscope up and see who else has the same problem. My friend Caroline Woolard, an artist who cofounded a barter economy school called Trade School, used to convene all the other artists who were starting radical education projects. It sounds simple, but relative to how busy and focused people get, it can be a revolutionary step.

Similarly, I often get asked by artists how to sell their work and get a gallery to represent them. It is a specific artistic variation on the more universal questions of how to make money and find support. Getting a gallery is not a goal with a repeatable path. Making it in the upper echelons of the art world is as idiosyncratic a process as making it in Hollywood. But if an artist uses the periscope move, she might find other artists—ones she admires—who are in her same shoes. And if those same artists were to organize an exhibition together with a few other people, it would help everyone. In fact, Damien Hirst, the incredibly successful British artist, got his start by organizing group shows for himself and his friends. Had he not, he likely would not have created the critical mass to entice the collector Charles Saatchi to visit the show and become a partner in Hirst's work.

In corporate circumstances the same kind of cooperative success happens when a group of manufacturers or growers get together to collaboratively build a market. The Milk Board creates national campaigns encouraging people to drink milk, which people buy generally through local or regional dairies. The group increases the total potential for success giving each member a greater share, but the members don't compete with each other directly because it is largely a regional market.

The periscope move works on any need for collective action: work-life balance, systemic low pay, or the particularities of wherever you find yourself. You may be able to develop a model collaboratively that far outstrips what you can build on your own.

Ultimately the design principle that all of business comes back to is the structural attempt to make price equal to value—while being able to define value as broadly as you want. As we have noted before, it is extremely hard to do that in the case of creative work because that value itself isn't known ahead of time. If you focus on the creation of value itself and design the risks and structures around it as well as you can, then you are building a house that can connect to the grid of a larger, thriving metropolis.

CHAPTER 7

To See the Whole

I love life. I always have. . . . But I don't love life because it is
pretty. Prettiness is clothes-deep. I am a truer lover than that. I
love it naked. There is beauty for me even in its ugliness. In fact,
I deny the ugliness entirely, for its vices are often nobler than its
virtues, and nearly always closer to a revelation. . . .

The people who succeed and do not push on to a greater
failure are the spiritual middle-classers. Their stopping at
success is the proof of their compromising insignificance.
How petty their dreams must have been!

—Eugene O'Neill

Having been in the weeds and used a lighthouse to navigate, we
have built with other tools to manage risk. We have built with
business itself, accepting the envelope of business as a parallel

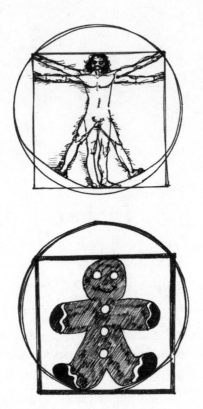

creative process to the letter of the underlying project itself, and we have tried that whole time to keep in mind a wide-angle view. To put those parts together into a whole, we need to return to the original question of Leonardo da Vinci and what he would be doing if he were alive today.

Compared to ours, the landscape of Leonardo's life was differently configured. When he was in the weeds, they were weeds he could name. When he asked a lighthouse question, he built the lighthouse too. The ultimate generalist, he inhabited the exact bleeding edge of human understanding. His capacity matched the speed of knowledge and let him discover what there was to know, then add to it, then discover it again.

That sets a high bar on the category of the artist, and leads to a final lighthouse question for this book: By collaboration and engineering, how do you create a modern Leonardo out of us all? What is at stake in the larger point-B world and also in the small but infinite one—creating each person by means of education? Our entry point is the story of an artist who took on a building in hopes of changing a city.

THE GINGERBREAD MAN VS. THE VITRUVIAN MAN

Christopher Miner is an artist by a literal definition. He has an MFA from the Yale School of Art and is represented by the New York gallery Mitchell-Innes & Nash. The art critic Ken Johnson wrote in the *New York Times* in 2009, "There's not enough real life in art these days. Christopher Miner's wonderfully humane, funny and deceptively simple videos are an exception."

Chris's latest art project is not a video but Crosstown, a 1.5-million-square-foot building in Memphis, Tennessee, that is being turned into an urban village and arts complex. Chris's first partner in the venture is Todd Richardson, a professor of northern Renaissance art history at the University of Memphis.

The building in question, Sears Crosstown, is a vast aircraft-carrier-size monument to peeling paint that has stood empty and shuttered since 1993. It is one of ten buildings that were rolled out all over the country by Sears, Roebuck & Company as regional superstores and catalog distribution centers beginning in the 1920s. Workers on roller skates would propel themselves down long, concrete-slabbed floors to find inventory that then traveled down baggage-claim chutes to packagers on the floor below, who sent out the shipments. In 1965, the building had the capacity to ship up to 45,000 catalog orders each day. It was an Amazon warehouse and shipping hub before Amazon. Many of these buildings have long ago been reclaimed for other uses. The Boston building houses a movie theater, stores, and medical office space. The Seattle building houses the world headquarters of the Starbucks Corporation.

Opened in February 1927, the Memphis building sits at a holy-grail crossroads of urban planning, atop the swath of the

city that was razed in the 1960s to make way for a highway
that was never built. In the quest to see Interstate 40 run coast
to coast, city planners bulldozed a large section of Memphis's
midtown—an area between the downtown skyline, which sits
on a bluff overlooking the Mississippi River, and the residential
neighborhoods that spread eastward into suburban shopping
centers and eventual farmland. The highway failed because it
was slated to cut through Overton Park, a haven of green in a
historic housing district. In a rare instance of park advocates
triumphing over eminent domain, the 1971 case, *Citizens to
Preserve Overton Park vs. Volpe*, went all the way to the U.S.
Supreme Court. The outcome saved the park but left Memphis
with a great scar across its middle. The building sits there like
a heavy Band-Aid, applying grave and now hollow pressure
to that original city-planning wound. The Sears Crosstown
building towers over a neighborhood of bungalow houses, next
to a soccer field–size, flattened pile of dirt left over from those
bulldozers. From the top of the dirt pile you can watch cars
whiz by on the rerouted interstate loop, an odd urban version
of sitting at the edge of the ocean watching the waves wash in.

If the Crosstown building could be reimagined, the site
could reconnect the downtown to the rest of the area and potentially transform the life of the city. Memphis has great bones—
the world headquarters of FedEx and AutoZone—but it is also
ranked the fourth-most-dangerous city in the United States,
with 1,500 violent crimes each year for every 100,000 residents.

A lot is at stake, and it hinges on both the artistic and financial success of Chris and Todd's project. They divided up the
work between them. Todd would connect with local businesses

and government leaders to find partner tenants for the larger building—schools and health care facilities and housing providers. Chris would build the anchor arts center, Crosstown Arts.

Conquering the sheer scale of a 1.5-million-square-foot building is like getting across the Atlantic Ocean safely in the dark. You need a 747 and not a bicycle. So Todd started working with a team of real estate professionals to build a financial model.

By that time, Chris and Todd had written a seventy-six-page operating manual memorializing everything he wanted Crosstown Arts to be. The manual was important enough to them that you could imagine it in a briefcase chained to the wrist of a Dan Aykroyd character in a throwback heist film of the 1980s. Some parts of their vision for the arts center *looked* like existing models—of galleries or artist-in-residence programs—but the way their minds worked, they weren't exactly copying those patterns. They were rebuilding them from scratch.

For example, Chris wanted to create an organic café that would feed artists in the live-in residency programs and also local businesspeople looking for a neighborhood lunch spot. Chris believed the café would be the most important part of the art center, the priceless anchor of hospitality for the whole gigantic aircraft carrier enterprise. But at first the finance team thought running a café was a terrible idea. From a business standpoint, managing a food joint when you are not a food business is a hassle and a time sink. They thought Chris should outsource the café to larger, specialized food providers who could make sandwiches much more cheaply than Chris ever could. But Chris didn't want *those* sandwiches, with their cellophane wrappers and their pale tomatoes. He wanted the nonplastic, unengineered purity of food made with love. If Chris's artistic vision was perfect and whole, like Leonardo's Vitruvian Man, his consultants wanted to squash it into the cookie cutter of a standard Excel model and have it emerge as a gingerbread cookie.

Crosstown is an inspiring idea but it can never happen without a financial model. Chris and Todd need the finance team, or else their vision will get stuck in the cul-de-sac of their own imaginations. For Chris and Todd to work with the finance team, they need to be able to talk in business and sketch in numbers. For the finance team to work with them, Chris and Todd need them to be able to protect enough space of "yes, and" to eventually be able to design around the "no." They are all in uncharted territory that none of them is equipped to navigate single-handedly.

Cities are more complex and less nimble than corporations, which are more complex and less nimble than small groups of people and individuals. In the case of the Crosstown project, the artist of the building is not a single person but a large and coordinated effort. The artist is as much the process itself as any person or team.

THE CONNECTIVE TISSUE
IN THE BODY OF KNOWLEDGE

The skills, information, and working methods they need will require them to take a page from the book of the Vitruvian Man's creator, Leonardo, and to build a generalist artist out of a team of many people. That places them squarely in the dilemma of how to picture Leonardo in modern times, beginning with the structure of education and the place of art within it.

Since Leonardo's time, our educational pathways have multiplied in number and narrowed in scope. In the eleventh century, the University of Cambridge, England, offered eleven degrees. In the eighteenth century, it offered thirteen. Now Cambridge offers sixty-seven different areas of study. (See Appendix.) Relative to an idea of the whole body of knowledge, we live in a gilded age of specialization.

At the same time, the quantity of information has multiplied. In 2010, Google chairman Eric Schmidt claimed that every two days we create as much new information as was ever created from the dawn of the history of man up to 2003. In 2003, the computer servers managing the world's corporations held what Microsoft estimated to be 0.005 zetabytes of data. By 2013, that number had risen to 4.2 zetabytes. The International Data Corporation predicts that by 2020 that number will rise to over 40 zetabytes.

To be a generalist now is not a solo sport but a personal practice of curiosity connected to collaborative conversation. It is also a David-and-Goliath battle between top-down categorization and bottom-up self-definition.

THE NEW META-GENERALIST

In the 1920s, a new product hit the market. It was a hobbyist kit that included a single drawing that looked like a page from a coloring book with numbers inside each partitioned area and a corresponding paint palette with a number for each color. In 1953, $80 million worth of these kits—called paint by number—were sold in the United States, at an average retail price of $2.50. By 1954, more American homes featured the product of these kits than original works of art.

On the one hand, you could say that paint-by-number kits were creative, letting people channel a desire to make something. On the other hand, the activity was templated. It asked you to answer a question and to complete a task without designing the task first. In curating an exhibition of these paintings at the National Museum of American History at the Smithsonian, William L. Bird Jr. described the kits as "an adult metaphor for the commercialization and mechanization of culture." At some point the mechanization of culture isn't culture. It is industry. Creativity gets used as a scrim to sell things. Standardization gets masked by a story about uniqueness, and life itself becomes a multiple-choice test, without an all-of-the-above option.

I happen to love paint-by-number kits. They have a nostalgia for me. I love them most when they are unfinished. They become beautiful in their detours and idiosyncrasies, in the unwavering ways we all project our humanity and our particularity even onto a standard form. Yet those kits alone are a totem for the idea of a preordained path. If you follow these instructions, you will succeed. If you keep your open-ended self in a box, you will rise up the ranks. What is heartbreaking is that increasingly, the process of education, which has the capacity to bring about the formation of the self—each person's own point B—has itself veered toward templated achievement over open-ended process.

In the fall of 2009, Bill Deresiewicz, a former English professor at Yale, gave a speech to the plebe class at the U.S. Military Academy at West Point. He published the talk a year later under the title "Solitude and Leadership." Deresiewicz argued that the constant need to achieve in school and extracurricularly to be eligible to attend elite colleges and universities was turning otherwise exceptional people into technocrats who couldn't be alone with their thoughts in the ways leaders are required to. One of his students had coined the term "excellent sheep" to describe these people. They were "world-class hoop-jumpers. Any goal you set them, they could achieve. Any test you gave them, they could pass with flying colors." Deresiewicz worried we would be grooming a generation of technocratic leaders, those who could answer questions but not ask them. That capacity to ask and not just to answer questions exists in everyone. The risk is in tapping into it.

The Williams College art history professor Michael Lewis describes something similar. When he gives exams, he offers a choice between a dryly analytic and a whimsical question, for instance: "Discuss the development of the monumental staircase from the Renaissance to the nineteenth century, citing examples," versus "General Meade overslept at Gettysburg and the South has won the Civil War; you are commissioner for the new national capital and must tell us which architects you will choose and what instructions you will give them."

Over his twenty-five years teaching, his students have shifted almost entirely from taking the imaginative one to taking the "dry and dutiful" one. As he wrote about it:

[T]oday's students are stronger than their predecessors; they are conspicuously more socialized, more personally obliging, and considerably more self-disciplined. To teach them is a joy, but *they will risk nothing*, not even for one facetious question on a minor exam.

Being able to ask a question, or respond to a large, open-ended one, is a core requirement of inventing point B. Education itself is not the filling of the person with knowledge but the creation of the person him- or herself. It is harder to ask broad questions in an increasingly specialized world, with that much more information to parse. What we need to articulate are the ways that being a specialist can still be an act of originality and expansiveness. We need a way to meld the open-endedness of the Gettysburg question and the narrowness of the history of the staircase. We need to define each person as a combination of their expertise and their particular worldview—their ability to recall the staircase and to entertain the hypothetical. We need to accept that everyone is a generalist but in a way that is self-defined and original. The construction of identity is an act not of design or engineering but of art.

ART AND SCIENCE, REDUX

In 2006, Stanford University—birthplace to many Silicon Valley start-ups and also home to the famous Hasso Plattner Institute for Design, better known as the D. School—decided that it wanted to champion not just design and entrepreneurship but the arts. What is now the Stanford Arts Institute grew out of a larger Stanford Challenge—a strategic planning and fund-raising platform built around the five themes of human health, the environment, K–12 education, international studies, and the arts.

To understand the arts initiative, you have to look at another project at Stanford at the time. From 2010 to 2012, Stanford convened a Study on Undergraduate Education, a committee of seventeen people tasked with a comprehensive review of the university's undergraduate curriculum. The committee was co-chaired by a woman named Susan McConnell, who is the Susan B. Ford Professor in biology.

McConnell is one of those people who reinforce the folk theory that those who are truly at the top of their fields are gracious. She goes by Sue and is an avid conservation photographer as well as neurobiologist. Her research concerns the ways in which circuits of neurons develop in the brain.

When Sue's committee released its report on the undergraduate curriculum, it concluded that the university's humanities requirement wasn't working. The report carried Sue's humble and curious tone when it read, "It is characteristic of faculty, on hearing all this, to condemn students for their cynicism, but the fault is more ours than theirs."

As a result, the university canceled the core humanities program and replaced it with a system of "Breadth Requirements." Students would take one to two courses in seven different areas: aesthetic and interpretive inquiry, social inquiry, scientific analysis, formal and quantitative reasoning, engaging difference, moral and ethical reasoning, and creative expression. That last one—"creative expression"—meant that all Stanford students would take a class in some form of making.

As part of the arts initiatives, two different programs developed in which students could do a capstone project in the arts. In one, Sue and a writer named Andrew Todhunter started a program in the sciences called Senior Reflection. In another, the Stanford Arts Institute began to run an Honors in the Arts initiative. Sue and Andrew's Senior Reflection stitches together art thinking as a process and science as a subject matter. The honors program champions academic research in art and science at the same time. Together, they tell a story about the connective tissue in the body of knowledge and about the idea of the artist as an intrepid explorer.

Since the Senior Reflection course began, more than seventy-five students have taken it. They spend a year developing an art project related to their scientific research and workshopping that project in intensive weekly seminars with their peers. In a university like Stanford, where one has to have been good at school and tests to be admitted, the Senior Reflection project is graded only on effort and methodology. That is to say it is structured around process and not outcome. As Sue said, "We love for them to be lost and confused because there's not enough of that."

The Stanford Art Institute's Honors in the Arts program is, in contrast, evaluated on artistic merit. Students must have a certain grade point average to apply and are selected through a competitive process. Their final projects are reviewed by a panel of experts before being awarded honors.

In 2014, one student, a senior named Jordan Bryan, built music visualization software as his honors project. To do that he had to solve a thorny mathematical problem. That solution became his math thesis and moved the needle forward in math research, full stop. Going river-deep in math doesn't tell you as much—even about math itself—as understanding math made visual through art.

Of the science majors in Senior Reflection, Sue observes that they find the art part so much harder than any of the science, but that they then feel pride of ownership having hit walls and gotten past them. When I suggested that their bravery and curiosity would serve them well as scientists, she said, "As people on the planet! Give it a try!"

When Sue was studying as an undergraduate herself, at Harvard, everyone she knew was majoring in art, what at Harvard is called "Visual and Environmental Studies." Sue said she was terrible at drawing but took one course. Every week she struggled. The last week, she drew a bicycle. "I just drew the spokes, in a crazy spontaneous way." Her teacher came by and said, "Finally you saw it, didn't you?"

There is something in that moment that is the essence of being an artist—the combination of acutely present observation and the receptiveness of an original, individual mind. As John Maeda, the former president of the Rhode Island School of Design (RISD) and the first design partner at the venture-capital firm Kleiner Perkins, once said, a work of art is like a kite. The wind is always already there but the kite shows you that it is.

Being an artist is fundamental to the liberal arts education: developing a worldview and learning foremost how to learn.

The self-perpetuating point-A world is full of test scores and metrics, of hoop-jumping. The point-B world is created by particular people. You start by noticing the world and go from there.

Stanford's arts programs echo the STEM to STEAM movement, started by John Maeda when he was the president of RISD from 2008 to 2013. The original STEM initiative champions grade school education in Science, Technology, Engineering, and Math. The STEM to STEAM initiative adds an A for Art. As John himself said of art and science in *Scientific American* in 2013, "Both are dedicated to asking the big questions placed before us: 'What is true? Why does it matter? How can we move society forward?' Both search deeply, and often wanderingly, for these answers."

Both of the Stanford programs point out the importance of conversation and synthesis across domains—the kind of learning that treats a whole university like a Leonardo brain and carves pathways between and across fields.

Building those points of connection is basic to the algorithm of the human mind. Also on the Stanford campus, a woman named Fei-Fei Li is the director of the artificial intelligence center. She trains computers to recognize images and, in the process, builds networks of connections. In a typical case, to get a computer to recognize a cat might take 24 million nodes, 140 million parameters, and 15 billion connections. (Fortunately, many people on the Internet like cats, so Li had less trouble crowdsourcing on the order of 62,000 cat images to do this.) There is a way in which the brain has the capacity for combinatorial computation that outstrips and can only inspire what a computer can do, and another way in which there is so much information that computers can remember it better. And, more often than not, any big question requires a lot of brains working together.

Where does that leave us? It leaves us to accept the necessity of specialization but on our own terms. To capture that cross section of your own particularity, you need to design your own metaphor, and then become as broadly conversant as you possibly can. Like the computer recognizing cat photos, you need to own your ability to synthesize information across many fields—but from the point of view of your unique cross section. The upshot is that professional identity becomes narrower and broader at the same time, and harder to categorize.

A QUESTION OF PROFESSIONAL IDENTITY

When I was in art school, I became obsessed with the idea of professional identity, probably because I didn't have one. If professional identity—the "So, what do you do?" party question—seems like a modern obsession, it is not. The great guild paintings—among them Rembrandt's *The Night Watch*, his 1642 masterpiece that hangs in the Rijksmuseum in Amsterdam—are really acts of announcing professional affiliation to the world. (Rembrandt's painting depicts a group of militiamen and, not unlike a class photo, they have their names emblazoned on a shield.)

The coherent construction of the professional self is a big part of how we understand other people, and tell ourselves who we are. If you think about your workplace, you can probably

easily come up with some of the things that would go in a guild painting—the props of your trade, the look of the places, the explicit or implicit uniforms people wear.

Despite appearances, professional affiliation is increasingly less clear. Marci Alboher wrote a book about the phenomenon of "slash" careers—people who were a "teacher slash saxophonist" ("teacher/saxophonist") or "lawyer slash minister." Our sense of which careers go together without requiring a slash—actress-model, or doctor-researcher—shifts over time. When Leonardo da Vinci finished his own professional training—after six years as an apprentice to the artist Andrea del Verrocchio—he was admitted into a guild that included artists alongside physicians and apothecaries. Doctor-artist would merit a slash today.

Very few people have a personal identity that coincides completely with their job category—an economist through and through, a prison warden in everything, and so on. We all know people who do see the world in a way that coincides with a job title, whether they have that actual job or not. Carl Djerassi, the polymathic inventor who was instrumental in the development of the birth control pill and also a novelist, was to his wife a chemist. She used to call him "Chemist" as a term of endearment, as in, reading one of his book manuscripts and looking up to say, "Chemist, this is good." As a label, "artist" is particularly fraught—a category performed by many, resisted by some, and open to everyone.

Christopher Miner of Memphis's Crosstown project is an artist the way that Carl Djerassi was a chemist. Chris is an outsize creative person—someone who built his house with his own hands and whose idea of a party is not passed hors d'oeuvres but a weekend at a Mississippi summer camp on the costume theme of famous NASA scientists. Still, there is a part of Chris that is much more general—simply a person trying to do something of value.

Instead of being a chemist or an actuary, what if we all got to choose our own metaphor? Building your own metaphor means becoming authentic and original by adding together areas that interest you and becoming larger than the sum of your parts. It means cutting your own pathway through the body of knowledge. It means accepting specialization as a necessary reaction to the overwhelming quantity of information but not accepting specialization as a label chosen by someone else.

DESIGNING YOUR OWN METAPHOR

There are many ways you can come up with your own metaphor. Your aim is to describe yourself with a shorthand story of your own making. You are not a metric. You are not a target demographic. You are not a job title. You are an amalgamation at any point in time that is snowflake-like in its irreproducibility. Your aim is to describe those contours, either by naming the core from which they emanate or by drawing the outline of the space they cover. Your primary aim is to have fun with it.

You can start by imagining a few of the most revealing snapshots from your life—the anecdotes someone might tell if they had to sum you up in one story. For example, my sister was singing with the band at her own wedding—not a few drinks in, but before the middle of the meal. At our brother's wedding, she caught the bouquet—lunging diagonally. Later she said, "I thought it was a competition." She is a lead singer and an athlete in other settings too. In contrast, I generally fear audience participation and avoid karaoke. My own metaphor would be about connecting things, something like a bridge.

If starting with a snapshot anecdote doesn't work for you, imagine yourself as a Barbara Walters–style interviewer, asking yourself unexpected questions to try to jog an insight:

- If you were in nature, what would you be or how would you spend your time—a log, a squirrel, an armadillo, a river, a distant galaxy?
- If you specifically had to be an obscure animal from middle school science class—perhaps a baleen whale,

massively imposing but only kind and plankton eating—
what would you be? (This question is perhaps closest to
the 1981 interview in which Barbara Walters famously
asked Katharine Hepburn what kind of tree she would
be.)

• If you had to be a character from a film, which one and why?
• Which part of the car is most similar to what you like to do?
A car works because of the core parts coming together—
fuel, engine turnover, horsepower, a foot on the gas. Do
you turn the engine over with ideas or with charm or enthusiasm? Are you able to gut it out pushing the stalled car?
Do you prefer to navigate? Is your nature more at the scale
of a bicycle or an airplane, not carlike at all?

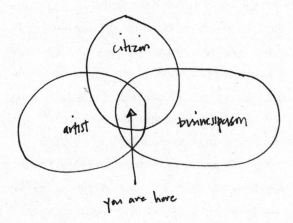

Those exercises should start to give you a sense of how you
show up in the world and how you thrive. You are trying to
give yourself a capsule story. If that doesn't yet come together
for you, you can break it down more into single questions. Go
for a walk or open a bottle with a friend and think about:

- What were some of the times when you were happiest?
- What was one of the last times you felt a great sense of accomplishment, and why was that?
- If you had to prepare a complicated project—a large dinner, a board meeting, a product launch—how would you go about it? Would you dive in, make a plan first, phone the experts you know who could do it for you, delegate, stress, or procrastinate?
- Are there particular words that people associate with you? If you were in a group of ten people and someone had to describe you with three words that didn't apply to everyone else, where might they start?
- And finally, what would you do with your day tomorrow if you could do anything you wanted to but it had to make a contribution to someone in some way?

You can also think about aspects of your metaphor in terms of currency conversion rates. What I mean is that usually you can do things that are a little outside your comfort zone, but they will take more of your energy. It's like converting money into a currency at a not very advantageous exchange rate—well over a unit of energy for a unit of output. For things that come easily to you, though, you might get one unit of output for a half unit of effort. Can you think of activities that are a real slog or that you approach with ease and lose yourself in? Those measures give you an indication of which activities you like and, over time, what suits you best.

To put these ideas into practice, take on the metaphor experiment in your workplace. Especially in cases where people have similar jobs, see if you can distinguish their unique methods. For example, I have a friend named Margaret who works in business development. Her colleague, let's call him Steve, is also in business development. But that is where their similarities end. Steve goes for huge new clients. He wrangles them like a big-game hunter. In contrast, Margaret scans a crowd and immediately can spot the individual people who can be cultivated. She is a gardener.

Another person, let's call him Sam, works at a large American company. He said that when he looks around the marketing and product teams he works with, he sees a lot of farmers but very few fishermen. Sam sees a lot of people who, like Margaret the gardener, can cultivate the land and weather the uncertainties, but very few people who take a big risk and cast a line out. He sees more guardians than risk takers.

Ultimately, making your own metaphor lets you be an artist in the very construction of your actual identity. It lets you put together the pieces of what motivates you, of how you approach problem solving, and of what you know and are curious to learn.

Technology is a part of making a metaphor in the following way: When we looked at ownership stakes in chapter 4, technology was making it possible to manage portfolios of microshares. It was making it easier to build out of pixels rather than out of large blocks. That capacity of technology to manage small pieces with less coordination cost is one of the hallmarks of the time we live in. Companies like Uber disintermediate transportation. Workers in many fields, including Uber drivers, become stand-alone freelancers brought together into networks instead of hired in as employees under the roof of one company. In building your own metaphor, similarly you get to gather your freely held interests under a roof of your own design. Technology itself becomes a metaphor for the capacity to create your own pixelated picture of who you are. Some people would call that the brand of you. It is also the substance of you, the way you navigate the most basic questions of how and why to live in the world.

There is a fundamental belief here in the possibility of particularity, the idea that each person is original. Even if you work in a job for which many different people are qualified, you do it differently, in a way that is particular to you, because that is an extension of how you individually show up in the world. The more nuance you can give to your ability to ask questions and to bring your whole person to work, the more the world, and your organization, can succeed.

UNIVERSAL SOCKET

In addition to your specific metaphor, there is also a set of skills that everyone needs to have to be as conversant as possible and as effective as possible in a world that increasingly asks us to talk to each other across large gulfs in understanding. This is not a body of knowledge to master but a set of skills for connecting with other people, for being conversant in other fields, and for understanding the methods by which other people believe things to be true. For a lawyer, that could mean the logic of making an argument. For a chemist, that could mean the scientific method. For a screenwriter, it could be the structure of stories.

If you picture a child's shape-sorter with the round peg that goes through the round hole or the square peg for the square hole, we need to become a marble that can go through both. And we need to be able to receive information from any field, to be a universal socket that's able to plug in anything. These are tools for portability and connection.

As you build the specificity of your own metaphor, consider the following habits to cultivate this receptivity and literacy in other fields. In your spare time, see if you can adopt a "divisional requirement" practice. In the same way that a liberal arts college curriculum asks you to take courses in the humanities, social science, and hard science, see if you can do this in your everyday life. The next time you are at the airport, instead of buying a business magazine or a lifestyle one, read *Scientific American*, or vice versa. My mother, the medievalist, reads the *Harvard Business Review* at the airport. The next time you meet a person who is interested in something you find boring or obscure or hard to understand, see if you can practice radical curiosity toward it. The next time you read the paper, start with a section you might normally skip.

One of the very real ethical responsibilities of living in a world that is so much more specialized is the responsibility that falls on the expert to explain his or her field. To what extent, as a specialist, do you have a responsibility to make your field—and the important questions in your field that concern everyone's welfare—comprehensible?

One of the things I always admired about my father was that although he was at some level a specialized, brilliant scientist, he seemed to take genuine pleasure in explaining his field to anyone. He really did have a favorite protein sequence in a favorite enzyme, but if you asked him what multiple sclerosis was—the disease he spent his life researching—he would explain it as a tree with a bark problem. It's true: a nerve cell looks like a tree and MS is a set of scars in the myelin, which is the insulation around what would be the neuron's tree trunk. The bark explanation was coming from a man who owned at least seven books called *Myelin*.

How much can we know about particle physics or the human circulatory system or artificial intelligence? We can champion the people who try to invite us in, who try to cover the first and second gears of explaining it, instead of asking us to start the car in a rolling third. The act of inviting people into other fields is one of kindness and graciousness as much as one of education. That sort of hospitality is what makes it possible to gather people from many different backgrounds to tackle large and complex questions.

With your own metaphor and our common marble nature, we become portable and porous, anchored by the core of what makes us original, and connected by the web of what lets us talk to each other. As Kwame Anthony Appiah said, "There is space where new thinking happens but it's not between anyone's ears."

ADAM SMITH WAS AN ARTIST

In all of this talk of professional identity, the Keyser Söze of this book is Adam Smith, the founder of economics himself. He was labeled an economist after the fact but he couldn't have been one before he invented the field. In that sense he was an artist and the field he invented was his point-B creation.

Smith's 1776 book, *The Wealth of Nations*, laid the groundwork for economics and introduced the metaphor of the "invisible hand" that guides markets if we all act in our own enlightened self-interest. But before that, Adam Smith was a Scottish moral philosopher. In a wonderful and obscure essay called "Adam Smith as a Person," Walter Bagehot, the

Adam Smith as an Artist

founding editor of the *Economist*, described Smith as "one of the most unbusinesslike of mankind." He was "an awkward Scottish professor, apparently choked with books and absorbed in abstractions. He never engaged in any sort of trade, and would probably never have made sixpence by any if he had been. His absence of mind was amazing." Once someone asked Smith to sign a document. Instead of writing his own name, he produced "an elaborate imitation" of the signature on the line above his. Another time, a stall worker at the Edinburgh fish market described Smith as apparently crazy if incongruously well dressed—"taking him for an idiot broken loose." Reflecting on an episode in Smith's childhood when he was kidnapped at the age of four by gypsies and later returned, Smith's biographer John Rae said, "He would have made, I fear, a poor Gypsy."

In the point-A world, Adam Smith did not look like the founder of economics. The book he had written twenty years before, *A Theory of Moral Sentiment*, was not about trade but about the importance of "sympathy"—the ability to imagine your way into other people's shoes. Smith argued for the importance of imagination and empathy as the glue in society. When he started to write *The Wealth of Nations*, his intention was not to write about economics but to construct a history of the progress of man—not exactly an unambitious project. As Bagehot wrote:

> [*The Wealth of Nations*] was in the mind of its author only one of many books, or rather a single part of a great book, which he intended to write. . . . He wanted to trace

not only the progress of the race, but also of the individual; he wanted to show how each man being born (as he thought) with few faculties, came to attain to many and great faculties. He wanted to answer the question, how did man—race or individual—come to be what he is?

Smith happened to be addressing that lighthouse question at a time of mercantilism, the nation-state equivalent of hoarding. It was the prevailing belief at the time that in order to be a wealthy country you had to keep the wealth you already had within your borders. Instead, Smith made an argument for trade, that all societies would be wealthier that way. In that process, he described a social science of markets. In inventing the point-B world that we now all live in, he was an artist. The very foundation of economics as a system was invented once, and could be invented again.

THE BIG QUESTIONS OF THE DAY

Like Smith, we all get to choose our own questions and—with as much eccentricity or particularity as we like—to engage in conversation about them. You don't have to be an artist or even an idealist. Inventing point B is necessary because whatever we make becomes our point A. Risking the extraordinary, the failed, the not yet proven is the way we bring into awareness the next ordinary circumstance.

The basis of our humanness is in our ability to create things. Our art—in the broadest sense—is whatever we make visible in the world. Each of us has to choose the scale at which we want to be artists of our own lives. It may be your family or your job or your neighborhood. You may be a captain of industry, or take on a great cause. You may collaborate with other people or work alone. It is true that everyone is an artist and a businessperson but it is also true that everyone is a citizen, in the broadest sense.

These fields all come together to answer the big questions of the day—questions of the environment and student debt, of the nature of mass incarceration and the structure of modern warfare, of the problems of escalating medical costs and the riddle of enacting campaign finance reform, to name a few.

If we applied the art thinking framework to university education we might come up with a whole new set of questions about what it is to learn, and we might even redefine what a university is. We might understand differently how a university's nonprofit status does not exempt it from capitalistic assumptions of growth—needing to get bigger and to provide more services to compete within university ranking systems. We might look at some of the recent university capital expansion projects, planned and realized, and imagine a world in which education barbelled and those universities with extremely large endowments survived and those that expanded so much they leveraged their financials folded. The idea of universities closing and becoming residential real estate may seem incomprehensible, but the future of New York's Soho as luxury real estate and high-end shopping might have felt equally incomprehensible to the factory workers who showed up there every day in the 1940s and the artists who bought their lofts in the 1960s and '70s.

We might understand differently the relationship of online learning and universities—the nature of how some massive open online courses—MOOCs—are appendages to the larger cost structure of physical-plant universities, and others are wistful tech-platform start-ups. We might watch universities continue to decentralize into networks of freelance adjunct professors—again barbelled against the distinguished and the tenured—who might, as free agents, eventually tip over into start-up education. Office buildings with daytime workers could allow their conference rooms to be bookable spaces for classes in the evenings. Education could become a problem of real estate. A university experience could become pixelated too, fitting into the interstitial spaces of physical occupancy and off-work hours. All that would be needed is a credential-izing service—a way of being able to know what someone had learned, a way to use technology to replicate the easy short-hand of a diploma, with a picture or diagram that mapped each student's skills and knowledge.

We could rethink the ways in which people pay for educa-tion. At a time of $1.2 trillion in student debt, we could watch the artistic inroads being made into that question. The Occupy Wall Street group Strike Debt has bought up more than $4 mil-lion in student debt for pennies on the dollar on the second-ary market and then forgiven it. The University of Oregon has proposed offering students the option of paying tuition now or paying the university 3 percent of their income for the first twenty years of their career. That rate is the same whether a student majors in engineering or art. Those solutions are ex-perimental and early stage but they hint at more to come. They may be the 4-minute-1.4-second mile that makes the 4-minute barrier look within reach.

In contemplating the environment as a big question of the day, we could consider the conundrum of collective action in a way that goes beyond low-wattage lightbulbs and recycling to ask, as the activist and writer Bill McKibben has, what would really happen to the world if the planet's temperature went up two degrees. Scientists believe the temperature could rise by much more than that if oil companies harvested their reserves. Yet the future income of those reserves is already included in those companies' stock prices. How do we square the analysis by which we arrived at those numbers, about global temperature and company valuations, with the collective imagination to move forward from them?

Technology is the area of greatest recent invention, but at the same time those inventions call up many other big questions of the day. If scalable technology is so important, how do we protect space for what is not scalable, so that we do not lose it altogether? If computers can learn and think algorithmically, what happens when we essentially allow math to train computers probabilistically, and the computer models start to perpetuate a majority viewpoint, in democratic countries that are founded on mechanisms to protect minority interests?

As a medium, technology allows for collective action that has never been possible before. If a politician shamelessly pretends to ask a tech entrepreneur his or her opinion as a front for then asking for money, that entrepreneur could post the experience to a website, and many other people could give five dollars to that politician's competitor. For every centralization of resources, technology makes it easier to stitch together collective action on the other side of the equation. The question of diffuse and concentrated interests can get rebalanced by technology's ability to more seamlessly coordinate many smaller actors. Those same platforms can help us all own small parts of what we create, and generally get closer and closer to being able to represent nonmonetary and holistic value alongside the way that price represents value in market terms.

Ultimately in that process we are all, alone and together, *makers*. We make things all the time. We make friendships and lives and mistakes and attempts and repairs and plans and schedules and babies and books and cards and pictures and reports and bridges and campaigns and arguments and efforts and experiences and events. And art. And a living. We are all deeply engaged in the creation of value and in the act of making a contribution, by presence or work or kindness or talent or collective effort on projects that are smaller or larger than ourselves. You may get credit or you may get paid. You may know or not know the impact of your own behavior. We rarely start with a blank slate; we just pull the lumbering, existent world closer to what we hope it can be.

The creative spark of art writ large exists in the work of database designers and tax structurers and firefighters and teachers, cops and clerks and auto repair workers, customer service agents and librarians and bricklayers, the people who know how to build stairs out of concrete, who can get dogs to sit still and pose for photographs, who are unafraid to uproot their grade school children to take a new job in a new city, who are themselves works in progress, not fully baked in habit.

REDEDICATION

On February 21, 2015, eighty-eight years to the day after the original Sears Crosstown building opened in Memphis, the new Crosstown hosted a groundbreaking. It was five years earlier when Christopher Miner and Todd Richardson—the artist and the art historian—had first gazed up at the hulking behemoth and wondered what they could do with it. In the intervening stretch, they had set up shop in a storefront across the street, received the backing of local philanthropists, banks, and public officials, and assembled a much larger team of experts—a Leonardo, out of the hands and minds of many different people. That team had come to include architects, designers, engineers, civic leaders, and even one doctor-theologian—which, in his art historian way, Todd said gave them the same rough mix as the group that built the dome of Florence Cathedral.

As the date approached, Memphis was in the middle of a week of spooky weather. The temperature had gone from balmy to below freezing. Sidewalks had frozen over in sheets of ice edged by fully verdant monkey grass. When the plane I took there from New York landed—after bobbing ominously the last half hour through a tunnel of sleet and no-visibility turbulence—the pilot touched down with such balletic precision, I almost cried.

The groundbreaking Saturday was the kind of day you would have wanted to stay home, but the energy of the project and the feeling of collective ownership brought everyone out. The building itself looked battered on the way to its redemption and reuse, many of its windows gone and its shell like a very strong linebacker in need of a physical therapist. For the ceremony, two large industrial-scale wedding tents stood behind the temporary storefront of the Crosstown offices. The main tent heaved with people old and young. As a line of Memphians streamed in, Chris stood outside, his jovial artistic eye scanning the crowd from underneath a giant blue and red golf umbrella.

As Todd got up to start the ceremony, he identified the question they had started with—a basic and universal sense of "Wouldn't it be cool if?" The collaboration that followed had resulted in a project to date that was porous and generous. Everyone had a handle on it. One of the most instrumental people in the project, a philanthropist who backed the very earliest stages, Staley Cates, was absent because his daughter was graduating from college that weekend—a set of values wholly championed by the crowd.

Chris and Todd had started in a similar whole-life fashion—within the wide-angle view of their own lives, Todd still working at the university and Chris a practicing artist. They had made a trajectory through the weeds, guided by a question, into terrain with many moving internal parts and external partners, to a point of groundbreaking. The building would be home to an art center and medical facilities, school resources and residential housing. It would, in its way, help to protect the life of the city and also be a place to get lunch and have a conversation.

The scale of the project was breathtaking—thousands of conversations, on the one hand, and then on the other enough masonry joints in the renovation that if you laid them end to end, they would reach 360 miles.

Chris and Todd and all their collaborators were standing on a precipice between art and industry—leisure and necessity, a grand idea and what would be asked of them economically, organizationally, and personally to pull it off. They had started to take their vision into financial reality in 2012, reaching out to prospective tenants of the building and to governmental and financial institutions to raise the money required to renovate it. Crosstown raised $200 million, from a mix of more than twenty different funding sources—public and private. SunTrust Bank led a consortium of lenders with $80 million in senior debt. SunTrust Community Capital led a $56 million transaction through the federal New Market Tax Credits program. The Goldman Sachs Urban Investment Group made a $35 million investment through the federal Historic Tax Credit program, and the City of Memphis contributed $15 million. As the Memphis mayor, A. C. Wharton, said, "On a massive project like this, there are not many green lights; the whole world is made up of red lights." But they did it anyway. In the span of five years, the project had gone from being "so outlandish that people were willing to take the call" to a shovels-in-the-ground start to realization.

The dignity and inventiveness of their work had brought them to that moment of pause and celebration. As Crosstown sat hollow and sturdy in the rain, the wind-whipped tents came to life with a choir and a brass band, not one but two mayors— one city and one county—and people from near and far speaking with the pride of locals.

What everyone had built was less a building and more a whole community. The bankers and the city—and partner tenants ranging from health service providers to a local university—joined in as co-creators of critical mass and, in some cases, fellow artists of elaborately inventive funding structures of a relatively recent vintage.

The groundbreaking was at once an ending and a beginning, a culmination of much work and the start of a new process. The team moved forward with that peculiar mix of will and faith, determination and belief, optimism and follow-through. Todd said, "We never lost hope that there is a path forward. We just have to find it." Their mantra was to "shine your light and walk to the end of what you can see" and then to keep going again after that.

ACKNOWLEDGMENTS

This book came into being surrounded by many people on both the letter and the envelope side—fellow travelers in the ideas and kind providers of space and time to write.

First, I am indebted to generous readers of work in progress. Ethan Kline, Sabrina Moyle, and Jeff Whitaker read the first full manuscript when I was decidedly in the weeds. Sabrina originally suggested the taxonomy of creativity and sent her own long notes on the subject.

Michael Joseph Gross was an infallible and wise guide through a heavy-lifting phase. He has taught me a lot, and although his current book is on physical strength, let me say he bench-presses a manuscript with real strength too.

Veronica Roberts is a true colleague-friend, and friend full stop, and also the source of my knowledge on Sol LeWitt and Eva Hesse. Heather Nolin provided extremely helpful bibliographic notes on Leonardo da Vinci and Florentine currencies. Judith Prowda shared her expertise in art law. Needless to say, errors are my own, and forays into hotly contested art historical territory are unintentional.

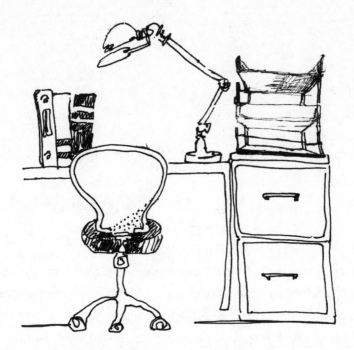

Other instrumental readers have included Matt Alsdorf, Marcia Connor, Natasha Degen, Christina Ferando, Stacey Gutman, Lisa Kicielinski, Sally Kline, Martha O'Neill, Emily Rubin, David Tze, Jonathan Tze, Evelyn Spence, and Elaine Whitaker. This manuscript has been read on a plane to Liberia, over a weekend in southern Georgia, at a neighboring beige cubicle, over drinks, and on the sidewalk outside Blue Man Group. Huge thanks all around.

On the envelope side of this book, I am very grateful to friends and family who generously gave me a place to hole up and write on breaks from my job: Heather Nolin and Herbert Allen, Harold Varmus and Constance Casey, Beverly Chapin, Rosie and Dick Gutman, and Darby English. Other friends made me feel like the luckiest foreign exchange student around,

inviting me over for holidays that fell across these writing so-
journs: Peter Murphy and Audrey Thier, Jonathan Cluett,
Cornelia Alden, Julie Carlo and Zoe Woo, and Jennifer Ponce.

It has been a privilege and a pleasure to work with the team
at HarperCollins: Hollis Heimbouch, a yoda of the publishing world, gave me a chance to write this book and guided me
through it. Stephanie Hitchcock understood what I hoped to do
and made it so much better, charting a wise and steady course.
Colleen Lawrie offered extremely thoughtful early edits. I am
incredibly grateful to many other people at HarperCollins,
including Cindy Achar, the managing editor, and Nikki Bal-
dauf, the production editor, for their miraculous shepherding
of the underlying material into a book; Sarah Brody for the
cover design and William Ruoto for the interior; and the copy-
editor Tom Pitoniak, an elegant and old-fashioned protector
of language and its form. Especially for a book that is about
how creative process happens within the structure of work, I
am thankful to the many people on the business side of how
this book has come into the world, including: Nick Davies
and Penny Makras, the senior publicist and senior marketing manager, respectively; Kathy Schneider, Doug Jones, and
Robin Bilardello, the sales team whom I met by chance on the
HarperCollins elevator; and Len Marshall, who, along with
my editors, holds the producer role for this project. I am also
grateful to Sheiva Rezvani for boundless patience and humor
taking author photos, and Pilar Queen, my agent, for believing
in the project and guiding this book into being.

This book began when I was a writer-in-residence in the
Lower Manhattan Cultural Council's Workspace program, with

thanks to LMCC and to Melissa Levin, Will Penrose, Sean Carroll, Clare McNulty, Sam Miller, Kay Takeda, and fellow Workspace residents, especially Dru Donovan, who suggested I try to meet the people I was writing about, leading to the Harper Lee adventure; and also to Tucker Veimeister, Beth Rosenberg, and their extended family for LMCC's Sarah Verdone Writing Award.

Editors of various articles gave me opportunities that helped shape my thinking—Chris Dannen at *Fast Company*, Kelly Schindler at *Art21*, Samantha Hardingham, who was a guest editor at *Architectural Design*, and C. Max Magee at *The Millions*—as did Chris Garvin, who invited me to speak on a College Art Association panel on design and business, as well as my coauthors of *The Social Life of Artistic Property*—Caroline Woolard, Bill Powhida, Michael Mandiberg, and Pablo Helguera—a group in which I first developed the ownership for artists argument.

I was lucky to speak with, correspond with, or formally interview many people, some who appear directly in these pages and all of whom were generous with their time: Anton Andrews, Natalie Balthrop, Carmen Bambach, Andreas Bechtolsheim, Neil Blumenthal, Bryan Boyer, Anna Counselman, Matthew Deleget, William Deresiewicz, Anthony Doerr, Carol Dweck, Ed Epping, Louise Florencourt, Thomas Fogarty, Dick Foster, Daniel Gilbert, Dave Girouard, Neil Grabois, Heidi Hackemer, Stephen Hinton, Dane Howard, Hisham Ibrahim, Claire Johnson, Jesse Johnson, Raza Khan, Michael Lewis, Fei-Fei Li, Matt Mason, Sue McConnell, Bill McKibben, Christopher Miner, Sean Moss-Pultz, Hugh Musick, Doug Newburg, Alexander von Perfall, Leslie Perlow, Ricardo Prada, Simon Pyle, Jefferson Rabb, Evan Ratliff, James Reddoch, Mamie Reingold, J. P.

Reuer, Todd Richardson, Dan Roam, Will Rosenzweig, Tom Sachs, Peter Scott, Melea Seward, Wesley ter Haar, Matthew Tiews, Jennifer Trainer Thompson, Eileen Tram, Amy Wrzesniewski, Jonathan Zittrain, Mary Zuber, and seemingly the entire town of Monroeville, Alabama, especially Dawn and Al Brewton, and also Chris Ard, Connie Baggett, Steve Billy, Patsy Black, Nathan Carter, Tonja Carter, Robert Champion, Harvey Gaston, Eric Gould, John "Doc" Grider, Robert Malone, Tim McKenzie, Crissy Nettles, K. T. Owens, and Conrad Watson.

I am grateful to Harper Lee, Roger Bannister, Thomas Fogarty, and everyone else whose story is told here. Prior research by others has also been incredibly helpful, especially Neil Bascomb's wonderful book on Roger Bannister, Wes Santee, and John Landy (*The Perfect Mile*); Charles Shields's book on Harper Lee (*Mockingbird*); Steven Levy's writing on Whitfield Diffie (in *Wired* and his book *Crypto*), and Ron Rubin's book on Fred Lebow and the New York City Marathon (*Anything for a T-Shirt*). I also wish to honor the late Donald Keough, whose book *The Ten Commandments of Business Failure* inspired me early on.

I am lucky to live in a constellation of generous people, including Sunny Bates, John Maeda, and Rory Riggs, who introduced me to a number of the people and topics I wrote about. Equally, I have been touched by the kindness of strangers, including Roger Bannister's former neighbor who mailed a package back across the Atlantic with a note, and Emily Forlund, who introduced me to Anthony Doerr even though I'd never met her and she is not his agent.

Many of my teachers come to mind both in the specifics of this book and in helping me learn how to teach and therefore also how to learn: Megan Busse, Ed Epping, James Forcier, Mike Glier, Eva Grudin, Gary Jacobsohn, David Leverett, Michael Lewis, Paul MacAvoy, Ted Marmor, Barry Nalebuff, Sharon Oster, Patricia Phillips, Nathan Shedroff, and Jessie Shefrin. And special thanks to Bruce McLean at the Slade, who encouraged me to start teaching business in the first place.

I have also learned tremendously from inspiring colleagues, students, and workshop participants at: Williams College, the Rhode Island School of Design, California College of the Arts Design Strategy MBA, the School of Visual Arts Products of Design MFA, the Sotheby's Institute of Art, LMCC, Creative Capital, MoMA, Assets for Artists, and the Joan Mitchell Foundation.

In addition to everyone above, I would like to thank: Julian Abdey, Greg Albers, Marci Alboher, John Alexander, Roshinee Aloysius, Casey Alt, Gail Andrews, Carlos and Liz Arnaiz, Christine Bader, Agathe de Baillencourt, Emilie Baltz, Lucy Bates-Campbell, Kathy Battista, Alex Beard, Trey Beck, Joanna Berritt, Johanna Blakely, Christa Blatchford, Steve Blood, Sara Bodinson, Mary Liz Brenninkmeyer, Nick Brown, Kristy Bryce, Irene Buchman, Christopher Burwell, Lesley Cadman, Timothy Cage, Bedford Carpenter, Amy Casher, Grey Cecil, Angelo Chan, Adrian Chitty, Allan Chochinov, Gregory Christianson, Jane Chu, Jonathan Clancy, Alex Clark, Jeanne Classe, Caitlin Condell, Peter Conklin, Elisabeth Conroy, Diane Cook, Abby Covert, Adam Crandall, Mark Crosby, Alex Darby, Chrissy Das, Virginia Davidson, Anna Dempster, Carla Diana, Nico Dios, Judith Dobrzynski, Dru Donovan, Brook Downton, Laura Edwards, Kari Elassal, Chuck Elliott, Oscar Estevez, Erik Fabian, Paulette Fahy, Heather Fain, Morgan Falconer,

Maria Figueroa, Eddie Fishman, Allison Fones, Marcus Fox, Renee Freedman, Gail Fricano, Jim Fricano, Adelaide Fuller, Jenny Gersten, Jessica Glaser, Alex Glauber, Adam Glick, Daniel Goldman, Marilyn J. S. Goodman, Erin Granfield, Timothy Gura, Olivia Gutman, Paul Gutman, David Haber, Elizabeth von Habsburg, Mark Hadley, Jonathan Haidt, Roger Hale, Nor Hall, Brad Hargreaves, Debbie Harris, Matt and Jessica Harris, Jeanne Heath, Jen Holleran, Jenny Holzer, Jason Huff, Catherine Ingman, Peter and Becky Ireland, Darby Jack, Gunnar Jakobsson, Pete Jensen, Anna Jobson, Jesse Johnson, Mary Tyler Johnson, Jorge Just, Julia Kaganskiy, Sewon Keng, Sara Kay, Gabrielle Kellner, Kibum Kim, Tom Kirk, Katy Kline, Charles Knapp, Erik Koelbel, Lori Kornigay, Molly Kurzius, Joshua Lachter, Beverly Layton, Tim Leberecht, Sandy Lee, Kati London, Bill Long, Sharon Louden, Steven MacIver, Guy Mallison, Albert, Penny, Lisa, Smith, and Hugh Mallory, Marko Martinez, Patty Marx, Laura McCarthy, Brenna Meade, Marina Mihalakis, Yoko Mikata, Andrew Miller, Corey Modeste, Sally Moir, Scott and Porter Montgomery, Marney Morris, Eames Moss-Pultz, Claire Muldoon, Mo Mullen, Wendy Mwandia, Sandy Nairne, Shervone Neckles, Jonathan T. D. Neil, Louise Mai Newberry, Carol Ockman, Kristin Ogdon, Gerry Ohrstrom, Amanda Oleson, Amee Olson, Heidi Olson, Barry O'Neill, Katie Orenstein, Sheff Otis, Geneva Overholser, Jane Panetta, Melissa Pearlman, Stephanie Pereira, Elizabeth Pergam, Veronica Pesantes, Lowell Pettit, Prish Pierce, Ulla Pitha, Daniel Polsby, Katy Polsby, Jan Postma, Alyson Pou, Kaki Read, Julie Reiter, Towson Remmel, Sarah Richardson, Jayne Riew, Esther Robinson, Paul Roossin, Jen Rork, Mary Rozell, John Rustum,

Duncan Sahner, David Sauvage, Alix Schwartz, Laurence Schwartz, Andie Sehl, Jill Selsman, Nicholas Serota, Dan Sevall, Rebecca Shaykin, Dewey and Teresa Sifford, Laura Silver, Ethan Slavin, Sinclair Smith, Tim Smith, Delores Snowden, Demy Spadideas, Frederick Speers, Juliette Spurtus, Michael Bungay Stanier, Alexander Stevenson, Dennis Stevenson, Barbara Strongin, Kirk Davis Swinehart, Carl Tashian, Mandy Tavokol, Kurian Tharakan, Ruthie Thier, Estelle Thompson, Joe Thompson, Corinna Till, Alex Trickett, Sarah Van Anden, Jen van der Meer, Leonel Velasquez, Rebecca Vollmer, Meg Vosburg, Bobbly Waltzer, Sean Watterson, Alison Weaver, Alicia Weschler, Alexi Whitaker, Jack Whitaker, Warren Woodfin, Gary Woodley, Susan Worthman, Gayle Karen Young, Li Jun Xian, Agnes Yen, and Alex, James, and William Abdey.

I owe a particular debt of gratitude to Thomas Fahey, Joseph Tjan, David Anderson, Erica Schlindra, Erin Hassett, Jessica Henry, Samuel Mann, Rosemerie Marion, Rochelle Katz, Andreas San Martin, Christopher Schultz, Joshua Zimm, Robert Muñoz, Jennifer Plascensia, Stephanie Jones, and Elizabeth Wagner. I would not have been able to write this book without them.

For my mother, Elaine, a beautifully rigorous academic, my aunt Beverly, a master of stories and a driving force in our lives, my sister Stacey, who practices business with real heart, and my brother Jeff, the original artist in the family—and for all the people we carry with us.

In the course of writing this book, there were people who saved my life and people who made me whole on the "worth saving" side. I thank you all.

Amy Whitaker

APPENDIX: AREAS OF STUDY

AT CAMBRIDGE UNIVERSITY

ELEVENTH CENTURY

Arts
    Grammar
    Logic
    Rhetoric
    Arithmetic
    Music
    Geometry
    Astronomy
Divinity
Law
Medicine

EIGHTEENTH CENTURY—DIDEROT
AND D'ALEMBERT'S *ENCYCLOPÉDIE*

History
  Sacred
  Ecclesiastical
  Civil, Ancient, and Modern
  Natural
Philosophy
  General Metaphysics
  Science of God
  Science of Man
  Science of Nature
Poetry
  Profane
  Sacred

TWENTY-FIRST CENTURY

Arts and Humanities:
  Faculty of Architecture and History of Art, Faculty
  of Asian and Middle Eastern Studies, Faculty of Classics, Faculty of Divinity, Faculty of English, Faculty of
  Modern and Medieval Languages, Faculty of Music, Faculty of Philosophy, Centre for Research in the Arts, Social
  Sciences and Humanities

Biological Sciences, including Veterinary Medicine:

Department of Biochemistry, Department of Experimental Psychology, Department of Genetics, Department of Pathology, Department of Pharmacology, Department of Physiology, Development, and Neuroscience, Department of Plant Sciences, Department of Veterinary Medicine, Department of Zoology, Wellcome Trust/Cancer Research UK Gurdon Institute, Sainsbury Laboratory, Wellcome Trust Centre for Stem Cell Research, Cambridge Systems Biology Centre

Clinical Medicine:

Clinical Biochemistry, Clinical Neurosciences, Haematology, Medical Genetics, Medicine, Obstetrics and Gynaecology, Oncology, Paediatrics, Psychiatry, Public Health and Primary Care, Radiology, Surgery

Humanities and Social Sciences:

Faculty of Archaeology and Anthropology, Faculty of Economics, Faculty of Education, Faculty of History, Faculty of Law, Institute of Criminology, Faculty of Politics, Psychology, Sociology and International Studies, Department of Land Economy, Centre of Latin American Studies, Centre of African Studies, Centre of South Asian Studies, Development Studies Committee

Physical Sciences:

Department of Applied Mathematics and Theoretical Physics, Institute of Astronomy, Department of Chemistry, Department of Earth Sciences, Department of

Geography (including Scott Polar Research Institute), Department of Material Sciences and Metallurgy, Isaac Newton Institute for Mathematical Sciences, Department of Physics, Department of Pure Mathematics and Mathematical Statistics

Technology:

Engineering, Chemical Engineering and Biotechnology, Computer Laboratory, Judge Business School, Cambridge Programme for Sustainability Leadership vii **"I don't remember":** Vik Muniz, Keynote Lecture for the Symposium "International Museum Education Institute: Focus Brazil—Pedagogy, Art, Participation," Museum of Modern Art, New York. July 22, 2011.

Introduction: Saving Lives vs. Making Lives Worth Saving

1 **"I just want":** Joseph Beuys, "Every Man an Artist: Talks at Documenta V," in *Joseph Beuys: The Reader,* edited by Claudia Mesch and Viola Michely (Cambridge, MA: MIT Press, 2007), 189. (Taken from an interview and recordings made by Clara Bodenmann-Ritter visiting Beuys's project at Documenta V, *Office for Direct Democracy.*)

2 **On January 17:** Tom Symonds, "The Mystery of Flight 038," BBC News, January 24, 2008, http://news.bbc.co.uk/2/hi/uk_news/england/london/7208126.stm.

3 **In describing the incident:** Nick Parker, Jamie Pyatt, Alex Peake, and Virginia Wheeler, "Wing and a Prayer," *Sun,* January 18, 2008, 4–5.

3 **"ordinary people":** Ben Webster, "First Officer Hailed as Hero for Nursing Stricken Boeing to Safety After Both Engines Fail," *Times* (London), January 19, 2008, 8.

4 **In 2004:** The HBR Editors, "Breakthrough Ideas for 2004," *Harvard Business Review,* February 2004, 2; Daniel H. Pink, "The MFA Is the New MBA," *Harvard Business Review,* February 2004, 11–12.

4 **James J. Cramer wrote:** James J. Cramer, "Analyze This," *New York,* March 14, 2004, 18.

6 **In 1926:** MaryKate Cleary, " 'But Is It Art?' Constantin Brancusi vs. the United States," Inside/Out: A MoMA/PS1 Blog, July 24, 2014, accessed September 14, 2015, http://www.moma.org/explore/inside_out/2014/07/24/but-is-it-art-constantin-brancusi-vs-the-united-states/.

The significance of the classification was that art had no import duty whereas utensils were taxed at 40 percent. Brancusi sued the U.S. government and won.

7   **In 1974:** "Joseph Beuys: Actions, Vitrines, and Environments, Room 4," Tate.org.uk, accessed September 14, 2015, http://www.tate.org.uk/whats-on/tate-modern/exhibition/joseph-beuys-actions-vitrines-environments/joseph-beuys-actions-4. The work is called *I Like America and America Likes Me,* 1974.

7   **In a testament:** The essay originates in a lecture Heidegger gave in 1935. He republished the essay in 1950 and 1960, and died in 1976.

7   **"A work of art is":** Martin Heidegger, "The Origin of the Work of Art," in *Basic Writings,* edited by David Farrell Krell (New York: HarperPerennial, 1993), 143–206. See essay overall, including the passage "Whenever art happens—that is, whenever there is a beginning—a thrust enters history; history either begins or starts over again" (201).

9   **In 1942:** Joseph A. Schumpeter, *Capitalism, Socialism, and Democracy,* 3rd ed. (1942; reprint, London and New York: Routledge, 2008), 81–86.

9   **The *Economist* magazine:** "Thanksgiving for Innovation," *Economist Technology Quarterly,* September 21, 2002, 13. "In this scheme of things, innovation accounts for any growth that cannot be explained by increases in capital and labour. . . . Governments worship at the altar of innovation these days for good reason. Far from being simply some missing factor in the growth equation, innovation is now recognized as the single most important ingredient in any modern economy—accounting for more than half of economic growth in America and Britain. In short, it is innovation—more than the application of capital and labour—that makes the world go round." This is an older citation but also the particular article I came across formatively while in art school.

9   **"In short":** "Thanksgiving for Innovation," *Economist,* September 21, 2002.

10 **In his 1776 book:** Adam Smith, *An Inquiry into the Nature and Causes of the Wealth of Nations, Books I–III,* edited by Andrew Skinner (1776; reprint, New York and London: Penguin Classics, 1999), 109–10. Ten men dividing up the work can make 12 pounds of pins, or 48,000—making that 4,800 per person per day. Compared to the single skilled laborer who makes twenty pins working alone, that is 240 times more.

10 **The story of the pencil:** Leonard E. Read, "I, Pencil: My Family Tree as Told to Leonard E. Read," *Library of Economics and Liberty,* December 1958, accessed September 1, 2015, http://www.econlib.org/library/Essays/rdPncl1.html.

10 **"magic of the price system":** Milton Friedman, "Power of the Market," *Free to Choose,* PBS, 1980, accessed September 1, 2015, https://www.youtube.com/watch?v=R5Gppi-O3a8. (See "the magic of the price system" at 1:58.)

11   **The successful fashion brand:** Seth Stevenson, "Polka Dots Are In? Polka
     Dots It Is!," *Slate*, June 21, 2012, http://www.slate.com/articles/arts/
     operations/2012/06/zara_s_fast_fashion_how_the_company_gets_new_
     styles_to_stores_so_quickly_.html. See also Nelson M. Fraiman, Medini
     Singh, Carolyn Paris, and Linda Arrington, "Zara," Columbia Business
     School Teaching Case, 2010.

13   **As in the case of Thomas Fogarty:** David E. Brown, *Inventing Modern
     America: From the Microwave to the Mouse* (Cambridge, MA: MIT Press,
     2002), 12–17.

13   **After it was completed:** Alexandra Alter, "Harper Lee, Author of 'To Kill
     a Mockingbird,' Is to Publish a Second Novel," *New York Times*, February
     3, 2015, http://www.nytimes.com/2015/02/04/books/harper-lee-author-of-
     to-kill-a-mockingbird-is-to-publish-a-new-novel.html?_r=0.

14   **three pairs of blue jeans:** Charles Shields, *Mockingbird* (New York: St.
     Martin's Griffin, 2006), 186, 200.

14   **Roger Bannister:** Harry Wallop, " 'I gave it everything': Sir Roger
     Bannister Marks 60 Years Since His Record," *Telegraph*, May 3, 2014,
     http://www.telegraph.co.uk/sport/othersports/athletics/10803219/I-gave-
     it-everything-Sir-Roger-Bannister-marks-60-years-since-his-record.html.

14   **In a film:** Daniel Noah, "The Major Dramatic Question," Gotham Writers'
     Workshop, accessed October 8, 2015, https://www.writingclasses.com/
     toolbox/articles/the-major-dramatic-question. First introduced to the author
     by Pete Jensen, faculty, Gotham Writers Workshop.

16   **Pixar:** Ed Catmull with Amy Wallace, *Creativity Inc.: Overcoming the
     Unseen Forces That Stand in the Way of True Inspiration* (New York:
     Random House, 2014).

20   **"big-C" and "little-c" creativity:** Mihaly Csikszentmihalyi, *Creativity:
     The Psychology of Discovery and Invention* (New York: HarperCollins,
     1996), 8.

20   **"the kind all of us share":** Ibid., 7.

20   **Starbucks:** "About Us," Starbucks.com, accessed February 2, 2015, http://
     www.starbucks.com/about-us/company-information.

21   **"to discover your own integrity":** Dror Benshetrit, "Design Outside the
     Lines," panel discussion organized by the New York City chapter of the
     Industrial Designers Society of America, held in the offices of FAB.com,
     New York, November 19, 2013.

22   **Leonardo da Vinci:** Martin Kemp, *Leonardo* (Oxford and New York:
     Oxford University Press, 2004).

23   **The most satisfying answer:** Frank Vitale, interview by author, July 6,
     2015.

25   **The British writer:** Read, "I, Pencil." See also Dale Ahlquist, "Who Is
     This Guy and Why Haven't I Heard of Him?," American Chesterton
     Society, accessed October 8, 2015, http://www.chesterton.org/
     who-is-this-guy/.

Chapter 1: From a Wide Angle

27   **"A human being":** Robert A. Heinlein, *Time Enough for Love* (New York: Ace Books, 1988), 248.

27   **owned a winery:** "Folks," Fogarty Winery, accessed October 8, 2015, http://www.fogartywinery.com/folks. The winery was founded in 1978 as more of a hobby interest by Fogarty, in partnership with the winemaker Michael Martella. They first produced wines commercially in 1981, hence the "Est. 1981" date on their bottles.

28   **was about five:** Thomas Fogarty, interview by author, December 12, 2011.

29   **saves three hundred thousand lives:** "Dr. Fogarty," Fogarty Institute for Innovation, accessed September 3, 2015, http://www.fogartyinstitute.org/about-fogarty.php.

29   **juvenile delinquent:** Thomas Fogarty, interview by author, December 12, 2001. See also Brown, *Inventing Modern America*, 12; and Jim Quinn, "Hall of Fame Interview: 'Failure Is the Preamble to Success,'" *Invention & Technology Magazine*, Winter 2004, accessed October 8, 2015, http://www.inventionandtech.com/content/"failure-preamble-success"-0.

29   **fly-fishing:** Thomas Fogarty, interview by author, December 12, 2011.

29   **"a sweatshop in every sense":** Ibid.

29   **in the eighth grade:** Ibid.

29   **only thirteen:** Quinn, "Hall of Fame Interview." The age of thirteen is an estimate based on Fogarty's recollections that he began work in a hospital in the eighth grade. Various accounts give ages ranging from twelve to fourteen or fifteen.

29   **eighteen cents:** David Cassak, "The Inventor's Inventor: An Interview with Tom Fogarty," *In Vivo: The Business and Medicine Report*, February 2003, 27–28.

29   **a new dishwashing agent:** Thomas Fogarty, interview by author, December 12, 2011.

30   **eye surgery:** Thomas Fogarty, interview by author, December 12, 2011.

30   **"holy cow":** Ibid.

30   **became a scrub technician:** Quinn, "Hall of Fame Interview."

30   **the eleventh:** Thomas Fogarty, interview by author, December 12, 2011.

30   **"'there has to be'":** Cassak, "The Inventor's Inventor," 28.

30   **seven or eight dollars:** Ibid.; Brown, *Inventing Modern America*, 12.

30   **personal handyman:** Brown, *Inventing Modern America*, 12.

31   **"smooth that transition":** Cassak, "The Inventor's Inventor," 28.

31   **Fogarty would remember:** Quinn, "Hall of Fame Interview."

31   **latex glove:** Cassak, "The Inventor's Inventor," 29.

31   **"I think I tried":** Ibid.

32   **By 1959:** Eileen Tram, Executive Assistant to Dr. Thomas J. Fogarty, email to author, October 31, 2014. Based on Eileen Tram conversation with Dr. Fogarty that day. See also "Profile: Thomas Fogarty," *Vascular News*, May 4, 2006, accessed September 3, 2015, http://www.vascularnews.com/

vn-archives/vascular-news-29-and-north-american-edition-12/profile-tom-fogarty. The profile includes a timeline of Fogarty's life, including medical school, 1956–60.

32 **"pronounce people dead":** Cassak, "The Inventor's Inventor," 28.

32 **"I'd always tied flies":** Brown, *Inventing Modern America*, 15.

32 **design challenge of adhesion:** "Dr. Fogarty," Fogarty Institute for Innovation, accessed September 3, 2015, http://www.fogartyinstitute.org/about-fogarty.ph.

33 **story of the fish:** David Foster Wallace, "David Foster Wallace on Life and Work," adapted from a commencement speech given by David Foster Wallace to the 2005 graduating class at Kenyon College, *Wall Street Journal*, September 19, 2008, accessed January 24, 2015, http://online.wsj.com/articles/SB122178211966454607.

34 **isolate this cultural difference:** Richard E. Nisbett, *The Geography of Thought: How Asians and Westerners Think Differently . . . and Why* (New York: Free Press, 2004), 89.

34 **context taken as given:** Ibid.

34 **and bubbles:** Ibid., 90.

35 **"like a pond":** Ibid. See also Takahiko Masuda and Richard E. Nisbett, "Attending Holistically vs. Analytically: Comparing the Context Sensitivity of Japanese and Americans," *Journal of Personality and Social Psychology* (2001): 922–34, accessed September 3, 2015, https://www.ualberta.ca/~tmasuda/index.files/Masuda&Nisbett2001.pdf.

36 **Pareto Principle:** Dave Lavinsky, "Pareto Principle: How to Use It to Dramatically Grow Your Business," Forbes.com, January 20, 2014, accessed February 2, 2015, http://www.forbes.com/sites/davelavinsky/2014/01/20/pareto-principle-how-to-use-it-to-dramatically-grow-your-business/.

36 *schole:* Richard Nisbett, "The Geography of Thought," *New York Times*, April 20, 2003, accessed January 25, 2015, http://www.nytimes.com/2003/04/20/books/chapters/0420-1st-nisbe.html?src=pm&pagewanted=2.

37 **In their 2003 book:** Jim Loehr and Tony Schwartz, *The Power of Full Engagement: Managing Energy, Not Time, Is the Key to High Performance and Personal Renewal* (New York: Free Press, 2003).

38 **changing to another:** Ibid., 7–8.

41 **"Amid the vastness":** Jean Paul Richter, trans., *The Notebooks of Leonardo da Vinci—Complete* (1888, reprint: Seattle, WA: Pacific Publishing, 2010), sec 1215, 219.

43 **"unexpected guest":** Will Rosenszweig, interview by author, August 22, 2014.

45 **Richard Drew:** Ernest Gundling, *The 3M Way to Innovation: Balancing People and Profit* (Tokyo: Kodansha International, 2000), 56–57. See also Virginia Huck, *Brand of the Tartan: The 3M Story* (New York: Appleton, 1955), 133–38.

46 **the whole idea of 20 percent time:** Kaomi Goetz, "How 3M Gave Everyone Days Off and Created an Innovation Dynamo," *Fast Company*, accessed February 1, 2011, http://www.fastcodesign .com/1663137/how-3m-gave-everyone-days-off-and-created-an -innovation-dynamo.

46 **AdSense to pay:** Ryan Tate, *The 20% Doctrine: How Tinkering, Goofing Off, and Breaking the Rules at Work Drive Success in Business* (New York: HarperBusiness, 2012), 15–17.

46 **Case Western in the 1990s:** Ibid., 18.

46 **pornographic:** Ibid., 27.

46 **targeted advertising:** Ibid.

46 **adapted porn filter:** Ibid., 25.

47 **"I expected that":** Paul Buchheit, The Technology Blog, July 30, 2014, accessed October 10, 2014, http://paulbuchheit.blogspot.com /2014/07/the-technology.html.

47 **forms of creative activity:** The idea for a taxonomy of creative activity first came about in conversation with my friend Sabrina Moyle, an early reader of this book and a creative force unto herself. I want to gratefully acknowledge her contribution here.

48 **In his 1962 book:** Geoffrey G. Jones, "Remembering Alfred Chandler," Working Knowledge, Harvard Business School blog, June 15, 2007, accessed September 6, 2015, http://hbswk.hbs.edu/item/5695?item=5695.html. See Alfred D. Chandler Jr., *Strategy and Structure: Chapters in the History of the Industrial Enterprise* (Cambridge, MA, and London: MIT Press, 1962).

49 **military offensives:** Generals David H. Petraeus and James F. Amos, *Counterinsurgency, Field Manual No. 3-24* (Washington, DC: Department of the Army, Department of the Navy, United States Marine Corps, December 15, 2006), accessed September 6, 2015, http://usacac.army.mil/ cac2/Repository/Materials/COIN-FM3-24.pdf.

49 **famine relief:** Tracy McVeigh, "Stars of 2014 Recreate Band Aid Spirit as Musicians Unite to Help Ebola Victims," *Guardian*, November 15, 2014, accessed September 6, 2015, http://www.theguardian.com/music/2014/ nov/15/-sp-band-aid-30-do-they-know-its-christmas.

49 **ONE Campaign:** In 2002, Bono, Bob Geldof, Jamie Drummond, Lucy Matthew, and Bobby Shriver cofounded DATA (debt, AIDS, trade, Africa), which in turn cofounded ONE in 2004 with ten other poverty-eradication charities. "ONE History," ONE Campaign website, accessed September 6, 2015, http://www.one.org/international/about/one-history/.

49 **Barack Obama:** David Talbot, "How Obama *Really* Did It," *MIT Technology Review*, August 19, 2008, accessed September 6, 2015, http:// www.technologyreview.com/featuredstory/410644/how- obama-really-did-it/.

50 **"infinitude":** Milan Kundera, *The Book of Laughter and Forgetting* (1978; reprint, New York: HarperPerennial, 1996), 225–26.

50   *Jeopardy*-style tournament: Frank Ryan, "Funny Man of God! Colbert's
      Faith," *New York Post*, September 6, 2015, 3.

50   **Dawn Wall:** William Langwiesche, "Meet the Two Men Who Free-
      Climbed Yosemite's Perilous Dawn Wall," *Vanity Fair*, April 2015,
      http://www.vanityfair.com/culture/2015/03/free-climb-yosemite
      -dawn-wall-tommy-caldwell-kevin-jorgeson.

51   **sex for the brain:** Roger von Oech, Ph.D., *A Whack on the Side of the
      Head: How to Unlock Your Mind for Innovation* (New York: Warner
      Books, 1983), 5.

52   **Mars Curiosity Rover:** Kenneth Chang and Jeremy Zilar, "NASA's
      Curiosity Rover Successfully Lands on Mars," The Lede blog, *New York
      Times*, August 5, 2012, accessed September 6, 2015, http://thelede.blogs.
      nytimes.com/2012/08/05/curiosity-is-set-to-
      land-on-mars/.

52   **Tyvek:** "Tyvek® Brand, Dupont.com, accessed September 6, 2015, http://
      www.dupont.com/products-and-services/fabrics-fibers-nonwovens/
      protective-fabrics/brands/tyvek.html.

52   **mushrooms:** Golda Arthur, "Making Houses Out of Mushrooms," *BBC
      News Magazine*, August 30, 2014, accessed September 6, 2015, http://www.
      bbc.com/news/magazine-28712940.

52   **"I think we are a region":** "Harper Lee," interview, in *Counterpoint*, edited
      by Roy Newquist (New York: Simon & Schuster, 1964), 407.

54   **Scottish illustrator:** Alexandra Alter, "Grown-Ups Get Out Their
      Crayons," *New York Times*, March 29, 2015, accessed July 22, 2015, http://
      www.nytimes.com/2015/03/30/business/media/grown-ups-get-out-their-
      crayons.html?_r=0.

55   **Abraham Maslow:** Abraham H. Maslow, "A Theory of Human
      Motivation," *Psychological Review* 50, no. 4 (July 1943): 370–96.

55   **the Grand Tour:** Jean Sorabella, "The Grand Tour" in *Heilbrunn Timeline
      of Art History* (New York: Metropolitan Museum of Art, 2000), accessed
      October 8, 2015, http://www.metmuseum.org/toah/hd/grtr/hd_grtr.htm.

55   **Laszlo Bock:** Laszlo Bock, "The Biggest Mistakes I See on Resumes,
      Part 2: Your Top 8 Questions," LinkedIn, January 26, 2015,
      https://www.linkedin.com/pulse/biggest-mistakes-i-see-resumes
      -part-2-your-top-8-questions-bock.

57   **"My Bonnie Lies":** AP, "Beatles Original for 90G," *New York Post*,
      September 20, 2015, 3.

58   **"Start to notice":** Tate, *The 20% Doctrine*, 17.

59   **"I live by the saying":** Brené Brown, "O's Experts Will Now Take Your
      Makeover Questions," *O, The Oprah Magazine*, September 2014, 124.

60   **typhoid fever:** "Orville Wright," Biography.com, accessed February 2,
      2015, http://www.biography.com/people/orville-wright-20672999; David
      McCullough, *The Wright Brothers* (New York: Simon & Schuster, 2015),
      22–25, 27–30.

60   **is now North Dakota:** National Parks Service, "Theodore Roosevelt and
      Conservation," http://www.nps.gov/thro/learn/historyculture/theodore-
      roosevelt-and-conservation.htm.

60   **taxidermizing animals:** "The National Parks: America's Best Idea:
      People—Theodore Roosevelt," PBS.org, accessed February 2, 2015, http://
      www.pbs.org/nationalparks/people/historical/roosevelt/. At age twelve,
      Roosevelt donated a number of his taxidermized creatures to the American
      Museum of Natural History in New York. A little over a decade later, he
      gave "622 carefully preserved bird skins" to the Smithsonian Institution in
      Washington, D.C.

61   **"regards man and his dignity":** Pope Francis, "Pope's
      Prayer Intentions for June Focus on Europe and Jobs Crisis,"
      transcript, Vatican Radio, May 27, 2014, accessed September
      3, 2015, http://en.radiovaticana.va/news/2014/05/27/
      pope's_prayer_intentions_for_june_focus_on_europe_and_jobs_/1101048.

61   **nightclub bouncer:** Robert Draper, "How Francis Is Remaking Rome,"
      New York Post, September 20, 2015, 8. See also David K. Li, "Pope
      Francis Worked as Nightclub Bouncer," *New York Post*, December
      3, 2013, accessed September 20, 2015, http://nypost.com/2013/12/03/
      pope-francis-i-worked-as-a-bouncer/.

61   **"Procrastinate":** Tom Sachs, interview by author and award acceptance
      speech, Louise Blouin Creative Leadership Summit, September 23, 2015.
      This list appeared as "10 Bullets for the *WSJ*," *Wall Street Journal*, September
      24, 2011, accessed January 25, 2014, http://www.wsj.com/news/interactive/
      TomSachsLttr102911. See also tenbullets.com. With thanks to Tom Sachs,
      who gave the author his own photocopy of the bullets after he read from them
      accepting an award at a party.

62   **The German neurologist:** Ferris Jabr, "Why Your Brain Needs More
      Downtime," *Scientific American*, October 15, 2013, http://www
      .scientificamerican.com/article/mental-downtime/.

63   **formation of the self:** Mary Helen Immordino-Yang, Joanna A.
      Christodoulou, and Vanessa Singh, "Rest Is Not Idleness: Implications
      of the Brain's Default Mode for Human Development and Education,"
      Perspectives on Psychological Science 7 (2012): 352. The title comes from a
      1894 book, *The Use of Life*, by John Lubbock.

63   **better able to perform:** Leslie A. Perlow and Jessica L. Porter, "Making
      Time Off Predictable—and Required," *Harvard Business Review*, October
      2009, https://hbr.org/2009/10/making-time-off-predictable-and-required.

63   **As of 2014:** Ibid.

64   **"enhanced productivity days":** Leslie A. Perlow, "Manage Your Team's
      Collective Time," *Harvard Business Review*, June 2014, https://hbr.
      org/2014/06/manage-your-teams-collective-time.

64   **"Patient first":** Thomas Fogarty interview by author.

66   **manufacture the device:** Cassak, "The Inventor's Inventor," 30.

66   **Twenty firms:** Ibid.

66   **"new things are tried":** Ibid.

66   **"Tom Fogarty's son":** Thomas Fogarty interview by author.

Chapter 2: In the Weeds

67   **"viewed from the inside":** George Orwell, "Benefit of Clergy: Some Notes in Salvador Dali," in *All Art Is Propaganda: Critical Essays*, compiled by George Packer, introduction by Keith Gersen (New York: Mariner Books/Houghton Mifflin Harcourt, 2009), 210.

67   **In 1949:** Charles J. Shields, *Mockingbird* (New York: St. Martin's Griffin, 2006), 15, for the year she moved to New York and sixteen for her age.

67   **British Airways:** Ibid., 20.

67   **"We didn't think":** Ibid., 22. Spoken by Louise Sims, wife of the saxophonist Zoot Sims. The fuller quotation: "Here was this dumpy girl from Monroeville. We didn't think she was up to much. She said she was writing a book and that was that."

68   **maybe two thousand copies:** Ibid., 14. Lee's editor at Lippincott was Tay Hohoff.

68   *Readers Digest*: Ibid., 12.

68   **"summer storm":** Newquist, ed., *Counterpoint*, 404.

68   **Pulitzer Prize:** Shields, *Mockingbird*, 182, 199.

69   **"working philosophies":** Newquist, ed., *Counterpoint*, 13, 15, 17. What he interviewed them about: 13. Location mostly at the Plaza: 15. For WQXR: 17. Tonja Carter, Harper Lee's attorney, did not respond to author correspondence to confirm these details.

69   **"I never expected any":** Ibid., 405.

70   **after the fact:** Shields, *Mockingbird*, 186.

71   **"know you're licked":** Harper Lee, *To Kill a Mockingbird* (1960; reprint, New York: Grand Central, 1982), 149; and Amy Whitaker, "The Obscure Early Lives of the Artists," *Millions*, January 2, 2013, accessed September 6, 2015, http://www.themillions.com/2013/01/the-obscure-early-lives-of-the-artists.html.

71   **In 1971:** Edward E. Jones and Richard F. Nisbett, *The Actor and the Observer: Divergent Perceptions of the Causes of Behavior*, (New York: General Learning Press, 1971).

72   **striking resemblance:** Newquist, ed., *Counterpoint*, 404.

72   **teacher mentored her:** Shields, *Mockingbird*, 63–64. Her teacher was Miss Gladys Watson.

73   **cart around everywhere:** Ibid., 50.

73   **When Lee transferred:** Ibid., 84, 85. She was a Chi Omega.

73   **Joy and Michael Brown:** Ibid., 24–25.

73   **Electrolux:** Ibid., 25; and Margalit Fox, "Michael Brown, 93, Dies; Industrial Musicals Gave Wings to 'Mockingbird,'" *New York Times*, June 29, 2014, accessed October 8, 2015, http://www.nytimes.com/2014/06/30/

arts/music/michael-brown-whose-industrial-musicals-gave-wings-to-to-kill-a-mockingbird-dies-at-93.html?_r=0.

73   **a year's salary:** Shields, *Mockingbird*, 25; and Fox, "Michael Brown, 93, Dies."

74   **"makes a nickel":** Shields, *Mockingbird*, 26.

74   *Go Set a Watchman:* Ibid., 114.

74   **galoshes:** Ibid., 131.

75   **Google X:** Ricardo Prada, interview by author, at Google X, August 25, 2014. See also Ricardo Prada, "Hi There," Ricardoprada.com, and Bryn Smith, "Getting Hired: How to Score a Job at Google X, the Secret Lab Behind Glass and Self-Driving Cars," *Core77*, January 21, 2014, accessed September 6, 2015, http://www.core77.com/posts/26282/Getting-Hired-How-to-Score-a-Job-at-Google-X-the-Secret-Lab-Behind-Glass-and-Self-Driving-Cars.

76   **"It's better than nothing":** Ricardo Prada, interview by author, at Google X, August 25, 2014.

76   **self-concept as smart:** Carol S. Dweck, Ph.D., *Mindset: The New Psychology of Success* (New York: Ballantine, 2006), 4.

78   **"If you stay doggedly":** Leonardo da Vinci, *Leonardo on Painting*, selected and translated by Martin Kemp and Magaret Walker (New Haven, CT: Yale University Press, 1989), 203. Kemp's concordance with other sources: BN 2038 28r (R530), Urb 131v-132r (McM 440).

79   **"drew so well":** Michael J. Gelb, *How to Think Like Leonardo da Vinci* (New York: Dell, 2000), 167. See also Kenneth Clark, *Catalogue of the Drawings by Leonardo da Vinci in the Collection of His Majesty the King, at Windsor Castle*, 2 vols. (New York: Macmillan, 1935); *Leonardo da Vinci: An Account of His Development as an Artist* (Baltimore: Penguin Books, 1939).

80   **"most curious man":** Gelb, *How to Think Like Leonardo*, 50.

80   **"'ugly babies'":** Ed Catmull, with Amy Wallace, *Creativity Inc.: Overcoming the Unseen Forces That Stand in the Way of True Inspiration* (New York: Random House, 2014), 131.

81   **MediaMonks:** Wesley ter Haar, presentation to NEW INC members, MediaMonks office, September 11, 2015.

82   **You can also absorb:** Anthony Doerr, interview by the author, August 18, 2015.

82   **"blind girl and a Nazi boy":** Anthony Doerr, interview by the author, August 18, 2015.

84   **"Man will not fly":** McCullough, *The Wright Brothers*, 208.

84   **two years later:** Arthur George Renstrom, *Wilbur & Orville Wright: A Reissue of A Chronology Commemorating the Hundredth Anniversary of the Birth of Orville Wright, August 19, 1871*, U.S. Centennial of Flight Commission and NASA: Monographs in Aerospace History, no. 32, September 2003, NASA publication SP-2003-4532, 7.

85   **Elvis Presley:** Joel Williamson, *Elvis Presley: A Southern Life* (New York: Oxford University Press, 2014), 30, 128. Elvis said he failed music class. Other reports say he received a C. See also "Elvis Presley: Biography," Sun Records, http://www.sunrecords.com/artists/elvis-presley.

85   **Oprah Winfrey:** David Zurawik, "From Sun Magazine: Oprah—Built in Baltimore," *Baltimore Sun*, May 18, 2011, accessed September 6, 2015, http://articles.baltimoresun.com/2011-05-18/entertainment/bs-sm-oprahs-baltimore-20110522_1_oprah-winfrey-show-baltimore-history-wjz.

85   **Fred Smith:** "Fred Smith: An Overnight Success," *Entrepreneur*, October 8, 2008, accessed September 6, 2015, http://www.entrepreneur.com/article/197542.

85   **Michael Jordan:** Bob Cook, "The Reality Behind the Myth of the Coach Who Cut Michael Jordan," *Forbes*, January 10, 2012, accessed http://www.forbes.com/sites/bobcook/2012/01/10/the-reality-behind-the-myth-of-the-coach-who-cut-michael-jordan-in-high-school/.

85   **Dr. Seuss's:** NPR Staff, "How Dr. Seuss Got His Start 'On Mulberry Street,'" NPR Books, January 24, 2012, accessed September 6, 2015, http://www.npr.org/2012/01/24/145471724/how-dr-seuss-got-his-start-on-mulberry-street.

86   **Fred Astaire:** "Fred Astaire: Biography," Biography.com, accessed September 6, 2015, http://www.biography.com/people/fred-astaire-9190991.

86   **Stephen King's:** Lucas Reilly, "How Stephen King's Wife Saved 'Carrie' and Launched His Career," Mental Floss, October 17, 2013, accessed September 6, 2015, http://mentalfloss.com/article/53235/how-stephen-kings-wife-saved-carrie-and-launched-his-career.

86   **"can't get a real job":** Paul Buchheit, The Technology blog, July 20, 2014, http://paulbuchheit.blogspot.com/2014_07_01_archive.html.

86   *Painting as a Pastime*: Christopher Klein, "Winston Churchill's World War Disaster," History in the Headlines, May 21, 2014, accessed September 6, 2015, http://www.history.com/news/winston-churchills-world-war-disaster. The essay "Painting as a Pastime" was first included in Sir Winston Churchill, *Amid These Storms* (New York: Charles Scribner's Sons, 1932). Published as a stand-alone book: Winston S. Churchill, *Painting as a Pastime* (New York: McGraw-Hill, 1950 and New York: Cornerstone Library, 1965).

87   **catastrophized:** Josephine Sykes, Monica Halpin, and Victor Brown, "Sir Winston Churchill: A Biography," Churchill College, Cambridge University, accessed September 6, 2015, https://www.chu.cam.ac.uk/archives/collections/churchill-papers/churchill-biography/.

87   **"finest hour":** Winston Churchill, "Their Finest Hour" (speech, House of Commons, London, England, June 18, 1940), accessed December 4, 2015, http://www.winstonchurchill.org/resources/speeches/233-1940-the-finest-hour/122-their-finest-hour.

87   **Alexander Graham Bell:** History.com Staff, "Alexander Graham Bell Patents the Telephone," "This Day in History," A+E Networks 2009, accessed September 7, 2015, http://www.history.com/this-day-in-history/alexander-graham-bell-patents-the-telephone.

87   **Barbie:** "Ruth Handler" (obituary), *Economist*, May 2, 2002, accessed September 7, 2015, http://www.economist.com/node/1109674. Ruth Handler was born in 1916. Barbie was released in 1959.

87   **Louise Bourgeois:** Holland Cotter, "Louise Bourgeois, Influential Sculptor, Dies at 98," *New York Times*, May 31, 2010, accessed September 7, 2015, http://www.nytimes.com/2010/06/01/arts/design/01bourgeois.html?_r=0. The exhibition was a 1982 retrospective at the Museum of Modern Art in New York.

87   **Aaron Sorkin:** Aaron Sorkin, "Remarks by Aaron Sorkin '83 at Syracuse University's 158th Commencement and the SUNY College of Environmental Science and Forestry's 115th Commencement," Syracuse University News Service, May 13, 2012. Sorkin failed a drama class in college. After college he was trying to become a writer and working variously as a bartender, telemarketer, and driver.

87   **Babe Ruth:** "Babe Ruth," actor listings on the Internet Movie Database, accessed September 7, 2015, http://www.imdb.com/name/nm0751899/?ref_=fn_nm_nm_1#actor.

87   **Raymond Chandler:** Carolyn Kellogg, "The Reading Life: Happy Birthday to Me—and Raymond Chandler," *Los Angeles Times*, July 17, 2011, accessed September 7, 2015, http://articles.latimes.com/2011/jul/17/entertainment/la-ca-raymond-chandler-20110717.

87   **David Seidler:** "David Seidler Profile," *Telegraph*, February 28, 2011, accessed September 7, 2015, http://www.telegraph.co.uk/culture/film/oscars/8352445/David-Seidler-profile.html.

88   **"barroom exchange":** Virginia Huck, *Brand of the Tartan: The 3M Story* (New York: Appleton-Centry-Crofts, 1955), 4, 16, and 23 (error in founding the mine, 16; 1901 share price, 4; whiskey quotation, 23). See also Ernest Gundling, *The 3M Way to Innovation: Balancing People and Profit* (Tokyo: Kodansha International, 2000), 50.

88   **$80 billion market cap:** The market capitalization of 3M was $87 billion as of September 19, 2015, https://www.google.com/finance?q=NYSE%3AMM&ei=naf9Vem2Gs7KmAHE-Z7wBg.

88   **"I'm Feeling Lucky'":** Thomas L. Friedman, "If Larry and Sergey Asked for a Loan . . . ," *New York Times*, Week in Review, October 26, 2008, 15, http://www.nytimes.com/2008/10/26/opinion/26friedman.html?_r=0.

89   **prime meridian:** The idea of longitude and latitude has existed for much longer but was only measured commonly from the prime meridian as a result of the International Meridian Conference in 1884, with the agreement of twenty-two governments (one opposing, two abstaining). "The Quest for Longitude and the Rise of Greenwich—A History," Greenwich Meridian, accessed September 7, 2015, http://www.thegreenwichmeridian.org/tgm/articles.php?article=9. See

also: "Greenwich and the Millennium," Royal Museums Greenwich, accessed September 7, 2015, http://www.rmg.co.uk/explore/astronomy-and-time/astronomy-facts/history/greenwich-and-the-millennium.

89 **landfill:** Snejana Farberov, "How Hurricane Sandy Flooded New York Back to Its 17th Century Shape as It Inundated 400 Years of Reclaimed Land," *Daily Mail*, June 15, 2013, http://www.dailymail.co.uk/news/article-2342297/Manhattans-original-coastline-revealed-Hurricane-Sandy-flooded-land-reclaimed-400-years.html.

89 **colonies:** Jeffrey Howe, "Boston: A History of the Landfills," Digital Archive of American Architecture, Study Guide to FA 267 from Saltbox to Skyscraper: Architecture in America, Boston College, accessed October 9, 2015, http://www.bc.edu/bc_org/avp/cas/fnart/fa267/bos_fill3.html.

89 **open sewer:** F. David 'Ferdie' Gilson, "South London Harriers: A Brief Club History," South London Harriers, last updated February 24, 2015, accessed October 9, 2015, http://www.southlondonharriers.org/about-us/club-history.html. "Sir Frederick Treves, a famous medical doctor of the time, calculated that a square mile of fog contained about six tons of soot."

90 **Mary Oliver:** Parker J. Palmer, *A Hidden Wholeness: The Journey Toward an Undivided Life* (San Francisco: Jossey-Bass/Wiley, 2004), 34. See also Mary Oliver, "Low Tide," *Amicus Journal*, Winter 2001, 34.

90 **In 1974:** Thich Nhat Hanh, *The Miracle of Mindfulness*, translated by Mobi Ho, translator's preface by Mobi Ho (1975; reprint, Boston: Beacon Press, 1987), vii–viii.

91 **"two ways to wash dishes":** Ibid., 4.

91 **"panflute accompaniment":** Dan Harris, *10% Happier* (New York: It Books, 2014), xiv.

92 **finger bowl:** Lady (Laura) Troubridge, *The Book of Etiquette: The Complete Standard Work of Reference of Social Usage* (1926; Surrey: Kingswood/World's Work, 1948), v–vi.

92 **meditation is rowing:** Author interview with Christopher Schultz, January 2014.

93 **In the past decade:** David Gelles, "A C.E.O.'s Management by Mantra," *New York Times*, March 1, 2015, Business, 1 and 6, http://www.nytimes.com/2015/03/01/business/at-aetna-a-ceos-management-by-mantra.html?_r=0. And author correspondence with Ethan Slavin, Aetna, January 19, 2016. See also "Ten Big Companies That Promote Meditation," OnlineMBA, February 1, 2012, accessed October 8, 2015, http://www.onlinemba.com/blog/10-big-companies-that-promote-employee-meditation/.

93 **skiing accident:** Gelles, "A C.E.O.'s Management by Mantra." The article was adapted from Gelles's book *Mindful Work: How Meditation Is Changing Business from the Inside Out* (Boston: Eamon Dolan Books/Houghton Mifflin Harcourt, 2015).

93 **stress levels** and **Piketty:** Ibid.

94 **dialectical:** "Dr. Marsha Linehan, Founder," Linehan Institute, accessed

September 20, 2015. Also see Marsha M. Linehan, *DBT Skills Training Manual*, 2nd ed. (New York and London: Guilford Press, 2015).

94   **"radical acceptance"**: Tara Brach, *Radical Acceptance: Embracing Your Life with the Heart of Buddha* (New York: Bantam, 2004).

95   **"peaks and valleys"**: Norman Lear, *Even* This *I Get to Experience* (New York: Penguin Books, 2014), 324.

95   **"Over and Next"**: Ibid., 327.

96   **"No daylight"**: Tate, *The 20% Doctrine*, 23.

96   **New York City Marathon:** Author correspondence with Lauren Doll, New York Road Runners, January 22, 2016. See also: Nicole Lyn Pesce, "26 New York City Marathon Facts from Its New City Museum Exhibit," *Daily News*, October 20, 2015, accessed January 24, 2016, http://www.nydailynews.com/life-style/26-facts-new-york-city-marathon-article-1.2403391; and "Going Green" Making Strides for the Environment," New York Road Runners, accessed January 24, 2016, http://www.tcsnycmarathon.org/about-the-race/going-green-making-strides-for-the-environment.

97   **2,000 runners:** Rubin, *Anything for a T-Shirt*, 45, 47.

97   **James Earl Jones's father:** Ibid.

97   **Diana Nyad:** "Diana Makes History," Diana Nyad website, accessed October 9, 2015, http://www.diananyad.com.

97   **towed during the race:** Rubin, *Anything for a T-Shirt*, 50, 52.

97   **newfangled:** Ibid., 44.

97   **Fiat X19:** Ibid., 41.

98   **old bowling trophy:** Ibid., 23; and "History of the New York City Marathon," TCS New York City Marathon, accessed October 9, 2015, http://www.tcsnycmarathon.org/about-the-race/marathon-facts/history-of-the-new-york-city-marathon#sthash.UbWLRq7S.dpuf. "Winners were given inexpensive wristwatches and recycled baseball and bowling trophies. The entry fee was $1 and the total event budget was $1,000."

98   **"crazy looking Long Johns":** Rubin, *Anything for a T-Shirt*, 19.

98   **cup of bourbon:** Ibid.

98   **three Dawns:** Amy Whitaker, "The Obscure Early Lives of the Artists."

99   **gift of participation:** Ibid.

99   **played Scout:** Ibid.

99   **much more interesting:** Ibid.

100   **famous author in 1961:** Ibid.

100   **"How often I found":** Lloyd Steven Seiden, ed., *A Fuller View: Buckminster Fuller's Vision of Hope and Abundance for All* (Studio City, CA: Divine Arts, 2011), 137. See also the R. Buckminster Fuller Collection, Stanford University Libraries, for recordings of Fuller's lectures and interviews, accessed December 7, 2015, https://library.stanford.edu/collections/r-buckminster-fuller-collection.

Chapter 3: To the Lighthouse

101   **"Failure is as exciting":** Roger Bannister, *The First Four Minutes*, 50th
       Anniversary Ed. (1955; reprint, Stroud, Gloucestershire: Sutton, 2004), 164.

102   **On May 6:** Ibid., 161, 167.

102   **In the 1860s:** Sir Montague Shearman, *Athletics* (1887; London: Longmans,
       Green, 1898), 107, 115. Describing Chinnery's run, 115. The half mile was
       run in under 2 minutes starting in 1872 (107), arguably laying ground for
       hopes of breaking the four-minute mile.

102   **By the 1940s:** Ibid., 31. Sydney Wooderson had broken the world record
       with a 4:06.4 mile in August 1937.

103   **nine-year tenure:** "The World Record for the Mile Run," MAA.org,
       accessed October 9, 2015, http://www.maa.org/sites/default/files/images/
       upload_library/3/osslets/100multiParameterAnimation/mile_record_
       scatter.html.

103   **"space-eating stride":** Neal Bascomb, *The Perfect Mile: The Race to Break
       the Four Minute Mile* (London: CollinsWillow, 2005), 7, 21.

103   **long preamble:** Ibid., 225.

104   **a 3:58 flat:** A.A.P., "Landy Now Through the 'Barrier,'" *Examiner*
       (Launceston, Tasmania), June 23, 1954, http://trove.nla.gov.au/ndp/
       del/article/96270699. Landy ran the 3:58 in Turku, Finland, on June 21,
       1954, the forty-sixth day after Bannister's May 6 run. Chris Chataway,
       one of Bannister's friends and pacers, was competing against Landy at
       the time. Landy credited the competition with Chataway, who finished
       approximately forty yards behind him, with spurring him to the record.

104   **Louis Zamperini:** Laura Hillenbrand, *Unbroken* (New York: Random
       House, 2010), xvii–xviii.

105   **two Swedes:** Bannister, *The First Four Minutes*, 30.

105   **At age eight:** Ibid., 16–17.

105   **At age ten:** Ibid., 17.

105   **as the roof crashed in:** Bascomb, *The Perfect Mile*, 14.

105   **came in eighteenth:** Bannister, *The First Four Minutes*, 19; and Bascomb,
       The Perfect Mile, 14.

105   **at age twelve:** Bannister, *The First Four Minutes*, 20–21.

106   **In 1945:** Bascomb, *The Perfect Mile*, 15.

106   **fall of 1946:** Ibid.; Bannister, *The First Four Minutes*, 27, 29.

106   **not finding an attendant:** Bannister, *The First Four Minutes*, 31, 32.

106   **compact physique:** Dylan Clever, "Athletics: Lovelock Enigma
       Continues," *New Zealand Herald*, May 17, 2009, accessed October
       9, 2015, http://www.nzherald.co.nz/sport/news/article.cfm?c_id=4&
       objectid=10572837/.

106   **"you'll never be any good":** Bannister, *The First Four Minutes*, 33.

106   **Finland:** Ibid., 205.

106   **third-string team:** Ibid., 34.

106   **ex-servicemen:** Ibid., 36.

106 **chain smoker:** Ibid., 34 and 35.

107 **Earls Court:** Bascomb, *The Perfect Mile*, 105–6.

107 **"the strain of first class competition":** Graham Tanner and Laurence Chandy, "The History of the Oxford University Athletic Club," 90, http://www.ouccc-oldmembers.co.uk/OUAC-History-Sep11.pdf. Tanner was an OUAC coach from 1976 to 2007. Chandy (Magdalen College) was OUAC president from 2001 to 2002. The history was first written by Tanner and then updated by Chandy.

107 **on his lunch break:** Bascomb, *The Perfect Mile*, 106.

108 **1952 Olympics:** Ibid., 138.

108 **two more years:** Bannister, *The First Four Minutes*, 138–39.

108 **Queen Elizabeth's coronation:** Ibid., 200.

108 **"challenge to the human spirit":** Ibid., 144.

108 **final lap on his own:** Bascomb, *The Perfect Mile*, 203–4. In the actual race, Brasher paced the first two and a half laps, and Chataway paced from there into the middle of the fourth lap (220–24).

108 **finishing kick:** Brian Oliver, *The Commonwealth Games: Extraordinary Stories Behind the Medals* (London: Bloomsbury, 2014), 164.

108 **uniformity of speed:** Malcolm Boyden, "3:59.4 Sir Roger Bannister Documentary," BBC Radio Oxford, May 9, 2014, 16:50–17:40 minutes, http://www.bbc.co.uk/programmes/p01ysrsq.

109 **took a break:** Bannister, *The First Four Minutes*, 158. By 4:04 mile, I am approximating the fact that they had their quarter-mile pace down to 61 seconds.

109 **behind the seats:** Bascomb, *The Perfect Mile*, 201.

109 **realize their luck:** Ibid., 203.

109 **four-minute range:** Bannister, *The First Four Minutes*, 159.

109 **polished floor:** Ibid., 160–61.

109 **British standards:** Ibid., 161.

109 **Eustace Thomas:** Ibid., 161, 163.

109 **North Sea:** Bascomb, *The Perfect Mile*, 170–71.

109 **"your only chance":** Ibid., 216.

110 **Felicity and Sally:** Bannister, *The First Four Minutes*, 163–64; Bascomb, *The Perfect Mile*, 215.

110 **false start:** Bascomb, *The Perfect Mile*, 218–19.

110 **newsreel:** "First Four-Minute Mile-HQ (Roger Bannister: 1954)," AthletixStuffChannel, YouTube, accessed October 9, 2015, https://www.youtube.com/watch?v=wTXoTnp_5sI.

110 **almost dizzying:** Harry Wallop, " 'I Gave It Everything': Sir Roger Bannister Marks 60 Years Since His Record," *Telegraph*, May 3, 2014, http://www.telegraph.co.uk/sport/othersports/athletics/10803219/I-gave-it-everything-Sir-Roger-Bannister-marks-60-years-since-his-record.html.

111 **"made success possible":** Bannister, *The First Four Minutes*, 165.

111 **"one thing supremely well":** Ibid., 166.

111 **collapsed and blacked out:** Roger Bannister, "Twin Tracks (excerpt)," *Telegraph*, March 30, 2014, http://www.telegraph.co.uk/sport/10731234/Roger-Bannister-The-day-I-broke-the-four-minute-mile.html.

111 **physically holding him up:** Bascomb, *The Perfect Mile*, 219, 224; Boyden, "3:59.4 Sir Roger Bannister Documentary," at 8:20 minutes.

114 **proudest contributions:** Boyden, "3:59.4 Sir Roger Bannister Documentary," at 22:30 minutes. Bannister has claimed this repeatedly. Here he talks about being a good father and grandfather and husband.

116 **"most revolutionary concept":** Levy, "Prophet of Privacy," *Wired*, November 1994, http://archive.wired.com/wired/archive/2.11/diffie_pr.html.

116 *The Space Cat:* Steven Levy, *Crypto: How the Code Rebels Beat the Government—Saving Privacy in the Digital Age* (New York: Penguin, 2001), 36.

117 **library's books:** Ibid., 7.

117 **admitted to the Massachusetts Institute of Technology:** Ibid., 8.

118 **pursuit of math itself:** Ibid., 9.

118 **department in 1965:** Although there had been a "Division of Computer Science" within the Math Department since 1961, and the Stanford Artificial Intelligence Project was begun in 1962, the Department of Computer Science was created in January 1965. "Department Timeline," Stanford Computer Science Department, Stanford University School of Engineering, accessed September 7, 2015, http://www-cs.stanford.edu/timeline.

118 **avoid the draft:** Levy, *Crypto*, 9. See also "Whitfield Diffie: 2011 Fellow Award Recipient," Computer History Museum, accessed September 7, 2015, http://www.computerhistory.org/fellowawards/hall/bios/Whitfield,Diffie/.

118 **consortium of research universities:** Levy, *Crypto*, 20. See also: "ARPANET Launch the World's First Packet-Switched Wide Area Computer Network," Centre for Computing History, accessed, September 7, 2015, http://www.computinghistory.org.uk/det/5613/ARPANET-launch-the-world-s-first-successful-packet-switched-wide-area-computer-network/. For an excellent general history of ARPANET, see: Roy Rosenzweig, "Wizards, Bureaucrats, Warriors, and Hackers: Writing the History of the Internet," *American Historical Review*, December 1998, 1530–52, accessed January 25, 2016, http://www.pne.people.si.umich.edu/PDF/ahrcwreview.pdf.

118 **Faustian bargain:** Levy, *Crypto*, 14–15.

118 **"are inseparable":** Ibid., 19.

119 **"untrustworthy people":** Ibid., 36.

119 **Datsun 510:** Ibid., 24–25.

119 **"cloak and dagger":** Ibid., 25.

119   **Konheim:** Ibid., 30–31.

120   **"downstairs to get a Coke":** Levy, "Prophet of Privacy."

121   **"apex of my career":** Letter from Miss Louise Florencourt to the author, February 24, 2015. Also from a conversation at Andalusia on September 26, 2009.

122   **"breath of the spirit":** Stephen Weil, *Rethinking the Museum and Other Meditations* (Washington, DC, and London: Smithsonian, 1990), 171. John Maynard Keynes, the first Chairman of the Arts Council, from a 1945 BBC Broadcast on the Arts Council's formation.

122   **palliative care nurse:** Bonnie Ware, *The Top Five Regrets of the Dying: A Life Transformed by the Dearly Departing* (Carlsbad, CA: Hay House, 2012).

125   **under brewer at Guinness:** Bascomb, *The Perfect Mile*, 168.

125   **Chataway finished second:** OUAC History, 67.

125   **set world records:** http://www.ouac.org/statistics/world-record-holders/.

125   **"running for a bus":** OUAC History, 63.

126   **"energy of the twins":** Bannister, *The First Four Minutes*, 160.

126   **announce split times:** Bascomb, *The Perfect Mile*, 220–21.

126   **"almost uninsurable risk":** Ibid., 192.

127   **"billion other men on earth":** Ibid., 8.

127   **cofound the London Marathon:** "In the Beginning," News & Media, Virgin Money London Marathon, accessed October 9, 2015, https://www.virginmoneylondonmarathon.com/en-gb/news-media/media-resources/history-london-marathon/in-the-beginning/.

127   **best-selling copyrighted book:** Bruce Watson, "World's Unlikeliest Bestseller," *Smithsonian*, 2005, http://www.smithsonianmag.com/science-nature/worlds-unlikeliest-bestseller-81732187/?no-ist.

127   **Ross was killed:** BBC News Staff, "Record Breakers' McWhirter Dies," BBC News, April 20, 2004, accessed September 7, 2015, http://news.bbc.co.uk/2/hi/entertainment/3643039.stm. See also Richard Cavendish, "The Guinness Book of World Records Was First Published on August 27th 1955," HistoryToday.com, vol. 55, no. 8, August 2005, accessed December 8, 2015, http://www.historytoday.com/richard-cavendish/publication-guinness-book-world-records.

128   **Softsoap was the brainchild:** Steven Greenhouse, "Minnetonka's Struggle to Stay One Step Ahead," *New York Times*, December 28, 1986, accessed September 7, 2015, http://www.nytimes.com/1986/12/28/business/minnetonka-s-struggle-to-stay-one-step-ahead.html.

129   **outside of use in public lavatories:** Kurian Tharakan, "Tiny Softsoap's Unconventional Strategy to Win Against the Industry," Duct Tape Marketing, September 29, 2012, accessed September 7, 2015, http://strategypeak.com/softsoaps-unconventional-strategy/.

130   **to outcompete him:** For related general strategies regarding vertical integration, see John Stuckey and David White, "When and When *Not* to

Vertically Integrate," *Sloan Management Review*, Spring 1993, 71–83.

130 **more than the company was worth:** Adam M. Brandenburger and Barry J. Nalebuff, "The Right Game: Use Game Theory to Shape Strategy," *Harvard Business Review*, July–August 1995, 66.

130 **took 38 percent:** Greenhouse, "Minnetonka's Struggle to Stay One Step Ahead."

131 **"legitimate challenges":** Bannister, *The First Four Minutes*, 201.

131 **Olympic Charter:** Ibid., 210.

133 **Some 1,300 runners:** Doug Robinson, "After 60 years, Sub-4-Minute Mile Still the Standard for Runners," *Deseret News*, May 6, 2014, accessed September 7, 2015, http://www.deseretnews.com/article/865602579/After-60-years-sub-4-minute-mile-still-the-standard-for-runners.html?pg=all.

133 **Hicham El Guerrouj:** "Fastest Run One Mile (Male)," Guinness World Records, accessed September 7, 2015, http://www.guinnessworldrecords.com/world-records/fastest-run-one-mile-(male).

133 **"the heroes around whom":** Bascomb, *The Perfect Mile*, 321.

135 **"I don't know how":** Ibid., 192–93.

135 **A French journalist:** Ibid., 1.

Chapter 4: To Make a Boat

137 **"The beginnings of all":** Sir William Gurney Benham, *Cassell's Book of Quotations* (London: Cassell, 1907), 628. Underlying citation: Cicero, *De Finibus* 5, 21, 68.

138 **one million square feet:** It was technically 1,076,390 square feet (100,000 square meters) and 9.7 miles of blue polypropylene rope. "Wrapped Reichstag," official website of Christo and Jeanne-Claude, accessed September 7, 2015, http://christojeanneclaude.net/projects/wrapped-reichstag?view=info#.Ve23vs4boZY.

138 **laundry line:** "The Gates," official website of Christo and Jeanne-Claude, accessed September 7, 2015, http://christojeanneclaude.net/projects/the-gates#.Ve24a84boZY.

139 **the sale of related drawings:** Jeanne-Claude, "Most Common Errors," official website of Christo and Jeanne-Claude, 1998, accessed December 5, 2015, http://christojeanneclaude.net/common-errors.

139 **In 1958:** "Wrapped Cans and Bottles," official website of Christo and Jeanne-Claude, accessed September 7, 2015, http://christojeanneclaude.net/projects/wrapped-cans-and-bottles?view=info#.Ve25U84boZY.

139 **In 1962:** "Wrapped Objects, Statues and Women," official website of Christo and Jeanne-Claude, accessed September 7, 2015, http://christojeanneclaude.net/projects/wrapped-objects-statues-and-women#.Ve25ms4boZY.

139 **from 1971 to 1995:** "Wrapped Reichstag," http://christojeanneclaude.net/
projects/wrapped-reichstag?view=info#.Ve23vs4boZY, and "The Gates,"
http://christojeanneclaude.net/projects/the-gates#
.Ve24a84boZY.

139 **Twitter listed on:** Vindu Goel, "Twitter Prices Its Initial Offering at $26
Per Share," *New York Times*, November 6, 2013, accessed September 7,
2015, http://www.nytimes.com/2013/11/07/technology/twitter-prices-ipo-
at-26-a-share.html?pagewanted=all&_r=0.

139 **It closed at:** David Gelles, "So Far, So Good for Twitter," Dealbook,
New York Times, November 7, 2013, accessed September 20, 2015,
http://dealbook.nytimes.com/2013/11/07/twitter-shares-surge-in
-a-smooth-start-to-trading/?_r=0.

139 **his Blogger platform:** Ryan Mac, "Who Owns Twitter? A Look at
Jack Dorsey, Evan Williams and the Company's Largest Shareholders,"
Forbes, October 4, 2013, accessed September 7, 2015, http://www
.forbes.com/sites/ryanmac/2013/10/04/who-owns-twitter-a-look-at
-jack-dorsey-evan-williams-and-the-companys-largest-shareholders/.

140 **For the first six months:** Stephen Gandel, "Twitter's Shady Accounting,"
Fortune, October 8, 2013, accessed September 20, 2015, http://fortune.
com/2013/10/08/twitters-shady-accounting/. Twitter was reporting
adjusted EBITDA, meaning earnings before interest, tax, depreciation, and
amortization, and also adjusted to take out accounting for grants of stock
to employees.

140 **without having any earnings:** Richard Costelo, "Twitter: Form S-1
Registration Statement," U.S. Securities and Exchange Commission,
12-14 and F-30, accessed September 7, 2015, http://www.sec.gov/
Archives/edgar/data/1418091/000119312513390321/d564001ds1.htm. See
also Gretchen Morgenson, "Earnings, Without All the Bad Stuff," *New
York Times*, November 9, 2013, accessed September 7, 2015, http://www.
nytimes.com/2013/11/10/business/earnings-but-without-the-bad-stuff.
html.

141 **"We lived in a nice apartment":** Harry M. Markowitz, "Biographical,"
Nobelprize.org, accessed September 7, 2015, http://www.nobelprize.org/
nobel_prizes/economic-sciences/laureates/1990/markowitz-bio.html.

141 **benefits of a diversified portfolio:** Ibid., and Harry M. Markowitz, "Prize
Lecture: Foundations of Portfolio Theory," Nobelprize.org, December
7, 1990, accessed April 4, 2016, http://www.nobelprize.org/nobel_prizes/
economic-sciences/laureates/1990/markowitz-lecture.pdf.

142 **Matthew Deleget is:** Matthew Deleget, interview by the author, and
presentation at Lower Manhattan Cultural Council Artist Summer
Institute, Governors Island, August 10, 2015.

143 **Mrs. Moneypenny:** "Books," Mrs Moneypenny, accessed October 9, 2015,
http://www.mrsmoneypenny.com/books.

144 **lucky economic container:** Thomas Fogarty interview by author.

144 **workouts on his lunch break:** Bascomb, *The Perfect Mile*, 106.

144 **house-sitting:** Levy, *Crypto*, 34–35.

144 **double-knit polyester suits:** Rubin, *Anything for a T-Shirt*, 12–13.

144 **a year's salary:** Shields, *Mockingbird*, 20, 25–26, 116.

145 **"fantastic gamble":** Harper Lee, "Christmas to Me," *McCall's*, December 1961, accessed September 7, 2015, http://heyboobooks.tumblr.com/post/2447111228/christmas-to-me-an-essay-by-harper-lee.

145 **saved $12,000:** Levy, *Crypto*, 25.

146 **David Kahn:** Ibid., 22.

146 **Snapchat:** Susanna Kim, "Meet People Who Were CEOs Living in Their Parents' Homes," ABCNews, November 13, 2014, accessed September 7, 2015, http://abcnews.go.com/Business/ceos-founders-lived-parents/story?id=26888490.

146 **Lebow personally paid:** Rubin, *Anything for a T-Shirt*, 22, 26.

151 **Historians believe that:** This date comes from Jack Wasserman, *Leonardo* (New York: Harry N. Abrams, 1975), 144. He cites Vasari. The dates also appear in the timeline of Leonardo's life in Ludwig Goldsheider, ed., *Leonardo da Vinci*, 3rd ed. (New York: Oxford University Press, 1948), 21.

151 **New Council Chamber:** Jane Roberts, "The Life of Leonardo," in Martin Kemp and Jane Roberts, *Leonardo da Vinci*, with a preface by E. H. Gombrich (London: Hayward Gallery, 1989), 35.

151 **Leonardo received the commission:** Ibid., 34.

151 **paid 35 florins:** "Contract for the Battle of Anghiari, May 4, 1504," in *Leonardo on Painting*, edited by Martin Kemp, selected and translated by Martin Kemp and Margaret Walker (New Haven, CT: Yale University Press, 1989), 270.

152 **the price of a salad:** William Arthur Shaw, *The History of Currency*, 1252 to 1894 (New York: Putnam, and London: Clement Wilson, 1896), 301–9, accessed September 7, 2015, https://books.google.com/books?id=GrJCAAAAIAAJ&pg=PR3&dq=The+History+of+Currency,+1252-1894+by+WIlliams+Arthur+Shaw&hl=en&sa=X&ved=0CB8Q6AEwAGoVChMI0MuH4cjlxwIVh52ACh1VEQVc#v=onepage&q=The%20History%20of%20Currency%2C%201252-1894%20by%20WIlliams%20Arthur%20Shaw&f=false. See also Julian Abagond, "Money in Leonardo's Time," Abagond, May 10, 2007, accessed September 7, 2015, https://abagond.wordpress.com/2007/05/10/money-in-leonardos-time/.

152 **As part of the arrangement:** Carmen C. Baumbach, et al., eds. *Leonard da Vinci, Master Draftsman* (New Haven, CT, and New York: Yale and Metropolitan Museum of Art, 2003), 234.

152 **By June 1505:** Jane Roberts, "The Life of Leonardo," 35, and Baumbach, *Leonardo, Master Draftsman*, 19.

152 **More than fifty years later:** Ibid.

153 **the king of France:** Michael White, *Leonardo: The First Scientist*

(New York: St. Martin's Press, 2000), 255, accessed September 7, 2015, https://books.google.com/books?id=-OmWWh2BqYkC&pg=PA254&lpg=PA254&dq=leonardo+patronage+king+of+france&source=bl&ots=M3kcEui1mm&sig=NpjlstNTu7tZaj5ngbsi_dvNPZo&hl=en&sa=X&ved=0CC8Q6AEwA2oVChMIkeearcvlxwIVRck-Ch3j4AJt#v=onepage&q=leonardo%20patronage%20king%20of%20france&f=false.

153   **ends justify the means:** Kemp and Walker, *Leonardo on Painting*, 271. *The Prince* was, historians believe, first distributed as a pamphlet in 1513 and then published in 1532.

155   **As Henderson wrote:** Martin Reeves, Sandy Moose, and Thijs Venema, "BCG Classics Revisited: The Growth Share Matrix," *BCG Perspectives*, June 4, 2014, accessed September 7, 2015, https://www.bcgperspectives.com/content/articles/corporate_strategy_portfolio_management_strategic_planning_growth_share_matrix_bcg_classics_revisited/.

158   **Google started with a:** John Battelle, "The Birth of Google," *Wired*, August 1, 2005, http://www.wired.com/2005/08/battelle/. See also John Battelle, *The Search: How Google and Its Rivals Rewrote the Rules of Business and Transformed Our Culture* (New York: Penguin, 2005), and Sara Kettler, "The Google Chronicles: 7 Facts on Founders Larry Page and Sergey Brin," Biography.com, August 19, 2014, http://www.biography.com/news/google-founders-history-facts.

158   **"merchants of death":** Andrew Glass, "Sen. Nye Assails 'Merchants of Death' on Sept. 4, 1934," *Politico*, September 4, 2007, http://www.politico.com/story/2007/09/sen-nye-assails-merchants-of-death-on-sept-4-1934-005614. See also: *Empires of Industry: Dupont Dynasty*, History Channel (New York: A&E Networks, 2000).

160   **In his 2000 book:** Hernando de Soto, *The Mystery of Capital: Why Capitalism Triumphs in the West and Fails Everywhere Else* (New York: Basic Books, 2003), 7.

161   **thirty times the monthly minimum wage:** Ibid., 18–21.

162   **The trajectory of the investor:** Andreas von Bechtolsheim, Oral History with William Joy, interviewed by Daniel S. Morrow, in conjunction with the 1999 MCI WorldCom Information Technology Leadership Award for Innovation, March 18, 1999, San Francisco, 8, accessed February 1, 2015, http://www.cwhonors.org/archives/histories/BechtolsheimandJoy.pdf.

162   **Intel 8080:** Ibid., and author correspondence with Andy Bechtolsheim, January 20, 2016.

163   **write a $100,000 check:** "#40 Andreas von Bechtolsheim & Family," in "The Richest People in Tech," *Forbes*, accessed September 7, 2015, http://www.forbes.com/profile/andreas-von-bechtolsheim/. See also Michael Knigge, "Von Bechtolsheim: I Invested in Google to Solve My Own Problem," *Deutsche Welle*, August 12, 2009, accessed September 7, 2015, http://dw.com/p/J7do.

163   **Fogarty met Albert:** Cassak, 30.

163   **artificial mitral valve:** Nicholas T. Kouchoukos, MD, "Dr. Albert Starr: A Historical Commentary," *Society of Thoracic Surgeons,* 2014, accessed September 7, 2015, http://www.sts.org/news/ dr-albert-starr-historical-commentary.

163   **Edwards had founded a company:** "About Us," Edwards Lifesciences, accessed September 7, 2015, http://www.edwards.com/sharedpages/pages/ ourhistory.aspx.

163   **"You've got to make this catheter":** Cassak, "The Inventor's Inventor," 30.

164   **That royalty became generative:** "Dr. Fogarty," Fogarty Institute for Innovation, accessed September 7, 2015, http://www.fogartyinstitute.org/ about-fogarty.php.

164   **At the famous Scull sale:** Amy Whitaker, "Ownership for Artists," in *The Social Life of Artistic Property* (Hudson, NY: Publication Studio, 2014), accessed September 7, 2015, http://www.thesociallifeofartisticproperty.com/ webVersion/ownership-for-artists/index.html.

164   **taxi magnate Robert Scull:** Patricia Cohen, "Artists File Lawsuits, Seeking Royalties," *New York Times,* November 2, 2011, page C1.

164   **But Rauschenberg didn't own:** Lindsay Pollock and Philip Boroff, "Crichton's $29 Million Jasper Johns Flag Boosts Christie's Sale," Bloomberg.com, May 12, 2010. See also Whitaker, "Ownership for Artists."

165   **He was paid a royalty:** Whitaker, "Ownership for Artists."

165   **only $325,000 total:** Judith Prowda, "Assessing Artists' Resale Rights Legislation," *New York Law Journal,* January 23, 2012, 1. See also Jori Finkel and Mike Boehm, "Sam Francis Foundation Sues Nine Galleries for Artist's Royalties," *Los Angeles Times,* November 2, 2011, accessed August 14, 2012, http://articles.latimes.com/2011/nov/02/entertainment/ la-et-artists-royalties-20111102/2.

166   **the website Guidestar:** http://www.guidestar.org/Home.aspx.

166   **their EDGAR database:** https://www.sec.gov/edgar/searchedgar/ companysearch.html.

166   **Bureau of Labor Statistics:** http://www.bls.gov/bls/blswage.htm.

168   **Matthew Blank:** Matthew C. Blank, "PGA East: SPARK! The Conversation: Matthew C. Blank & Tom Fontana," May 13, 2015, Paley Center for Media, New York.

170   **plastic ukuleles:** "Ruth Handler: Marketing Toys," *Who Made America?,* PBS.org, accessed February 1, 2015, http://www.pbs.org/wgbh/ theymadeamerica/whomade/handler_hi.html.

170   **immigrant and entrepreneur:** "ABC Nightly News Report: Bratz vs. Barbie," December 23, 2006, accessed February 2, 2015, https://www. youtube.com/watch?v=lIdlHcZmniI.

171   **Mattel alone had paid:** John Kell, "Bratz Doll Maker MGA Entertainment Sues Mattel," *Wall Street Journal,* January 13, 2014, accessed September 7, 2015, http://www.wsj.com/articles/SB1   00014240527023035954045793

18680190603384.

171   **incarceration in a legal process:** Gina Keating, "Bratz Doll Creator
Tells of Origins at Mattel Trial," Reuters, June 13, 2008, accessed
September 7, 2015, http://www.reuters.com/article/2008/06/14/
mattel-bratz-bryant-idUSN1328758120080614.

171   **"fair use":** For the fair use factors, see the United States Code, Title 17,
section 107, accessed online December 7, 2015: http://www
.copyright.gov/title17/92chap1.html#107. For a discussion of fair use applied
in the fine arts, see Judith B. Prowda, *Visual Arts and the Law* (Surrey,
England, and Burlington, VT: Lund Humphries, 2013), 82. For a discussion
of how the fair use factors are applied with different emphasis in different
cases, see Judge Easterbrook's opinion in *Kienitz v. Sconnie Nation LLC*,
United States Court of Appeals, Seventh Circuit, No. 13-3004, 2014 WL
4494825 (2014), which specifically critiques the treatment of "transformative
use" in *Cariou v. Prince*.

172   **negotiated licensing fee:** Amy Adler, Dale Cendali, and Judith Prowda,
Esq. (moderator), Panel Discussion, Sotheby's Institute of Art, New York,
October 16, 2013. See also Nicholas O'Donnell, "Free Speech, Fair Use, and
Meaning—Recapping an Evening of Copyright and the Visual Arts at the
Sotheby's Institute," *Art Law Report*, October 17, 2013, accessed September
7, 2015, http://www.artlawreport.com/2013/10/17/free-speech-fair-use-and-
meaning-recapping-an-evening-of-copyright-and-the-visual-arts-at-the
-sothebys-institute/.

172   **the heirs to Marvin Gaye:** Ben Sisario and Noah Smith, " 'Blurred
Lines' Infringed on Marvin Gaye Copyright, Jury Rules," *New York
Times*, March 10, 2015, accessed September 7, 2015, http://www.nytimes.
com/2015/03/11/business/media/blurred-lines-infringed-on-marvin-gaye-
copyright-jury-rules.html. See also Prowda, *Visual Arts and the Law*, 80,
for a discussion of George Harrison's 1969 song "My Sweet Lord," which
was found to copy Ronald Mack and The Chiffons' 1963 song "He's So
Fine" but not to be infringing.

173   **In 2000:** Nicholas O'Donnell, "No Infringement in Cariou v. Prince—
Second Circuit Plays Art Critic and Finds Fair Use," *Art Law Report*,
April 25, 2013, accessed September 7, 2015, http://www
.artlawreport.com/2013/04/25/no-infringement-in-cariou-v-prince-second
-circuit-plays-critic-and-finds-fair-use/download case; http://www.google.
com/url?sa=t&rct=j&q=&esrc=s&source=web&cd=1
&ved=0CCAQFjAA&url=http%3A%2F%2Fcyber.law.harvard
.edu%2Fpeople%2Ffisher%2Fcx%2F2013_Cariou
.docx&ei=ldWhVImPDI_7gwS_lIPYCg&usg=AFQjCNEK55P
bxXbXQdikpGKP9CjA7qC_1Q&sig2=2CYmRNuD3TlBelvnCY
PK5w&bvm=bv.82001339,d.eXY. With thanks to Judith Prowda, art law
faculty, Sotheby's Institute.

173   **received about $8,000:** *Patrick Cariou v. Richard Prince*, United

States Court of Appeals, Second Circuit, 714 F.3d 694 (2013), accessed September 7, 2015, http://cyber.law.harvard.edu/people/tfisher/cx/2013_Cariou.pdf.

174   **decided in both directions:** Brian Boucher, "Landmark Copyright Lawsuit Cariou v. Prince Is Settled," *Art in America*, March 18, 2014, http://www.artinamericamagazine.com/news-features/news/landmark-copyright-lawsuit-cariou-v-prince-is-settled/.

174   **Prince sold several of the paintings:** Brian Boucher, "Richard Prince Wins Major Victory in Landmark Copyright Suit," *Art in America*, April 25, 2013, http://www.artinamericamagazine.com/news-features/newsrichard-prince-wins-major-victory-in-landmark-copyright-suit/.

176   **two related cancer drugs:** Filgrastrim and Pegfilgrastrim, respectively. "Royalty Pharma Acquires a Portion of the Memorial Sloan-Kettering Cancer Center's US Royalty Interest in Neupogen.Neulasta," January 22, 2004, accessed September 7, 2015, http://www.royaltypharma.com/press-releases/royalty-pharma-acquires-a-portion-of-memorial-sloan-kettering-cancer-center-s-us-royalty-interest-in-neupogen-neulasta; author email correspondence with Alexander von Perfall, February 5, 2015. Rory Riggs, the chairman of Royalty Pharma, is a former colleague of the author.

177   **BitTorrent takes a far lower:** Author interview with Matt Mason, then chief content officer for BitTorrent, January 12, 2015.

177   **In 2015:** Evie Nagy, "Most Creative People 2015, #11, Matt Mason, Chief Content Officer, Bittorrent," *Fast Company*, June 2015, accessed September 7, 2015, http://www.fastcompany.com/3043911/most-creative-people-2015/matt-mason.

178   **never pass his music collection:** Author interviews, Sean Moss-Pultz, 2014–15. Christopher Hall, Casey Alt, Lê Quý Quốc Cuông, and Sean Moss-Pultz, "Bitmark: A Decentralized Property System," https://bitmark.com/bitmark.pdf. The author discloses a small financial interest in Bitmark. See also Josh Constine, "Monegraph Uses Bitcoin Tech So Internet Artists Can Establish 'Original' Copies of Their Work," *TechCrunch*, May 9, 2014, accessed September 7, 2015, http://techcrunch.com/2014/05/09/monegraph/.

178   **unique and unpirated:** Hall, Alt, et al., "Bitmark: A Decentralized Property System."

179   **own a small piece of it:** Division of Trading and Markets, "Jumpstart Our Business Startups Act: Frequently Asked Questions About Crowdfunding Intermediaries," Securities and Exchange Commission, February 5, 2013, accessed September 7, 2015, https://www.sec.gov/divisions/marketreg/tmjobsact-crowdfundingintermediariesfaq.htm. The JOBS Act itself instructed interpreting these rules within 270 days of the April 5, 2012, signing of the act into law. Those rules have not yet been codified as of the

time of writing.

Chapter 5: To Be in the Fray

181 **"a failure of imagination":** Donald R. Keough, *The Ten Commandments of Business Failure* (New York: Portfolio/Penguin, 2008), 111.

182 **"not a good day":** Author interview with Ed Epping, July 3, 2015.

185 **"a comic tradition":** Adam Phillips, *Winnicott* (Cambridge, MA: Harvard University Press, 1988), 14.

185 **Winnicott had many ideas:** Ibid., 31. "[H]is work, in a sense, initiates a comic tradition in psychoanalysis."

185 **from illusion to disillusionment:** D. W. Winnicott, *The Maturational Process and the Facilitating Environment: Studies in the Theory of Emotional Development*, edited by M. Masud Khan (Madison, CT: International Universities Press, 1965), available at http://www.abebe.org. br/wp-content/uploads/Donald-Winnicott-The-Maturational-Process- and-the-Facilitating-Environment-Studies-in-the-Theory-of-Emotional- Development-1965.pdf; *The International Psycho-Analytical Library* (London: Hogarth Press and the Institute of Psycho-Analysis, 1965), 64:1–276. See "The Theory of the Parent-Infant Relationship" (1960), beginning on 37.

186 **The idea of the holding environment:** Winnicott, "The Theory of the Parent-Infant Relationship," in Winnicott, *The Maturational Process and the Facilitating Environment*, 44–45, 47–48.

186 **"Only the true self":** James F. Masterson, *The Narcissistic and Borderline Disorders* (New York and London: Brunner-Routledge, 1981), 104.

186 **Dalio favors:** John Cassidy, "Mastering the Machine," *New Yorker*, July 25, 2011, accessed July 29, 2015, http://www.newyorker.com/ magazine/2011/07/25/mastering-the-machine.

188 **In eulogizing Kirk Varnedoe:** Adam Gopnik, "Last of the Metrozoids," *New Yorker*, May 10, 2004, 90.

189 **In 2006:** Jori Finkel, "Tales from the Crit: For Art Students, May Is the Cruelest Month," *New York Times*, April 30, 2006, accessed February 1, 2015, http://www.nytimes.com/2006/04/30/arts/design/30fink.html?_r=0.

189 **violently grooved:** Michael J. Lewis, "The 'New' New Brutalism," *New Criterion*, December 2014, accessed August 11, 2015, http://www. newcriterion.com/articles.cfm/The-new-New-Brutalism-8018; and Michael J. Lewis "American Art and Architecture," course lecture on this topic at Williams College, November 18, 2014.

190 **"nude on a scale":** Finkel, "Tales from the Crit."

191 **"I am amenable to criticism":** Robert Giroux, "The Supernatural Grace of Flannery O'Connor," FSG Work in Progress Blog, http://www.fsgworkinprogress.com/2015/03/the-supernatural -grace-of-flannery-oconnor/.

191 **"I see my role":** Finkel, "Tales from the Crit."

191   **"examine the dynamics":** Laura Montini, " 'Brain Trust': The Stellar Creative
       Process Designed by Pixar," Inc.com, June 4, 2014, accessed July 1, 2015,
       http://www.inc.com/laura-montini/how-pixar-s-creative-process-has-
       evolved.html.

191   **all of their movies "suck":** Catmull, with Wallace, *Creativity, Inc.*, 90.

191   **"That's a blunt assessment":** Ibid., 91.

192   **"tinkering with the edge":** Author interview with Ed Epping.

193   **The Buddhist teacher:** Matthieu Ricard, " 'Empathy Fatigue'—1,"
       blog, October 3, 2013, http://www.matthieuricard.org/en/blog/posts/
       empathy-fatigue-1.

193   **Those who have compassion:** Ibid., and Matthieu Ricard, "Empathy
       and the Cultivation of Compassion," blog, May 4, 2009, http://www
       .matthieuricard.org/en/blog/posts/empathy-and-the-cultivation-of-
       compassion. See also O. M. Klimecki, S. Leiberg, M. Ricard, and T. Singer,
       "Differential Pattern of Functional Brain Plasticity After Compassion and
       Empathy Training," *Social Cognitive and Affective Neuroscience* 9, no. 6
       (2014): 873–79.

194   **"I wanted to do something":** Veronica Roberts, "Converging Lines: Eva
       Hesse and Sol LeWitt," from the catalog *Converging Lines: Eva Hesse
       and Sol LeWitt* (New Haven, CT: Yale University Press, 2014), 13. With
       thanks to Veronica Roberts for further conversations about Sol and Eva's
       friendship.

195   **That decision rippled:** Ibid., 13.

195   **"I have much confidence":** Ibid., 18.

196   **If you threw it back:** Bascomb, *The Perfect Mile*, 105–6.

199   **The opposite of the colleague-friend:** Kevin Wade, *Working Girl*, directed
       by Mike Nichols (Century City, CA: 20th Century Fox, 1989), DVD, 2001.

199   **Gore Vidal:** Gore Vidal, "Gore Vidal Quotes: 26 of the Best," *Guardian*,
       August 1, 2012, accessed September 21, 2015, http://www.theguardian.
       com/books/2012/aug/01/gore-vidal-best-quotes.

199   **"a triple back flip":** Catmull, with Wallace, *Creativity, Inc.*, 98.

200   **Docter's film *Inside Out*:** Pete Docter, *Inside Out* (Pixar, 2015), http://
       www.imdb.com/title/tt2096673/.

200   **grossed almost $300 million:** http://www.boxofficemojo.com/movies/
       ?id=pixar2014.htm, accessed July 1, 2015: $90.4 million opening weekend,
       second place.

200   **Somewhere around the three-year mark:** Lisa Miller, "How *Inside Out*
       Director Pete Docter Went Inside the 11-Year-Old Mind," Vulture.com, June
       16, 2015, accessed August 11, 2015, http://www
       .vulture.com/2015/06/pete-docter-pixar-inside-out.html.

200   **found the film's center:** Lisa Miller, Vulture.com, June 16, 2015. See also
       Andy Greenwald, "Grantland Q&A: Talking with Director Pete Docter
       About Pixar's Terrific 'Inside Out,' " Grantland.com, June 19, 2015,
       accessed September 7, 2015, http://grantland.com/hollywood-prospectus/

pixar-inside-out-pete-docter-podcast-andy-greenwald/; and Brook Barnes, "'Inside Out,' Pixar's New Movie From Pete Docter, Goes Inside the Mind," *New York Times*, May 20, 2015, accessed September 7, 2015, http://www.nytimes.com/2015/05/24/movies/inside-out-pixars-new-movie-from-pete-docter-goes-inside-the-mind.html.

201   **film producers are great models:** Lynda Obst, *Sleepless in Hollywood: Tales from the NEW ABNORMAL in the Movie Business* (New York: Simon & Schuster, 2013).

201   **Through no particular fault:** Helen O'Hara (interviewer), "Rachel Winter & Robbie Brenner on *Dallas Buyers Club*," Empire Online, undated, circa 2013, accessed August 11, 2015, http://www.empireonline.com/interviews/interview.asp?IID=1837.

202   **A year and a half before:** Borys Kit, "The Actor Turned Down 'Magnum, P.I.,' Choosing Small Roles like the Lead of 'Dallas Buyers Club' in His Impressive Tapdance to Stay on the New A-List," *Hollywood Reporter*, September 11, 2013, accessed August 11, 2015, http://www.hollywoodreporter.com/news/dallas-buyers-club-matthew-mcconaughey-625407.

202   **After declining the role:** Ibid.

202   **he agreed to direct:** O'Hara, EmpireOnline.com. See also "Rachel Winter, Producer," Cast and Crew: Dallas Buyers Club, http://www.focusfeatures.com/film/dallas_buyers_club/castncrew?member=rachel_winter, and "Robbie Brenner, Producer," Cast and Crew: Dallas Buyers Club, http://www.focusfeatures.com/dallas_buyers_club/castncrew?member=robbie_brenner.

202   **Rachel Winter to coproduce:** O'Hara, EmpireOnline.com.

202   **near-starvation diet:** Craig Borten and Melisa Wallack, *Dallas Buyers Club*, directed by Jean-Marc Vallée (Santa Monica, CA: Focus Features), DVD, 2014. See also A. O. Scott, "Taking on Broncos and a Plague: Matthew McConaughey Stars in 'Dallas Buyers Club,'" *New York Times*, October 31, 2013, http://www.nytimes.com/2013/11/01/movies/matthew-mcconaughey-stars-in-dallas-buyers-club.html.

202   **roughly 38 of 40 pounds:** E! Online, http://www.eonline.com/news/365424/skinny-matthew-mcconaughey-dishes-on-his-shocking-weight-loss (38 pounds); Julie Miller, "Matthew McConaughey Considering Releasing His Dallas Buyers Club Weight-Loss Diary to the Public," *Vanity Fair*, February 18, 2014, http://www.vanityfair.com/hollywood/2014/02/matthew-mcconaughey-dallas-buyers-club-weight-loss-diary (47 pounds); Theo Merz, "Should I Try the Matthew McConaughey Diet?," *Telegraph*, February 6, 2014, http://www.telegraph.co.uk/men/active/10616932/Should-I-try-the-Matthew-McConaughey-diet.html (38 pounds).

202   **delay production:** Producer's Guild of America (PGA East) Screening Q&A, October 23, 2013, AMC Loews Lincoln Square 13, New York.

203   **no artificial lighting:** Ibid.

203   **roughly $4 million:** Ibid.

203   **more than $50 million worldwide:** http://www.boxofficemojo.com/ movies/?id=dallasbuyersclub.htm.

203   **unicorn-like occurrence:** Obst, *Sleepless in Hollywood*, 37, interviewing Peter Chernin, who estimates that the DVD business accounted for half of movie profits.

204   **It is the diagonals:** Vijay Kumar, *101 Design Methods: A Structured Approach for Driving Innovation in Your Organization* (Hoboken, NJ: Wiley, 2012), 8.

204   **first given this diagram:** Interview of Hugh Musick, by the author, January 25, 2013.

204   *101 Design Methods:* Kumar, *101 Design Methods*, 8.

204   **creative and commercial arts:** Barry Bergdoll and Leah Dickerman, *Bauhaus 1919–1933: Workshops for Modernity* (New York: Museum of Modern Art, 2009), 58–60.

205   **indoor pollution:** "Acumen Makes First Cookstove Investment with BURN Manufacturing," Acumen blog, June 11, 2015, http:// acumen.org/blog/acumen-makes-first-cookstove-investment -with-burn-manufacturing/.

206   **off of an electrical grid:** Ibid.

206   **a winding and weedy one:** Author interview with Peter Scott, BURN Manufacturing CEO, August 12, 2015.

206   **north of Nairobi:** Ibid.

207   **invented to solve:** "Acumen Makes First Cookstove Investment with BURN Manufacturing."

208   **cut down for kindling:** Ibid.

211   **"Why is programming fun":** Frederick Brooks Jr., *The Mythical Man Month: Essays on Software Engineering* (1975; Reading, MA: Addison Wesley Longman, 1995), 7.

211   **"not accustomed to being perfect":** Ibid., 8.

212   **start a Scrum movement:** "Ken Schwaber" and "Jeff Sutherland," Scrum Guides, http://www.scrumguides.org/ken.html and http:// www.scrumguides.org/jeff.html. For a Scrum Guide, see http://www. scrumguides.org/docs/scrumguide/v1/Scrum-Guide-US.pdf#zoom=100.

212   **faster horse and buggy:** The quotation is often attributed to Henry Ford: "If I had asked people what they wanted, they would have said a faster horse." Many people dispute whether Ford ever actually said that. See Patrick Vlaskovits, "Henry Ford, Innovation, and That 'Faster Horse,'" *Harvard Business Review*, August 29, 2011, https://hbr.org/2011/08/henry-ford-never-said-the-fast/; "Henry Ford's Quotations," Henry Ford Blog, March 12, 2013, http://blog.thehenryford.org/2013/03/henry-fords-quotations; and http:// quoteinvestigator.com/2011/07/28/ford-faster-horse/.

214   **"knife-edged sharpness":** Brooks, *The Mythical Man Month*, 154.

215   **"verifiable by the boss":** Ibid., 155.

216   **"ladder of inferences":** Karen Christensen, "Thought Leader Interview: Chris Argyris," *Rotman Magazine*, Winter 2008, 13, accessed September 21, 2015, https://www.rotman.utoronto .ca/-/media/Files/Programs-and-Areas/Rotman%20Magazine/ Thought%20Leader%20Articles/ThoughtLeader_Argyris.pdf.

218   **Carol Dweck's research:** Carol Dweck, *Self-Theories: Their Role in Motivation, Personality, and Development* (Philadelphia: Taylor & Francis Psychology Press, 2000).

219   **a rubric:** David Grant, *The Social Profit Handbook* (White River Junction, VT: Chelsea Green, 2015).

221   **Lisa Yuskavage:** Thomas Gebremedhin, "Good World to Be In: Interview with Lisa Yuskavage," Daily blog, *Paris Review*, April 29, 2015, http://www. theparisreview.org/blog/2015/04/29/good-world-to -be-in-an-interview-with-lisa-yuskavage/. "When I first came to New York City, I had this painting show that was the culmination of a lot of ideas I'd had as a student, and it was a big flop. I don't mean a big flop commercially. It was a big flop for me because I walked into the opening and I hated the show. And I stopped painting for a year. . . . It didn't represent what I felt. It was like a show for a person I was pretending to be and not my real self. I was trying to ape to something that I was supposed to be doing. I come from a working-class family. I kind of have a potty mouth. I have a lot of crazy energies that I didn't know you could put into art. I thought art was for classy people, and I was going to try to be one of those people. That's when I put on my painting beret, my little pinkie went up, and I was a fake. I was a fraud. And I didn't know how to do it any other way."

222   **"Luckily we failed":** David A. Garvin, "How Google Sold Its Engineers on Management," *Harvard Business Review*, December 2013, https://hbr. org/2013/12/how-google-sold-its-engineers-on- management.

223   **relatively flat organization:** Ibid.

223   **Barr's mythology:** Amy Whitaker, *Museum Legs* (Tucson, AZ: Hol Art Books, 2009), 160. See also Harriet S. Bee and Michelle Elliott, eds., *Art in Our Time: A Chronicle of the Museum of Modern Art* (New York: Museum of Modern Art, 2004), 81.

225   **"cold towel around your head":** Said by Nicholas Serota in a strategic planning meeting, summer 2000. With permission.

225   **defrosting a freezer by hand:** Amy Poehler, *Yes Please* (New York: Dey St., 2014), x.

226   **ill-fated costume:** Anthony Doerr, interview by the author, August 18, 2015.

226   **"faint suggestion of bad parenting":** Anthony Doerr, "Costume Drama," *Real Simple*, October 2014, 58. Author interview with Anthony Doerr, August 18, 2015.

227   **"Every day I fail":** Doerr, *Real Simple*, 59.

227   **"down before a typewriter":** Shields, *Mockingbird*, 186.

Chapter 6: To Build a House

229   **"Being good in business":** Andy Warhol, *The Philosophy of Andy Warhol (From A to B and Back Again)* (1975; reprint, London: Penguin Books, 2007), 88. See also Natasha Degen, ed., *The Market* (Cambridge, MA: MIT Press, 2013), 184.

231   **in a computer lab at Wharton:** Anne Freedman, "Making Waves on Their Own Ship," *Wharton Magazine*, Winter 2012, http://whartonmagazine. com/issues/winter-2012/making-waves-on-their-own-ship/.

231   **Then Neil told him:** Maureen Callahan, "The Right Frame of Mind," *Vanity Fair*, October 2012, accessed September 7, 2015, http://www .vanityfair.com/style/2012/10/warby-parker-glasses-frames.

231   **"the production line right next door":** Neil Blumenthal interview with author, February 26, 2013.

232   **owns LensCrafters:** Halah Touryalai, "Ray-Ban, Oakley, Chanel or Prada Sunglasses? They're All Made by This Obscure $9B Company," *Forbes*, July 2, 2013, accessed September 7, 2015, http://www.forbes .com/sites/halahtouryalai/2013/07/02/ray-ban-oakley-chanel-or -prada-sunglasses-theyre-all-made-by-this-obscure-9b-company/.

232   **"from a businessman's perspective":** Neil Blumenthal interview with author, February 26, 2013.

232   **the envelope maker's craft:** Ibid.

233   **In 2015:** Max Chafkin, "Warby Parker Sees the Future of Retail," *Fast Company*, March 2015, accessed September 21, 2015, http:// www.fastcompany.com/3041334/most-innovative-companies-2015/ warby-parker-sees-the-future-of-retail.

234   **"Now we hire":** Neil Blumenthal interview with author, February 26, 2013.

234   **history of labor safety:** Ibid.

234   **"Volunteer hours on the weekends":** Ibid.

235   **dance kaleidoscopically:** To my recollection, this project with the McDonald's cup lids was done by a classmate named Eddie Ferrell.

235   **coated piece of metal:** Robert M. Pirsig, *Zen and the Art of Motorcycle Maintenance: An Inquiry into Values* (New York: HarperTorch, 2006).

236   **The firm Nutrinsic:** "Company Overview of Nutrinsic Inc.," *Bloomberg Business*, accessed October 9, 2015, http://www.bloomberg.com/research/ stocks/private/snapshot.asp?privcapid=36826619. See also Bob Rosenberry, "Oberon FMR: The 'FMR' Stands for Fish Meal Replacement," *Shrimp News International*, June 17, 2011, accessed October 9, 2015, http://www. shrimpnews.com/FreeReportsFolder/FeedsFolder/OberonFMR62011.html.

237   **"violent Vase Madness":** Jane Gleeson-White, *Double-Entry: How the Merchants of Venice Created Modern Finance* (2011; New York: W.W. Norton, 2012), 137 (quoting Wedgwood).

238   **"move like clockwork":** Ibid., 137–38.

240   **credit crisis of 1772:** Richard B. Sheridan, "The British Credit Crisis of 1772 and the American Colonies," *Journal of Economic History*, June 1960, 161–86.

243   **In 2004:** Chris Anderson, "The Long Tail," *Wired*, October 2004 (expanded into a book in 2006), http://archive.wired.com/wired/archive/12.10/tail.html?pg=3&topic=tail&topic_set=.

243   **Airbnb was founded:** Christine Lagorio-Chafkin, "Brian Chesky, Joe Gebbia, and Nathan Blecharczyk, Founders of AirBnB," 30 Under 30: 2010, Inc.com, July 17, 2010, accessed October 9, 2015, http://www.inc.com/30under30/2010/profile-brian-chesky-joe-gebbia-nathan-blecharczyk-airbnb.html.

245   **sole bidder:** Mark Gongloff and Andrew Stein, "Halliburton Job Bigger Than Thought," *CNN Money*, May 7, 2003, accessed September 21, 2015, http://money.cnn.com/2003/05/07/news/companies/halliburton_iraq_con/.

246   **expertise in staffing:** See also Halliburton's annual financial statement, Form 10-k, 2014, accessed September 21, 2015, https://www.sec.gov/cgi-bin/viewer?action=view&cik=45012&accession_number=0000045012-15-000040&xbrl_type=v#.

247   **venture capitalist Peter Thiel:** Peter Thiel with Blake Masters, *Zero to One: Notes on Startups, or How to Build the Future* (New York: Crown Business, 2014), 7–8.

249   **"not mere utility":** Jeré Longman "Lionel Messi: Boy Genius," *New York Times*, May 21, 2011, http://www.nytimes.com/2011/05/22/sports/soccer/lionel-messi-boy-genius.html?_r=0.

249   **As Neil said:** Neil Blumenthal interview with author, February 26, 2013.

250   **In 2009:** Evan Ratliff, "Vanish," *Wired*, accessed November 11, 2014, http://archive.wired.com/vanish/2009/11/ff_vanish2/all/.

251   **"lazy roadie":** Ibid.

251   **"fax machine":** David Carr, "Long-Form Journalism Finds a Home," *New York Times*, March 27, 2011, accessed November 11, 2014, http://www.nytimes.com/2011/03/28/business/media/28carr.html?_r=1&.

251   **Evan complained:** Evan Ratliff, interview with author, April 11, 2013; and Jeff Rabb, interview with author, December 1, 2014.

252   **"ordering another round":** Carr, "Long-Form Journalism Finds a Home."

252   **"third weekend in October":** Amy Whitaker interview with Evan Ratliff.

252   **number-one season:** Ray Glier, "Lineman's Arms Save No. 1 Title," *New York Times*, October 24, 2009, accessed October 8, 2015, http://www.nytimes.com/2009/10/25/sports/ncaafootball/25alabama.html/.

252   **tiny devices:** Carr, "Long-Form Journalism Finds a Home."

253   **version of the platform:** The publicly available platform was originally called the Creatavist, and then renamed the Atavist. The content part of the Atavist's business was renamed the *Atavist Magazine*. Both the magazine and the platform formerly known as the Creatavist are referred to herein

as the Atavist for simplicity. Evan Ratliff, correspondence with the author, October 12, 2015.

255   **"worst form of government":** Walter John Raymond, *Dictionary of Politics: Selected American and Foreign Political and Legal Terms*, 7th ed. (1978; Lawrenceville, VA: Brunswick, 1992), 124.

255   **"black swan":** Nasim Taleb, *The Black Swan: The Impact of the Highly Improbable*, 2nd ed. (New York: Random House, 2010).

257   **TARP bailout:** ProPublica, "The Bailout Scorecard," last updated October 2, 2015, accessed October 7, 2015, https://projects.propublica.org/bailout.

257   **Edgar Bronfman:** Matthew Herper, "Do the Richest Make Money Fastest?," *Forbes*, September 27, 2001, http://www.forbes.com/2001/09/27/wager.html.

261   **all . . . made of corn:** Michael Pollan, *The Omnivore's Dilemma: A Natural History of Four Meals* (New York: Penguin, 2007), 18–19.

266   **organizing group shows:** Katherine Markley, "25 Years of YBAs," *artnet News*, June 19, 2013, https://news.artnet.com/market/25-years-of-ybas-52819.

266   **largely a regional market:** For more on this topic I recommend Adam Brandenberger and Barry Nalebuff, *Co-opetition* (New York: Crown, 1996). It is about conjoined competitive and cooperative strategies.

Chapter 7: To See the Whole

269   **"I love life":** Eugene O'Neill, "To Malcolm Mollan, December 1921," in *Selected Letters of Eugene O'Neill*, edited by Travis Bogard and Jackson R. Bryer (1988; reprint, New York: Limelight Editions, 1994), 160.

269   **the people who succeed:** Eugene O'Neill, "Eugene O'Neill's Credo and His Reasons for His Faith," *New York Tribune*, February 13, 1921, B1, accessed through ProQuest Historical Newspapers, *New York Tribune* (1911–1922).

271   **New York gallery:** Christopher Miner, Mitchell-Innes & Nash, accessed February 2, 2015, http://www.miandn.com/artists/christopher-miner/works/1/.

271   **"wonderfully humane":** Ken Johnson, "Art in Review: Christopher Miner, 'Easter for the Birds,'" *New York Times*, February 13, 2009, http://query.nytimes.com/gst/fullpage.html?res=9C05E0D81331 F930A25751C0A96F9C8B63.

271   **latest art project:** "Eyesore Cured in Memphis," *Construction Equipment Guide*, Southeast Edition, August 18, 2015, http://www.constructionequipmentguide.com/Eyesore-Cured-in-Memphis/25998/. The building was, at its full original construction size, 1.5 million square feet. After its renovation, with added atria, it will be closer to 1.1 million square feet.

272   **In 1965:** "Amazon Before Amazon," Crosstown Concourse blog, May 18, 2015, http://crosstownconcourse.com/amazon-before-amazon.

272   **Boston building:** Thomas Baily Jr., " 'Founding Partners' Commit to Lease Most of Memphis' Sears Crosstown Building," *Memphis Commercial Appeal*, August 19, 2012, accessed October 8, 2015, http://www.commercialappeal.com/business/founding-partners-commit-to-lease-most-of-memphis-sears-crosstown-building-ep-514683878-323870221.html. Called Landmark Center, the Boston building was completed in 2000.

272   **Seattle building:** Lee Moriwaki, "Old Sears Named Starbucks Headquarters," *Seattle Times*, June 7, 1997, http://community.seattletimes.nwsource.com/archive/?date=19970607&slug=2543322.

273   **the 1971 case:** *Citizens to Preserve Overton Park, Inc., et al., v. John A. Volpe, Secretary, Department of Transportation, et al.*, 401 U.S. 402 (91 S.Ct. 814, 28 L.Ed.2d 136).

273   **great bones:** "The Ten Most Dangerous U.S. Cities," *Forbes*, accessed October 8, 2015, http://www.forbes.com/pictures/mlj45jggj/4-memphis/.

274   **throwback heist film:** For a brief period around 2011, the author worked for Crosstown as a consultant, to build with Chris an Excel model of the different parts of the arts complex and how they came together.

275   **gingerbread cookie:** Christopher Miner, interviews with author, spring and summer 2011. Todd Richardson, correspondence with the author, October 13, 2015.

276   **Since Leonardo's time:** Bryan Boyer, Justin Cook, and Marco Steinberg, *In Studio: Recipes for Systemic Change* (Helsinki, Finland: SITRA, 2011), 30.

276   **dawn of the history of man:** *TechCrunch*, August 4, 2010. Some people have disputed the second half of this statistic, about the amount of information up to 2003. See also Robert T. Moore, "Was Eric Schmidt Wrong About the Historical Scale of the Internet?," RJMetrics blog, February 7, 2011, http://readwrite.com/2011/02/07/are-we-really-creating-as-much.

276   **zetabytes:** Anton Andrews, Program at PopTech Conference, October 2014, Camden, Maine. See also: Vernon Turner, John F. Gantz, David Reinsel, Stephen Minton, "The Digital Universe of Opportunities: Rich Data and the Increasing Value of the Internet of Things," International Data Corporation (IDC) White Paper, EMC Corporation, April 2014, accessed January 24, 2016, http://idcdocserv.com/1678.

277   **paint by number:** William L. Bird Jr., *Paint By Number* (New York: Princeton Architectural Press in association with Smithsonian Institution, National Museum of American History, 2001), 3.

277   **"mechanization of culture":** Ibid., 3.

278   **In the fall of 2009:** William Deresiewicz, "Solitude and Leadership," *American Scholar*, March 1, 2010, accessed September 7, 2015, https://theamericanscholar.org/solitude-and-leadership/, and interviews by the author, February 3, 2012, and November 3, 2014.

278   **"pass with flying colors":** Deresiewicz, "Solitude and Leadership."

278   **but not ask them:** Ibid.

279   **"facetious question":** Michael J. Lewis, "Children Who Never Play,"
First Things, September 23, 2014, accessed September 7, 2015, http://
www.firstthings.com/web-exclusives/2014/09/children-who-never-play;
interview by the author, November 18, 2014.

280   **From 2010 to 2012:** Angela Zhang, "Stanford Arts Institute to Pilot New
Interdisciplinary Honors Program," *Stanford Daily*, August 8, 2013, accessed
September 7, 2015, http://www.stanforddaily.com/2013/08/08/stanford-
arts-institute-to-pilot-new-interdisciplinary-honors-program/. Also author
interview with Susan McConnell, July 21, 2015.

280   **in biology:** Margaret Rawson, "Faculty Senate Hears, Debates SUES
Report," *Stanford Daily*, January 27, 2012, accessed September 7,
2015, http://www.stanforddaily.com/2012/01/27/faculty-senate-hears
-debates-sues-report/.

280   **circuits of neurons:** Author interview, Susan McConnell, July 21, 2015.

280   **"more ours than theirs":** Rawson, "Faculty Senate Hears, Debates SUES
Report."

281   **"creative expression":** Ibid.

281   **some form of making:** Author interview with Stephen Hinton, Denning
Family Director of the Stanford Arts Institute and Avalon Foundation
Professor in the Humanities and Professor of Music, July 21, 2015.

281   **In another:** Zhang, "Stanford Arts Institute to Pilot New Interdisciplinary
Honors Program"; author interview with Susan McConnell, July 21, 2015.

281   **"lost and confused":** Author interview with Susan McConnell, July 21,
2015.

282   **"people on the planet":** Ibid.

282   **bicycle:** Ibid.

282   **like a kite:** John Maeda, talk at Creative Mornings, August 4, 2011. See
also CreativeMornings/Findings, accessed September 7, 2015, http://
findings.creativemornings.com/post/8477645882/i-think-of-artists
-as-kitemakers-the-wind-is.

283   **STEM to STEAM:** Sophia Hollander, "STEAM Blends Science and the
Arts in Public Education," *Wall Street Journal*, December 2, 2013, accessed
September 7, 2015, http://www.wsj.com/news/articles/SB10001424052702
3047470045792240037212627927. See also: http://stemtosteam.org.

283   **"wanderingly":** John Maeda, "Artists and Scientists: More Alike
than Different," *Scientific American*, July 11, 2013, accessed July 8,
2015, http://blogs.scientificamerican.com/guest-blog/artists-and
-scientists-more-alike-than-different/.

283   **recognize a cat:** Fei Fei Li, "How We're Teaching Computers to
Understand Pictures," TED2015 Conference, Vancouver, British Columbia,
March 17, 2015, accessed September 7, 2015, http://www
.ted.com/talks/fei_fei_li_how_we_re_teaching_computers_to_under
stand_pictures/transcript?language=en, see transcript especially at 8:40 and

9:40.

284   **militiamen:** "Militia Company of District II Under the Command of Captain Frans Banninck Cocq, Known as the 'Night Watch,' Rembrandt Harmensz. van Rijn, 1642," Rijksmuseum, accessed September 7, 2015, https://www.rijksmuseum.nl/en/collection/SK-C-5.

284   **on a shield:** "The Night Watch," Museum Het Rembranthuis, accessed September 7, 2015, http://www.rembrandthuis.nl/en/rembrandt/belangrijkste-werken/de-nachtwacht.

285   **"slash" careers:** Marci Alboher, *One Person/Multiple Careers: A New Model for Work/Life Success* (New York: Hachette, 2007), xi–xvi.

285   **apothecaries:** Michael Gelb, *How to Think Like Leonardo da Vinci* (New York: Delta/Random House, 1998), 25.

286   **"Chemist":** Edward Carr, "The Last Days of the Polymath," *Intelligent Life*, Autumn 2009, accessed September 7, 2015, http://moreintelligentlife.com/content/edward-carr/last-days-polymath.

286   **famous NASA scientists:** Author interview and email with Christopher Miner, July 2011.

288   **baleen whale:** Cynthia Littleton, "Barbara Walters: Probing Questions and a Tall Tale of the Tree," *Variety*, April 8, 2014, http://variety.com/2014/tv/news/barbara-walters-probing-questions-and-a-tall-tale-of-the-tree-1201152684/.

293   **"between anyone's ears":** Paola Antonelli, Kwame Anthony Appiah, Linda Shearer, and Philippe de Montebello (moderator), "Keynote Panel: Looking Forward Ten Years: What Is the Museum of 2021?," Association of Art Museum Curators Conference, Metropolitan Museum of Art, New York, May 16, 2011. Panel description accessed September 7, 2015, http://c.ymcdn.com/sites/www.artcurators.org/resource/resmgr/keynote_panel.pdf.

294   **Keyser Söze:** *The Usual Suspects*, directed by Bryan Singer (MGM, 1995).

295   **"idiot broken loose":** Walter Bagehot, "Adam Smith as a Person," in *Biographical Studies* (London: Henry Holt, 1899), 267–69.

295   **gypsies:** Adam Smith, *The Essential Adam Smith*, edited by Robert L. Heilbroner (New York: Norton, 1987), 4, originally in John Rae, *Life of Adam Smith* (London: Macmillan, 1895), 5.

296   **"come to be what he is":** Bagehot, "Adam Smith as a Person," 268–69.

297   **artists who bought their lofts:** Susan Zukin, *Loft Living: Culture and Capital in Urban Change* (New Brunswick, NJ: Rutgers University Press, 1982); and Ann Fensterstock, *Art on the Block* (New York: Palgrave Macmillan, 2013).

298   **then forgiven it:** "Rolling Jubilee Student Debt Buy," Strike Debt, September 16, 2014, accessed September 7, 2015, http://strikedebt.org/debtbuy4/.

298   **University of Oregon:** Tara Siegel Bernard, "Program Links Loans to Future Earnings," *New York Times*, July 19, 2013, http://www.nytimes

.com/2013/07/20/your-money/unusual-student-loan-programs-link
-to-future-earnings.html?pagewanted=all&module=Search&mab
Reward=relbias%3Ar%2C%7B%221%22%3A%22RI%3A7%22%7D;
Dave Girouard, "How the Market Can Reign in Tuition," *Wall Street Journal*,
October 4, 2013, A23.

299 **Bill McKibben:** Bill McKibben, "Global Warming's Terrifying
New Math," *Rolling Stone*, July 19, 2012, accessed September 7,
2015, http://www.rollingstone.com/politics/news/global-warmings
-terrifying-new-math-20120719.

299 **harvested their reserves:** Bill McKibben, correspondence with the author,
October 11, 2015.

299 **politician's competitor:** I had this idea while watching Lawrence Lessig
answer an audience question at the event: "Design and Violence Debate
IV: The Internet, Open Wide," Gabriella Coleman (for) and Larry Lessig
(against), moderated by Paola Antonelli and Jamer Hunt, May 19, 2015.
Someone asked Lessig if politicians consulted technologists as experts and
he said that he often heard that these conversations were a preface to asking
for money. See also Paola Antonelli, "Design and Violence Debate IV: The
Internet, Open Wide," Design and Violence, Museum of Modern Art, May
19, 2015, accessed September 7, 2015, http://designandviolence.moma.org/
design-and-violence-debate-iv-the-internet-open-wide/.

301 **groundbreaking:** "Groundbreaking Event Feb. 21 for Sears Crosstown
Redevelopment," *Commercial Appeal*, January 17, 2015, accessed
September 7, 2015, http://www.commercialappeal.com/news/local-news/
groundbreaking-event-feb-21-for-sears-crosstown-
redevelopment_47604183.

301 **art historian way:** Todd Richardson, "The Dilemma of Discovery,"
TEDx Memphis, August 29, 2015, https://www.youtube.com/
watch?v=1LyIddnW67w. One particularly instrumental member of the
expanded team not mentioned in detail here is McLean Wilson, who joined
Todd as a co-leader, Crosstown Development Team, while Christopher
Miner focused on running Crosstown Arts.

303 **masonry joints:** "Eyesore Cured in Memphis," *Construction Equipment Guide*,
Southeast Edition, August 18, 2015, http://www.constructionequipmentguide.
com/Eyesore-Cured-in-Memphis/25998/.

303 **$200 million:** Joel Halpern, "Crosstown Project Secures $200M Financing;
Announces New Name; Holds Groundbreaking Celebration," Press
Release, Low Income Investment Fund, January 21, 2015, accessed January
25, 2016, http://www.liifund.org/news/post/crosstown-project-secures-
200m-financing-announces-new-name-holds-groundbreaking-celebration/.
The exact amount of the debt transaction led by SunTrust Bank was $80.5
million.

303 **consortium of lenders:** Ibid.

303 **$56 million transaction:** Ibid.

303 **Goldman Sachs Urban Investment Group:** "Impact Investing: Sears Crosstown, Memphis, TN," GoldmanSachs.com, accessed January 25, 2016, http://www.goldmansachs.com/what-we-do/investing-and-lending/impact-investing/case-studies/sears-crosstown-memphis.html. The exact amount of the Goldman Sachs investment was $36.5 million.

303 **City of Memphis:** Adam Hammond, "City Pays Up for Sears Crosstown Project Despite Questions," WREG Memphis News Channel 3, December 4, 2013, accessed January 25, 2016, http://wreg.com/2013/12/04/city-pays-up-for-sears-crosstown-project-despite-questions/.

303 **"not many green lights":** Halper, "Crosstown Project Secures $200M."

303 **"so outlandish":** Todd Richardson, "Welcome and Opening Remarks," Crosstown Groundbreaking Ceremony, Memphis, Tennessee, February 21, 2015, author notes.

303 **shovels-in-the-ground:** "Your Itinerary: Crosstown Groundbreaking Program," February 21, 2015. Speakers included Mayor Mark Luttrell, Shelby County; Mayor A. C. Wharton, city of Memphis; Jim Howard, Dudley Ventures; Annie Donovan, director, Community Development Financial Institutions; Johnny Moore, CEO, Suntrust Bank Memphis; David Gorleku, Goldman Sachs Urban Investment Group; McLean Wilson, co-leader, Crosstown Development Team; Todd Richardson, co-leader, Crosstown Development Team.

303 **brass band:** Katie Fretland, "Crosstown Concourse Groundbreaking Marked with Stories, Music, and Rain," *Commercial Appeal,* February 21, 2015, http://www.commercialappeal.com/news/crosstown-concourse-groundbreaking-marked-with-stories-music-and-rain-ep-947395517-324457351.html.

304 **keep going after that:** Todd Richardson, Remarks, Crosstown Groundbreaking Ceremony, Memphis, Tennessee, February 21, 2015. See also "Breaking Ground," Crosstown Concourse blog, March 3, 2015, http://crosstownconcourse.com/breaking-ground.

ABOUT THE AUTHOR

Amy Whitaker is a writer, artist, and teacher working at the intersection of creativity, business, and everyday life. She holds an MBA from Yale and an MFA in painting from the Slade School of Fine Art at the University College London. She is currently an entrepreneur-in-residence at the New Museum Incubator, and principal in the curriculum development company Eggshell Knight. She was the recipient of the Sarah Verdone Writing Award from the Lower Manhattan Cultural Council. She lives in New York City.